The Call of the Holy

T&T Clark Studies in **Fundamental Liturgy** offer cutting edge scholarship from all disciplines related to liturgical study. The books in the series seek to reintegrate biblical, patristic, historical, dogmatic and philosophical questions with liturgical study in ways faithful and sympathetic to classical liturgical enquiry. Volumes in the series include monographs, translations of recent texts and edited collections around very specific themes.

Edited by

Laurence Paul Hemming
Susan Frank Parsons

Forthcoming Titles in the series:

The Banished Heart. Origins of Heteropraxis in the Catholic Church
Being Liturgical: The Subject of Worship. The Practice of the Love of God
Collects of the Roman Missal. A Study in Liturgical Reform

The Call of the Holy

Heidegger – Chauvet – Benedict XVI

Hal St John

B L O O M S B U R Y

LONDON • NEW DELHI • NEW YORK • SYDNEY

Bloomsbury T&T Clark

An imprint of Bloomsbury Publishing Plc

50 Bedford Square	1385 Broadway
London	New York
WC1B 3DP	NY 10018
UK	USA

www.bloomsbury.com

Bloomsbury is a registered trade mark of Bloomsbury Publishing Plc

First published 2012
Paperback edition first published 2014

British Library Cataloguing-in-Publication Data
A catalogue record for this book is available from the British Library.

ISBN: HB: 978-0-567-56620-1
PB: 978-0-567-20514-8

Library of Congress Cataloging-in-Publication Data
A catalog record for this book is available from the Library of Congress.

Typeset by Newgen Imaging Systems Pvt Ltd, Chennai, India
Printed and bound in Great Britain

Contents

Preface

Laurence Paul Hemming

Fr. Louis-Marie Chauvet's *Symbol and Sacrament* was published in French in 1987 and in an English translation in 1995. It remains one of the most important engagements in English or in French with sacramental theology, a field that has, since the early twentieth century, been marked by a certain anxiety, especially for Catholics. The anxiety expresses itself in the following way: how is it possible to reconcile the claims of faith, of the presence of Jesus Christ in the sacraments, and in the Holy Eucharist especially, with the claims of the physical and material sciences – and the demands those latter claims make on the materialism (and atheism) of contemporary philosophical thought? Chauvet's book steps into the very midst of the attempt to disengage Catholic theology from a problematic inheritance of not a theologically, but it would now seem a philosophically, redundant, language. Nowhere does that redundancy seem more perilous than in the language of transubstantiation.

Chauvet's ambitions for the book are stated right at the beginning: in this work he sought to develop '*a foundational theology of sacramentality*', 'that is to say, a theology which permits a *sacramental reinterpretation*, specific in its point of view, but global in its extension, *of the entirety of the Christian existence*'.[1] The phrase explicitly recalls a parallel remark of Martin Heidegger's, from the only formal engagement Heidegger ever took up of his mature thought with Christian theology, the lecture entitled *Phenomenology and Theology*, given in Tübingen around the time of the publication of *Being and Time*.[2] In this lecture Heidegger held out before Christianity the need for a theology that was 'non-objectifying', not captivated by the present and emerging danger 'that the scientific-technological

---

[1] Louis-Marie Chauvet, *Symbole et Sacrement*, pp. 7–8. '*Une théologie fondamentale de la sacramentalité*. [. . .] c'est-à-dire une théologie qui permette une *relecture sacramentelle*, partielle de son point de vue, mais globale quant à son extension, *de l'ensemble de l'existence chrétienne*.' Translation modified from that of Patrick Madigan SJ and Madeleine Beaumont, as Louis-Marie Chauvet, *Symbol and Sacrament: A Sacramental Reinterpretation of Christian Existence*, Collegeville, Pueblo/Liturgical Press, 1995, p. 1. (Chauvet's emphases)

[2] See Martin Heidegger, *Phänomenologie und Theologie* in *Wegmarken* (GA9), pp. 45–77. The lecture was first published in 1969. The phrase in question is repeated several times, but is summed up on p. 53 as 'das ganze Dasein als christliches, d,h. kreuzbezogenes vor Gott gestellt' ('The entire existence posited as Christian, that means, bound to the cross before God').

manner of thinking will spread out over all areas of life' – including the theological.[3]
Theology, Heidegger had argued in concluding, is not a natural science 'because
presumably it need not be a science at all'.[4] In this sense the thought of Martin
Heidegger promises at least the possibility of settling the anxiety I have named.
Moreover no-one could better know the claims of a Catholic understanding than
Martin Heidegger, the former Catholic seminarian, the self-described 'Catholic
philosopher' (at least until the age of 28).

The science of theology has been, or so it seems, certainly since Suárez, and
perhaps since St Thomas Aquinas, the science of metaphysics. The significance
of Chauvet's ambitious desire to free Catholic theology from the language of
metaphysics, above all as it has been deployed in sacramental theology, cannot
be underestimated. It is unsurprising that Chauvet should have turned to assist
him in his desire to Heidegger, the philosopher who promised to destructure
the history of philosophy down to its roots, whose later work promises a new
beginning, and who above all has pointed up the danger and ubiquity of the
technological as a universal way of thinking.

Although there have been a few, and very important, engagements with
Chauvet (Fr Bernard Blankenhorn's being one, discussed in the pages that follow),
there has been no really major study of Chauvet's engagement with Heidegger
until the publication of this book. This is hardly surprising – Heidegger's
thought itself is still in the process of being understood and fully received – but
the breadth of Chauvet's own reach, and that of Heidegger's, are huge, and the
erudition required for such a study is not inconsiderable.

Does Chauvet succeed in pointing a way forward for theology to free itself
from its entanglement with metaphysics? The entanglement with metaphysics
is, at the very least, the entanglement with the history of philosophy as a history
of thinking in itself. There are marks in Chauvet's text which suggest that, in
bringing to the fore the entanglement with part of this history, he has done no
more than entangle theology with metaphysics' more contemporary ends: his
emphasis on *praxis*, as that mode of thinking derived from Hegel's confrontation
with Marx, does not, it would seem, free theology from metaphysics so much
as show the extent to which theology has accompanied metaphysics right up to
the end. We should recall that it is not Nietzsche who first proclaims the death

---

[3] Martin Heidegger, *Phänomenologie und Theologie* in *Wegmarken* (GA9), p. 76. 'Aber heute besteht
und wächst die Gefahr, daß die wissenschaftlich-technische Denkweise auf alle Gebiete des Lebens
sich ausbreitet.'
[4] Martin Heidegger, *Phänomenologie und Theologie* in *Wegmarken* (GA9), p. 76. 'Weil sie vermutlich
überhaupt nicht eine Wissenschaft sein darf.'

of God, but Hegel, in his discussion with the 'speculative Good Friday', an idea which Hegel introduces with his essay *Faith and Knowing* of the Jena years of 1802–3, developed further in the final sentence of the *Phänomenologie* as the 'Calvary of absolute Spirit'.[5]

It is Hegel's resolute and unswerving materialism, a materialism upon which Marx utterly depends and on which he builds (even while refusing ever adequately to acknowledge the debt), which drives the revolution in thinking that brings to an end any possibility of metaphysics speaking of a 'supersensible', a 'beyond' to being, and that inaugurates that period in the history of philosophy which glories in the triumph of becoming over being – which itself, marks the eclipse of the metaphysical talk of being as the absolute, as God, as First Cause, as what is most beingful in all things (all particular beings). Hegel's materialism inaugurates and completes the very epoch of absolute subjectivity that is the motor for Chauvet's thinking and the epoch which theology as a discipline has to confront. This epoch, which is also the epoch of the absolute triumph of the 'scientific-technological manner of thinking' is one in which theology itself will stand and fall, either by relegating itself to becoming no more than (yet another) social science, or by overcoming its scientific pretensions and turning back to its origins, free from the history of philosophy as metaphysics, and learning again to reflect on what it means to know and speak of faith in the triune God who reveals himself to man in the person of Jesus the Christ. In this we must applaud Chauvet, as having been so central a part of theology's desire to confront the demands of the age and to free itself from every metaphysical determination. In this Chauvet does not stand alone, but stands with those other French thinkers – Lacoste, Marion and others, who have taken these initial steps.

The research that appears in Hal St John's book has been a long-needed engagement of the deepest and most serious kind with Chauvet's thought. We could read this book as a confrontation with Chauvet, and at times, it would seem, that is how St John presents his case: but to do so would be a mistake. For even as Chauvet has not himself exhausted the engagement of sacramental theology either with the anxiety I have indicated marks its contemporary forms, or the challenges of scientific-technological thinking, so St John both shows what has been achieved and the direction in which theology, if it is to rise up to these challenges, needs to go. The care and perspicacity which St John

---

[5]   G. W. F. Hegel, *Glauben und Wissen*, Hamburg, Felix Meiner, 1962 (1802–3), p. 123f, citing B. Pascal, L. Brunschwicg (eds), *Pensées*, Paris, Hachette, 1897, p. 441. 'La nature est telle qu'elle *marque* partout un Dieu *perdu* et dans l'homme et hors de l'homme.' See also G. W. F. Hegel, *Phänomenologie des Geistes*, Hamburg, Felix Meiner, 1988 (1807), p. 531. 'Schädelstätte des absoluten Geistes.'

has brought to this task are a mark of the utmost respect for Chauvet's initial provocation, and should be read as such.

Is it, as both Chauvet and St John suggest, even possible to propose a non-metaphysical understanding of the Holy Eucharist? Under what name could it be described? Could we speak of transubstantiation and not speak metaphysically? Let us first ask: what guarantee does metaphysics offer theology, that put so many theologians in its thrall? Transubstantiation was a term forged to counter a Eucharistic heresy, and to show that there was a reasonable way to claim that there was an 'objective' presence of Christ in the Holy Eucharist. 'Objective' means, taken in one way, undeniable, and in another, 'universal'. 'Undeniable' does not mean 'shown by an invincible proof', but rather the opposite – that anything we wanted to say of the Holy Eucharist was consistent and at peace with the highest thinking of the age. 'Universal' meant only 'in every conceivable way' – speaking of the being of the Holy Eucharist in the broadest, highest, most general terms.

Transubstantiation received its fullest formal definition at the Council of Trent. This definition says: 'If anyone should deny that wonderful and singular conversion of the whole substance of the bread into the Body, and of the whole substance of the wine into the Blood – the species only of the bread and wine remaining – which conversion indeed the Catholic Church most aptly names transubstantiation, he should be anathema.'[6] Whatever else this canon says, it stresses that the word transubstantiation is not a doctrine, nor a dogma, nor a technical term of a theological science, but a way of naming.

As a name, it has come, especially in recent years, to signify either the anxiety that the presence of Jesus Christ in the sacrament of the altar is not understood to be sufficiently objective, or (and following Fr de Certeau's reading of Henri Cardinal de Lubac) it names precisely the opposite – the over-objectification of that presence in the 'physicality', the materialities, of the Holy Eucharist. The name transubstantiation first appeared in the earlier part of the twelfth century, perhaps in Tours, and its first official use was in 1215 at the Fourth Council of the Lateran, as the first of its 70 canons.[7] Because even in 1215 the language used

---

[6] Definitions of the Council of Trent, Session XIII, 11 October, 1551, Canon 2. 'Si quis negaverit mirabilem illam et singularem conversionem totius substantiæ palis in corpus, et totius substantiæ vini in sanguinem, manentibus dumtaxat speciebus panis et vini, quam quidem conversionem Catholica Ecclesia aptissime transsubstantiationem appellat, anathema sit.'

[7] Definitions of the Fourth Council of the Lateran, 11–30 November, 1215, Canon 1. 'Firmiter credimus et simpliciter confitemur . . . in [Ecclesia] qua idem ipse sacerdos est sacrificium Iesus Christus, cuius corpus et sanguis in sacramento altaris sub speciebus panis et vini veraciter continentur, transsubstantiatis pane in corpus, et vino in sanguinem potestate divina' ('Firmly we believe and simply we trust . . . in [the Church in] which there is the same priest and sacrifice, Jesus Christ, whose body and blood are truly contained in the sacrament of the altar under the species of bread and wine; the bread being transubstantiated by divine power into the body, and the wine into the blood').

speaks of substance and species, to which St Thomas Aquinas later added the Aristotelian twist of 'accidents',[8] the suspicion has always been that what is at issue is a kind of Eucharistic physics, a formal, scientific guarantee of the objectivity sought. Gary Macy, whose careful work on transubstantiation spans 30 years, has been an impressive and important historian of this name and of theologies of the Eucharist in general.[9] He has pointed out more than once that transubstantiation is not a unitary term, and names a whole family of understandings of the Holy Eucharist.

We should begin by understanding that the two objects of a metaphysical rendering of a metaphysical account of what transubstantiation names – undeniability, and universality – need to be abandoned for us really to understand the Holy Eucharist at all. For the truth of the materialities of the Holy Eucharist is such, that irrespective of what we who have faith *know* to be true (namely that Christ himself is fully and entirely present, body and blood, soul and divinity, in the Holy Eucharist *and in its very materialities*), because these materialities still *look and behave* like bread, *look and behave* like wine, the unbeliever is, and must always be, free, *not* to believe what we know and hold to be true. And secondly, what transubstantiation names can never be detached from its holy context, which is the sacred liturgy, for if the materialities of the Holy Eucharist are not marked by the reverence and sacrality which the sacred liturgy indicates for them, even when the sacrament is reserved in a tabernacle (on an altar, veiled, marked by a light, handled only by those wearing a stole and in sacred dress, etc.), then even if we who believe were to stumble across a consecrated host, not knowing that it had been consecrated, we could *ourselves* mistake it for mere bread, or at the very least be troubled by doubt as to its real nature, no matter how great our firmness of faith and clarity of resolution.

The three troublesome terms at the heart of the name transubstantiation are substance, species and accident. It is unsurprising that the word 'accident' made no appearance in 1215, but its absence from the Tridentine definition suggests an unwillingness formally to commit the Catholic Church to a use derived from Aristotle, and the need to connect what was said at Trent with the earlier formulation. Accident, *per accidens*, renders Aristotle's term *kata sumbebēkos*: 'with respect to that which falls out alongside and together with'. 'Accident', the accidental, is (thought in this way) simply 'the apparent', the way something

---

[8] Cf. St Thomas Aquinas, *Summa theologiæ*, IIIa, q. 77, art. 2, corp., *et passim*.
[9] See Gary Macy, *The Theologies of the Eucharist in the Early Scholastic Period*, Oxford, Clarendon Press, 1984; Gary Macy (ed.), *Treasures from the Storeroom: Medieval Religion and the Eucharist*, Collegeville, Pueblo/The Liturgical Press, 1999.

presents a face or mien of itself, such that this face is the inevitable and genuine face of what it *is*. In this sense, it says no more than the word 'species', the word employed both at Trent and in the Lateran canon. Species, from *specere*, to behold, indicates what is given to sight, namely the form, the appearance, the face or mien. Finally, if substance has a long history as 'that which underpins', Aristotle's *ousia*, at the same time it means no more than the being of a thing, what it *is*. Thought like this there is no particular commitment to metaphysical essence in the use of the word substance.

What is it that is metaphysical about the use of the word 'substance'? Precisely, that metaphysics goes out after the *whatness*, the 'quiddity', the 'very being' or inner 'essence' of the thing in question each time. It is this pursuit of the constant *whatness* – the whatness that is always there, in every form of the face, every look that the mien bears, that binds the appearance, the faces presented, of the materialities of the Holy Eucharist – these materialities that begin as bread and wine – to the 'inner being', the substance or essence, and that makes the 'doctrine' of transubstantiation appear like a pseudo-physics. For metaphysics itself goes out after the very objectivity that transubstantiation seems to guarantee: that in each case the *essence*, the inner being of a thing can be found out and exhibited, irrespective of the manner and place, the 'how', of its appearing. Essences are always the same, they are at the same time, universals. The secret 'promise' of an adequate 'doctrine' of transubstantiation is that it adequately discloses the objective, universal, truth of the Eucharist, such that it cannot, or should not, be doubted.

Except that the unbeliever, by definition, can never grant the objectivity of the presence of Christ, body and blood, soul and divinity, in the Holy Eucharist. Indeed, this is the very essence of the problem. For Christianity, to be authentic to God's own initiative of freedom, must defend and guarantee and even protect the unfaith of the unbeliever. To do otherwise is to act contrary to God's own action, in permitting freedom of will. And here lies the difficulty in every 'doctrine' of transubstantiation: its explanation of the objective presence of the Christ founders in the freedom of the unbeliever *not* to believe. Whereas the proof of real physics lies in a certain kind of testing, such that the strength of a bridge can be tested not just because it spans a river theoretically, but that it practically allows traffic to pass across it without failing, no such test exists for the materialities of the Holy Eucharist. St Thomas insists that it is by faith alone (*sola fide* – what better place for this phrase to originate than in a discussion of transubstantiation?), which is initiated by divine authority (and so not by the choice of the believer *to* believe), and therefore *not* by means of the senses, that

Christ's body and blood are truly in the sacrament.[10] We will not know for sure whether the Eucharist has saved us until the end of time, and we stand before the judgment throne of God. Metaphysics, however well it speaks of essences and universals, cannot, it seems, always help us in matters of faith and final judgment.

And here is where those who reject the name of transubstantiation as a metaphysical name seem to fall. For, it would seem, that when we say that Christ really is present in the materialities of the Holy Eucharist, it depends in some way on who 'we' are. And inasmuch as it depends on who we are, to the modern, materialistic mind, it seems that it depends *for its very truth* on our will and subjective disposition. We modern Christians so often interpret faith, belief, as 'what I will to be the case'. But in the case of the Holy Eucharist, this is not so. For if Christ really is present in the materialities of the Holy Eucharist, body and blood, soul and divinity, then it depends on *whether* I believe it or not, not one jot. The Holy Eucharist *is*, which means, *makes present*, this reality *not* because I, or anyone else, should or do believe it, but because, and *only* because, *God in His Christ has revealed and commanded that it be so*. It depends on who 'we' are for recognition of its truth, but not for the truth itself. Its truth, its very being, does not depend on me, or us, at all. It depends for its very truth on God alone. When Jesus Christ said 'this is my body', 'this is my blood', these things were revealed by the one who is alone the way to the Father and so who alone knows and wills what the Father knows and wills – and that is *all* that is required. St Thomas Aquinas says no less, when he says that it is by the infinite power of God (and so by no other means) that these appearances of bread and wine *are* (here is the reference to being, *are*, because they *have the power to make present*) the body and blood, soul and divinity of Jesus the Christ, the Only Son of the Father.[11] God says that this is so, and such is God's power, it *is* so, and we who have been given grace by the divine initiative to believe, *know* that it is so, and witness to it accordingly.

If the truth of the perfect presence of Christ in the materialities of the Holy Eucharist does not, in any way depend on my will, my subjective disposition, or what I desire, then how am I to be with the Eucharist, and who am I before it? In the Mediaeval schools a simple set of questions made this relation plain. The questions began as follows: 'if the sacred host were thrown into the mire, is the

---

[10] St Thomas Aquinas, *Summa Theologiæ*, IIIa, q. 75, art. 1, corp. 'Verum corpus Christi et sanguinem esse in hoc sacramento, non sensu deprehendi potest, sed sola fide, quæ auctoritati divinæ innititur.'

[11] See St Thomas Aquinas, *Summa Theologiae*, IIIa, Q. 77, a. 1, resp.

body of Christ thereby dishonoured?' The surprising answer to this question was 'no'. We find in St Thomas Aquinas the response that even in the case of a sacred host cast into the mire, 'neither does this turn to the detriment of the dignity of Christ, who willed to be crucified by sinners without detriment to his dignity'.[12]

The corollary is not, however, that it *does not matter* if the sacred species is cast into the mire. Indeed it does, and we who know what the sacred species is, and who have been given by grace and baptism understanding to recognize and know the divine presence in the Holy Eucharist, are required to defend the dignity of the body of Christ and his abiding presence on earth, even to the forfeit of our own bodies and blood, souls and mortality. If an unbeliever were to attempt to desecrate the sacred species, we should have to oppose that desecration, even to the forfeiture of our lives. We must witness in our very lives to what is revealed through this holy sacrament.

There is a connection indicated in the text of the canon of the Fourth Lateran Council that stands only in the background at Trent: the connection is between transubstantiation and the priesthood of Christ. Neither is intelligible without the other: for if it is by the divine command alone that this bread and wine becomes the body and blood of Christ, that divine command is repeated and effected by the action of priesthood (and so by all ordained into the priesthood of Christ). The priest speaks, and so fulfils the command, of the consecration of the sacred species, in the person of the Christ who is both priest and victim. What is required to understand this is not a metaphysics, but rather our own insertion into the revelation which is given in Adam, and fulfilled in Christ, and which the Sacred Liturgy in its ongoing action continues to extend over all time and all places on the earth. Here we find the need to understand, not the meaning of the words 'substance', 'accident' and 'species', but rather the how, the manner of the being, of Christ, the new Adam who overcomes the necessary fault of the old, who fulfils and completes the eternal priesthood of Melchisedech, he whom the inheritors of Levi, the priests and bishops, make present in the life of the Church. Here we can understand the whole history of revelation, not only as a theology bound to the cross before God, but even as bound to the cross as the representation of the tree of life, that original and promised life before God which is our origin and destiny: eternal life before the throne of the divine and triune God in his majesty.

---

[12] St Thomas Aquinas, *Summa Theologiæ*, IIIa, q. 80, art. 3, ad. 3 'Nec hoc vergit in detrimentum dignitatis Christi, qui voluit a peccatoribus crucifigi absque diminutione suæ dignitatis.'

For this a quite different kind of theology is required to any entanglement with metaphysics, a theology rooted in the interpretation of the whole history of revelation, a theology recognizing its former attachment to, and now its being detached from, metaphysics; a theology where the understanding of being has nothing to do with employing the word 'being' as a predicate for God. Indeed, 'on this point one would have to establish wholly new distinctions and delimitations'.[13] It is for the sake of these wholly new distinctions and delimitations that this book lies open in your hands.

---

[13] Martin Heidegger, *The Reply to the Third Question at the Seminar in Zurich, 1951* in *Seminare* (GA15), p. 437. 'Hier braucht es ganz neue Unterscheidungen und Abgrenzungen.'

Foreword

This book began as a PhD thesis at the University of London's Heythrop College. My initial research interest was driven by a desire to explore the theological roots of *caritas* (charity). This general idea became more sharply focused into an investigation into Eucharistic presence and how this, conceived after metaphysics, may contribute to a postmodern understanding of charity.

A version of Chapter 4 was published in 2007 under the title *Being-in-Love: an Enquiry Into the Ontological Foundation of Ethics*[1] and Chapter 5 in 2011 under the title *Obeying the Voice of the Lord . . . Sacrifice and Worship.*[2]

This foreword gives me a very welcome opportunity to express my thanks. Especially to Dr Laurence Paul Hemming who has been unflinching in his support and rigorous in his supervision from the very beginning. Likewise to Dr Susan Parsons for her enthusiasm and encouragement. Thanks are due to Dr M. Lourdes and Cherrie Maya for their contributions to the ideas developed here. The book is much improved for the efforts of these three, but all remaining mistakes are my own. I am indebted to the staff at Heythrop College and the British Province of the Society of Jesus who have facilitated my studies in various ways.

[1] Hal St John, 'Being-in-Love: An Enquiry Into the Ontological Foundation of Ethics', in *Studies in Christian Ethics,* 20 December (2007), pp. 345–63.
[2] Hal St John, 'Obeying the Voice of the Lord . . . Sacrifice and Worship', in *Usus Antiquior,* Vol. 2, No.1, January (2011), pp. 13–31.

Introduction

Catholic orthodoxy, in particular within Eucharistic theology, does not require a metaphysical God to sanction and legitimize its various claims. In Eucharistic theology, until recently, orthodoxy has been defended by an appeal to metaphysics. God as First Cause produces grace which in turn is mediated to humanity, following the consecration of the Eucharistic species, through the Blessed Sacrament.[1] With Nietzsche's exclamation *God is dead!*,[2] which he understands to be the basic explanation of our contemporary condition, this sequence of causes however is turned upon its head. Now that 'the holiest and the mightiest thing the world has ever possessed has bled to death under our knives',[3] God, metaphysically construed, no longer exists to originate grace and the stark if not disquieting question of the future of the sacraments raises itself. If God, as the principle of causality and originator of grace, is no longer alive to ensure or guarantee its bestowal, from whence does 'grace' emerge and do the sacraments in fact have a future?

While Martin Heidegger does not treat the subject of the sacraments in any of his writings, since for him 'philosophical research is and remains atheism',[4] nevertheless he offers theology a way forward beyond metaphysics that suggests

---

[1] B. Blankenhorn OP, maintains that 'Aquinas clearly teaches that sacramental efficacy essentially involves an instrumental action fully subordinated and dependent on the divine principal cause' [The Instrumental Causality of the Sacraments: Thomas Aquinas and Louis-Marie Chauvet, *Nova et Vetera*, English Edition, Vol. 4, No. 2 (2006), p. 263].

[2] F. Nietzsche, *The Gay Science* (2007), p. 120.

[3] F. Nietzsche, *Die Fröhliche Wissenschaft* (1999), p. 141. 'Das Heiligste und Mächtigste, was die Welt bisher besaß, es ist unter unseren Messern verblutet.'

[4] M. Heidegger, *Prolegomena zur Geschichte des Zeitbegriffs* (GA20) (1979), pp. 109–10. 'Philosophische Forschung ist und bleibt Atheismus.' In *Heidegger's Atheism* (2002) Hemming observes that, in spite of Heidegger's apparent indifference towards the question of God, 'there is hardly a text of Heidegger's, long or short, that does not mention God, gods or divinity' (p. 2).

'grace's' provenance and raises the possibility of a future for the sacraments. The key question directing this research is whether, following Heidegger and taking theology in this direction, it is possible to preserve an orthodox view of sacraments. This book argues that it *is* possible to be orthodox following the death of God without conceding anything to the secularizing force of current post-metaphysical thinking. Sacraments, it is maintained, do not need a metanarrative, with 'its functors, its great hero, its great dangers, its great voyages, its great goal',[5] to have legitimacy in the wake of 'the crisis of metaphysical philosophy'.[6] This research is an investigation into where sacramental legitimacy resides once the grand narrative, with 'its great hero' the metaphysical God, has lost its credibility.[7]

Having delineated the field of enquiry in these general terms, my question may be articulated as follows: do the canons of Catholic orthodoxy disintegrate when surveyed from the domain that opens up in the overcoming of metaphysics, when God as the cornerstone (*causa sui*) upholding the universe of beings is unchained causally from beings and held thus no longer to be a being among beings, even if the highest?[8] If contemporary ways of thought are held to be post-metaphysical we might rephrase the question: is it possible to be orthodox today, or do the long-standing claims of orthodoxy need to be reconsidered afresh to take into account, if not to accommodate, a post-metaphysical view of the world? These questions presuppose orthodoxy to be a metaphysical construction which, as such, deconstructs with the implosion of onto-theology. This research does not rely on such presuppositions but rather enquires into the question: if orthodoxy is not inextricably bound up with metaphysics then where are its roots to be found?

---

[5] J.-F. Lyotard, *La Condition postmoderne: rapport sur le savoir* (1979), p. 7, 'ses foncteurs, le grand héros, les grand périls, les grands périples et le grand but'.

[6] J.-F. Lyotard, *La Condition postmoderne: rapport sur le savoir* (1979), p. 7, 'la crise de la philosophie métaphysique'.

[7] J.-F. Lyotard, *La Condition postmoderne: rapport sur le savoir* (1979), p. 63, 'a perdu sa crédibilité'. What we have here, echoing Lyotard's words in his reflection on the *la condition postmoderne*, is 'a process of delegitimation fuelled by the demand for legitimation itself' [(1979), p. 65, 'un procès délégitimation qui a pour moteur l'exigence de légitimation'].

[8] Heidegger understands the being of God to survive after the collapse of its metaphysical construals for 'when one proclaims "God" the altogether "highest value", this is a degradation of God's essence' [M. Heidegger, *Brief über den Humanismus (1946)* in *Wegmarken*, (GA9), p. 349. 'Wenn man vollends "Gott" als "den höchsten Wert" verkündet, so ist das eine Herabsetzung des Wesens Gottes']. The evaluation of God, Hemming concurs, 'is itself a devaluation of a most dreadful kind' (2005, p. 240). Negative theologians do not rely on metaphysical constructions in their reflections on God's essence which is not really an 'is' or 'essence' at all. We will come to see how the *nihil* of *das Nichts* allows God to be glimpsed (not evaluated) in the excessive plenitude of his not-being. It is in this sense that we might say that God 'is' not.

To examine this question, the thoughts of a theologian are explored who, following an exegesis of Heidegger's writings, questions the aptness of orthodox doctrines to denominate and thereby interpret modern religious experience. This book examines how the French theologian Louis-Marie Chauvet has deployed Heidegger's writings to overcome what he believes to be the foundational thinking that has been an impediment to the development of sacramental theology in recent times. Chauvet presents himself because, it has been claimed, he 'is a major representative of a significant theological movement'[9] which attempts to think through the question of sacramentality within the framework of an emerging postmodern theology.[10] In a review of the English translation of his major work *Symbole et Sacrament* Joseph Martos highlights Chauvet's importance and place within the universe of sacramental theologians when he says of the text:

> It is the first radically different sacramental theology to come out of Europe since the existential-phenomenological transformation of neo-scholastic thinking wrought by Rahner and Schillebeeckx over thirty years ago, and for that reason alone it deserves serious attention.[11]

Chauvet does not claim to be offering a new interpretation of Heidegger's writings for his concern is theological. He wants to apply Heidegger's thought (in particular Heidegger's critique of onto-theology) to 'a theology which opens up a *sacramental reinterpretation*, initially modest but ultimately global in its potential extension, of what it means to *lead a Christian life*'.[12] His project is one that has been broadly accepted by mainstream European sacramental theologians witnessed at a recent major conference in 2001 on sacramental presence organized and hosted by the University of Leuven in Belgium. However, it will become clearer as the research unfolds that, in dismissing negative theology generally, Chauvet foregoes the prospect of understanding Heidegger in greater depth, as one who has thought through *das Nichts* and who thinks from out of this region.

It seems reasonable to assume that Chauvet's interpretation of Heidegger will be constrained and coloured by the intellectual milieu within which he

---

[9] B. Blankenhorn OP, The Instrumental Causality of the Sacraments: Thomas Aquinas and Louis-Marie Chauvet, *Nova et Vetera*, English Edition, Vol. 4, No. 2 (2006), p. 257.

[10] Jean-Luc Marion's *God Without Being* is offered as an example of Heidegger's growing influence on postmodern theology. Although he does not deal with sacramental theology to the same technical degree it provides a context within which Chauvet's theologizing can take place.

[11] J. Martos, *Book Reviews*, Horizons, 23 No. 2, Fall 1996, p. 345.

[12] L.-M. Chauvet, *Symbole et Sacrament: Un relecture sacramentelle de l'existence chrétienne* (1987), pp. 7–8. '... une théologie qui permette une *relecture sacramentelle*, partielle de son point de vue, mais globale quant à son extension, *de l'ensemble de l'existence chrétienne*' (emphasis in original).

conducts his researches so that the context determines (to some degree) the text. One possible approach therefore might have been to examine how Heidegger's thought has been received within French academic circles and then to extrapolate any findings to Chauvet himself. This possibility has been resisted for the simple reason that Chauvet, although he is not advancing a unique interpretation of Heidegger, nevertheless works directly from Heidegger's texts and relies very little on secondary sources in his interpretation. Chauvet in fact struggles to extricate himself from a conventional French hermeneutic of Heidegger. This observation is alluded-to in Vincent J. Miller's review of *Symbole et Sacrament* when he writes of Chauvet's 'purely optimistic reading of the *later* (my emphasis) Heidegger' with its tendency to overlook 'Heidegger's concern about the fallenness of traditions'.[13]

For instance, Chauvet repeatedly makes use of anthropological insights into human nature and the interaction between human beings. To add an empirical dimension to his otherwise philosophical theology, he appeals to ethnological data to corroborate his thesis that the giving of gifts from one human being to another functions as the glue binding individuals into social groups. Chauvet believes that 'the system of symbolic payments in traditional societies . . . *reveals our own archaisms*',[14] if not something primordial about the human condition. The exchange of objects that have neither use nor economic value mirrors the existential sharing of one person's '*lack-in-being*' with another's. This is because *it is subjects who exchange themselves* through the object; who exchange, he says, *under the agency of the Other*, their *lack-in-being* and thus come before each other in the middle of their absence deepened by their exchange, in the middle of their difference experienced radically as otherness because of their exchange.[15]

Chauvet sees nothing incongruous about aligning Heidegger's understanding of being, which in his interpretation speaks of an absence implicit in presence, with anthropology's characterization of human nature. In this he shows the extent to which he has come under the influence of the French convention of interpreting Heidegger's writings as philosophical anthropology or anthropological humanism and so fails to see Heidegger's own challenge to social anthropology. Chauvet's appeal to anthropology is not an innovation for,

---

[13] Vincent J. Miller, *An Abyss at the Heart of Mediation: Louis-Marie Chauvet's Fundamental Theology of Sacramentality*, Horizons, 24/2 (1997), p. 240.

[14] L.-M. Chauvet, *Symbole et Sacrament*, p. 112. '. . . le système de prestations symboliques des sociétés archaïques . . . *révélateur de nos propres archaïsmes* . . .'

[15] L.-M. Chauvet, *Symbole et Sacrament*, p. 107. We will see in subsequent chapters how Chauvet uses this model of exchange to rescript the meaning of Eucharistic presence.

as Tom Rockmore shows in his *Heidegger and French Philosophy*, the French have consistently tried to reduce Heidegger's writings[16] to a kind of philosophical anthropology. Heidegger, Rockmore forewarns, is neither anthropological or metaphysical, nor a post-metaphysical humanist, in fact not a humanist at all; and the French reading, based as it was on the letter but not the spirit of the theory, misperceived 'a similarity between it and Heidegger's nonhumanistic thought'.[17]

Chauvet could have detected Heidegger's position with respect to anthropology (and humanism) from a reading of *Being and Time*, a text to which Chauvet refers on only one occasion in his major work *Symbole et Sacrament*. Heidegger states here that anthropology fails to give 'an unequivocal and ontologically adequate' answer to the question about the *kind of Being* which belongs to those entities which we ourselves are. These ontological foundations, for Heidegger, can never be disclosed by subsequent hypotheses derived from empirical material, but they are always 'there' already, even when that empirical material simply gets *collected*. If positive research fails to see these foundations and holds them to be self-evident, this by no means proves that they are not basic or that they are not problematic in a more radical sense than 'any thesis of positive science can ever be'.[18]

Heidegger maintains that since ethnology operates within 'definite preliminary conceptions and interpretations of human Dasein in general',[19] it can make no contribution to fundamental ontology; it merely recapitulates what previously has been 'ontically discovered'.[20] Chauvet has not heeded Heidegger's warning that the scientific structure of anthropology is today thoroughly questionable and needs to be attacked in new ways, ways which must be sourced from the 'problematic of ontology'.[21]

Structure of this book

In Chapter 1 Chauvet's direct citations from Heidegger's corpus of writings are examined and re-situated in the texts from which they were drawn. This allows

---

[16] Especially Heidegger's *Letter on Humanism* which was written in response to a series of questions formulated by Jean Beaufret, one of Heidegger's earliest interpreters in France.

[17] T. Rockmore, *Heidegger and French Philosophy . . . Humanism, Antihumanism and Being*, Routledge (1995), p. 188.

[18] M. Heidegger, *Sein und Zeit* (GA2) (1962), p. 50, 'je eine These der positiven Wissenschaft sein kann'.

[19] M. Heidegger, *Sein und Zeit* (GA2) (1962), p. 51, 'bestimmten Vorbegriffen und Auslegungen vom menschlichen Dasein überhaupt'.

[20] M. Heidegger, *Sein und Zeit* (GA2) (1962), p. 51, 'des ontisch Entdeckten'.

[21] M. Heidegger, *Sein und Zeit* (GA2) (1962), p. 45, 'ontologischen Problematik'.

Heidegger's original meaning to be glimpsed. With this in mind, Chauvet's reading is appraised to evaluate whether Chauvet has arrived at an adequate interpretation. An alternative reading of those writings of Heidegger, pertinent to Chauvet's argument, is then presented.

In Chapter 2 the contours of Chauvet's sacramental theology, starting from his reading of Heidegger, is sketched. This exercise brings to the foreground other possible starting points for an alternative sacramental theology premised on a more inflected reading of Heidegger. Chapter 2 involves a consideration of Henri de Lubac's *Corpus Mysticum* which, in charting the development of Eucharistic devotion since the Middle Ages, highlights St Augustine's perspective that became obfuscated in the Church's reaction to the Berengarian controversy. It is shown how, for Chauvet, the overcoming of metaphysics implies the recovery of the Augustinian tradition and the symbolic imagination. Chauvet looks to Heidegger's discourse on the fourfold (*das Geviert*) to justify philosophically this rekindling of the symbolic approach to the sacraments.

Chapter 3 explores in further detail the region of *das Nichts* which Chapter 1 identified as a key area in Heidegger's thought glanced over perfunctorily by Chauvet. The assertion, which this chapter endeavours to corroborate, that Heidegger was influenced in demonstrable ways by Otto, permits the conclusion that Heidegger's writings on *das Nichts* have to do with divinity and as such have an application to worship generally and Eucharistic theology in particular. This becomes especially relevant in Chapter 5 where, drawing on my reading of Heidegger, it is suggested that post-metaphysical thinking supports orthodoxy rather than subverts it. The question Chapter 3 sets out to answer is whether, following a close reading of Rudolph Otto, Heidegger's *das Nichts* and Otto's *das Heilige*, as the Wholly Other, speak from out of a common domain, the mystery of being.

Chapter 4 aims to demonstrate where my reading of Heidegger might lead in respect of established Catholic teaching. It offers a way forward showing how, in fact, what Heidegger pointed to can be taken up, even without self-consciously doing so. Pope Benedict's first encyclical, *Deus Caritas Est*, is read closely to establish whether it is congruous with Heidegger's thought with a particular emphasis on ethics. If it can be established that Heidegger's philosophy is consistent with Catholic teaching we will receive a first confirmation that orthodoxy need not be lost or re-inscribed, as Chauvet maintains, to accommodate a post-metaphysical view of the world. This will provide a basis for the need to reconsider how Heidegger's thought, correctly understood, can in fact be deployed as a propaedeutic to sacramental discourse.

Chapter 5 draws together the strands of the preceding chapters to revisit the question of ecclesial symbolism. It relies heavily on Heidegger's writings and suggests, through a consideration of sacrifice, a way forwards for a genuine Eucharistic theology. Heidegger's thoughts on death and *das Nichts* allow Eucharistic presence to be conceived in an orthodox way after metaphysics.

1

Chauvet and Heidegger

In the Introduction it was suggested that one way to test the central thesis of this book, such that the claims of orthodoxy are sufficiently well grounded to survive the death of God as 'moral God' or as a being metaphysically construed, is to examine the work of an influential Catholic theologian, Louis-Marie Chauvet, who takes the opposite view, namely that the doctrines constituting Catholic orthodoxy cannot survive the intensive glare of postmodern scrutiny. His position is no more clearly set out than in his suspicion of the concept of substance which he claims, with the connected doctrine of transubstantiation, is no longer apt to denominate the event that occurs in the consecration of the Eucharistic species. This book, although taking seriously Chauvet's claim, nevertheless demonstrates that it is grounded on a misreading of Martin Heidegger, a thinker whose writings help to articulate postmodernity's self-understanding. What we show here, against Chauvet's counterargument, is that transubstantiation, a later name for a doctrine that even Jesus' earliest disciples themselves found hard to accept,[1] nevertheless expresses theologically the integral content of Eucharistic presence. When that which comes to presence in the Eucharistic moment is understood phenomenologically, as the outcome of the holy's call resounding from the formless void of the nothing, not only are traditional doctrines reaffirmed in the light of mankind's earliest and therefore primordial experiences but, in addition, the event of our salvation is concretely realized *now* in the everyday circumstances of our present lives. It is no longer postponed to a *later* after-life. In other words, acceptance of transubstantiation opens up the possibility of a present existential transformation foregone when it is deemed too hard to accept.

---

[1] Jn 6.60.

This chapter examines how Chauvet arrives at his conclusions by assessing his reading of the German philosopher, Martin Heidegger, whose writings underpin Chauvet's sacramental theology. In showing that Chauvet has missed something essential to Heidegger's thought, Chauvet's theological conclusions, for example, that the sacraments require reinterpretation after the demise of grand narratives and with the retrocession of a metaphysical God, become questionable. Our proposal, that orthodoxy does not require a metaphysical God to guarantee its claims, begins to look plausible following the demythologization of Chauvet's thought. It gives support to Jean-Luc Marion when he says:

> the Christian religion does not think God starting from the *causa sui*, because it does not think God starting from the cause, or within the theoretical space defined by metaphysics.[2]

and to Bossuet's assertion that:

> our God . . . is infinitely above that first Cause and prime mover known by philosophers.[3]

To accomplish the aim this chapter sets itself the main headings Chauvet formulates in the early stages of *Symbole et Sacrement* to interpret key themes from Heidegger's writings, will be reinvoked to give a recognizable structure to the enquiry. The direct citations Chauvet relies upon to support his exegesis will be taken and re-situated in the particular texts of Heidegger's from which they were extracted. Texts altogether overlooked by Chauvet, but which nonetheless may contribute to an understanding of the theme being discussed, will also be considered. By this method the extent and success of Chauvet's appropriation of Heidegger's thought will be determined in the light of my own understanding of Heidegger's writings.

Before this can be done, however, it is necessary to present briefly Chauvet's account of the putative metaphysical bias (a by-product of scholasticism) germane to present-day sacramental theology. In so doing it will become clear why Chauvet turns to Heidegger's writings on the overcoming of metaphysics to unfold his post-metaphysical sacramental theology.

---

[2] J.-L. Marion, *Dieu Sans L'Être*, p. 57, 'la religion chrétienne ne pense pas Dieu à partir de la *causa sui*, parce qu'elle ne le pense pas à partir de la cause, ni à l'intérieur de l'espace théorique défini par la métaphysique.' (Unless otherwise stated italicized words in a footnote citation reflect emphases in the original text.)

[3] J.-L. Marion, *Dieu Sans L'Être*, p. 57, ' notre Dieu [. . .] est infiniment au-dessus de la Cause première et de ce premier moteur que les philosophes ont connu . . .'

1.1 Chauvet's critique of St Thomas Aquinas'
Platonic presuppositions

The initial question directing Chauvet's enquiry is how the category 'cause' came to be used by the Scholastics (in particular Thomas Aquinas) to think theologically about the term 'grace' in the setting of the believer's sacramental relation with God. What thought processes lay behind the belief that God's sacramental presence as 'grace' could somehow be engineered by human ingenuity or conjured up simply by mortal intention?

Chauvet begins a tentative answer by demonstrating that the philosophical traditions since Socrates, which set the parameters within which the theological researches of St Thomas were conducted, contained disguised and therefore unchallenged assumptions. The Scholastics were unable to think independently of these onto-theological presumptions while they continued to think within a traditional philosophical frame. This inability to step back into a region from whence these otherwise invisible presuppositions or biases would come into view, gave these thinkers a family resemblance allowing us to speak of the metaphysical.

Perhaps the most significant unexamined presumption inhering in these traditions is that the condition of mutual and ever open exchange, required for the beloved to be loved by the lover, is ruled out by Socrates (and by extension those thinking within the Western tradition). The notion of the good as permanently incomplete is anathema in the logic of platonic discourse. Fleeting pleasures, such as love and joy, are set in opposition to the permanency and perdurance of 'existence' (*ousia*) because, as passing states, they never arrive at a destination being continuously in 'process' (*genesis*) or underway. Unconcerned with a higher *telos* they do not reach a final resolution within the limited universe of human ideas. Unbounded by anthropomorphizing categories of ordinary human thinking that confer existence to being, they are thereby without limits and unconstrained by the finite. Escaping the grasp of the entitative they flourish precisely by being non-existent, no-thing or not-being. For Plato however, any thought which fails to arrive at a finite term, by virtue of which it is invested with a final significance or crowned with the laurel-wreath of existence, is altogether unthinkable. Guy Lafon interprets Plato, Chauvet states, to say:

> The infinite is the enemy; if humankind is to survive, it must be wiped out.[4]

---

[4]   L.-M. Chauvet, *Symbole et Sacrement*, p. 29. 'L'infini, voilà l'ennemi: pour vivre, il faut l'abattre.'

Chauvet, following Eberhard Jüngel, claims that this project, the elimination of the infinite, the unbounded, the limitless, is the premise (if not the ultimate idea) of metaphysics which characterizes itself as theo-onto-logical. *The elimination of the infinite is the forgotten basis of Western thought.* As such the infinite's subtle and near-undetectable influence, rumbling underground as faintly audible background noise, occasionally breaking through the roar of ordinary living, must be guarded against at all times.

We will come to see that for Chauvet the way to break down this defensive strategy against incursions of the infinite into human thinking is to think beyond metaphysics. Thinking conducted within the realm of symbols will, for Chauvet, push the infinite into the foreground once again driving subterranean supernaturalism out into the open: what before was a barely detectable murmur becomes now a clearly discernable voice. In short, symbols for Chauvet will allow a reinstatement of the infinite; they will revive what Western thinking has conspired so determinately to eliminate; they will allow a recalling of what has been forgotten since the dawn of Western civilization; they will enrichen contemporary understandings of what constitutes the real. Chauvet cites Lafon to support this position:

> [there are] happenings, such as love, and joy, and pleasure, which do not produce existence or come to an end in the sense of a distinct term. There are many other realities of this nature and these all attest in one way or another to the presence of the symbolic order.[5]

Inextricably bound up with Platonic categories of thought, St Thomas could not think in any other way than the metaphysical. For him every impermanent condition was *negatively* valorized so that, inevitably, the characteristic dignity of a 'passing' that is also a 'becoming' passed by unnoticed being pushed underground. In place of this fundamental desire to eliminate as far as possible whatever pertains to a becoming without end, the Good, as achieved perfection, self-sufficiency or that which is perfectly measurable and proportioned, is favoured. Everything falls under the dominion of 'value', of calculation, of the cause that measures, of what is '*worth more*', of what offers more advantages and greater usefulness. These distinctions arise when

---

[5] Citation from Guy Lafon, *Esquisses pour un christianisme*, p. 88, in L.-M. Chauvet, *Symbole et Sacrement*, p. 30, '[il est] des avènements qui ne sont pas producteurs d'existence, qui ne s'achèvent pas dans l'existence comme dans un terme: l'amour est de ceux-là, est aussi la joie et le plaisir, et sans doute bien d'autres avènements, qui tous, chacun à sa façon, attestent la présence du champ symbolique'.

our wisdom and intellect are oriented towards the Good understood in this narrow metaphysical way.

This failure in St Thomas' thinking accounts, Chauvet contends, for the thomist emphasis on causality and St Thomas' mechanical understanding of the sacraments. It answers the question Chauvet was eager to answer: why is the category 'cause' singled out for privileged consideration when the sacramental relation with God through grace is discussed in (scholastic) theology? With the devaluation, subordination or suppression of '*genesis*', occurring when being is expressed solely and exclusively in terms of '*ousia*', things can not merely 'be' as such in the fulsomeness of uncompromised possibility. To exist at all they must have a reason or a cause or else be held out as no thing at all.[6]

In his writings on the sacraments St Thomas oscillates between two positions: on the one hand, sacraments merely signal what is present and on the other they actually cause the presence they signify. Chauvet describes St Thomas' movement between these two poles in his various writings and finally asserts that Thomas' great achievement in sacramental theology is found in his attempt to reduce (insofar as this could be done at all) the heterogeneity between sign and cause, a reduction which nevertheless acknowledges the impossibility of a complete homogeneity.

Although, Chauvet admits, Thomas' understanding of sacramental causality underwent several important changes between the composition of the *Commentary on the Sentences* (1254–6) and that of the Third Part of the *Summa Theologica* (1272–3) nevertheless, St Thomas was unable to step back from the unconscious assumptions of platonic discourse with their neglect of the transient, the fleeting, the passing. This position is best illustrated in St Thomas' later claim that the sacraments 'cause grace' if only *per aliquem modum* (in a certain way). Even though St Thomas purports to be using 'cause' in an analogous sense Chauvet nevertheless concludes that scholastic terminology leads to a *technical or productionist* view of Eucharistic presence: sacramental signs and symbols cause the grace they simultaneously signify. Having described the broad range of interpretations of the meaning of sacrament in St Thomas' writings, from pure sign to efficient causality, Chauvet moves (almost in frustration it seems) to bind St Thomas to an exclusively *metaphysical* position: the sacraments are for Aquinas, according to Chauvet, a form of 'technology' that manufacture grace within a productionist scheme.

---

[6]   Heidegger's interest in the term *das Nichts* arises precisely because it allows phenomena to present themselves to human understanding not as manipulable useful things but as things that exist in their own right without reference to disfiguring metaphysical structures of significance.

Following this move,[7] the stage is now set in *Symbole et Sacrement* for a conversation between a traditional scholastic view of sacraments, with its presumed metaphysical bias, and Heidegger's philosophy which, addressing its reader from a region beyond metaphysics, provides a space for him to step back into so that the possibility of metaphysics' overcoming opens up. In other words Heidegger's thought offers the promise of thinking sacraments outside the productionist scheme of representation which, perpetuating the platonic tradition of thinking within anthropomorphizing categories, brings the infinite to rest in a higher *telos* conferring upon it a final significance. Aspects of Eucharistic presence, formerly concealed and covered up because passing silently by without going out and alighting upon a fixed term, are potentially now accessible as a result of the perspective presented by Heidegger's philosophy. These aspects have evaded theological consideration and, as such, have been unthinkable until now. In short, Heidegger's thought promises to extricate the infinite from its representations which paradoxically, in revealing the nature of the divine, nevertheless muffle God's call more than they amplify it. His thinking promises to release the holy from scholastic confinement so that, escaping the snares of the fowler, it is at last free to effect the final and definitive transfiguration of everything, reviving what is withered, replenishing what is spent and refreshing what is exhausted.

Chauvet sets out his reading of Heidegger under various headings in Part I of chapter Two of *Symbole et Sacrement*, in a section bearing the title *Overcoming Metaphysics According to Heidegger*. The following discussion concentrates on:

- *Thinking Metaphysics: Not as Fall but as an Event* and
- *Overcoming Metaphysics: An Unachievable Task*[8]

as these offer a glimpse into the philosophical underpinnings of Chauvet's theology of sacramental presence.

1.2 Thinking Metaphysics: Not as Fall but as an Event

We have seen what metaphysics means in a theological sacramental setting, that is sacraments in the productionist scheme are not merely the sign of something

---

7 It is outside the scope of this research to present an alternative interpretation of St Thomas' thinking on the sacraments. Others have critically assessed Chauvet's interpretation of Aquinas, for instance Bernhard Blankenhorn, OP, in his article *The Instrumental Causality of the Sacraments: Thomas Aquinas and Louis-Marie Chauvet* [*Nova et Vetera*, English Edition, Vol. 4, No. 2 (2006), p. 263].

8 L.-M. Chauvet, *Symbole et Sacrement*, p. 52f. 'Le Dépassement de la Métaphysique Selon Heidegger . . . Penser la métaphysique non comme une faute, mais comme un événement . . . Dépasser la métaphysique: une tâche inachevable . . .'

that presents itself of its own accord but are rather instead the very cause of the presence that comes to be eventualized in the signification. Causality finds its principle in the establishment of a 'stasis' over the restless fluctuation of otherwise unresolved existence. We must now ask ourselves the question what metaphysics signifies in philosophy, with particular reference to the thought of Martin Heidegger.

In his *Introduction to 'What is Metaphysics?'* Heidegger makes the same enquiry:

> . . . the question 'What is metaphysics?' might well remain what is most needed of all that is necessary for thought . . . in order to prepare the transition from representational thinking to *das andenkende Denken* (a thinking that recalls), nothing becomes more necessary than the question: What is metaphysics?[9]

Tracing its genealogy back to Greece, Chauvet asserts that metaphysics came to prevail at the same time as the forgetting of the ontological difference, that is the difference between being (*genesis*) and entities (*ousia*). But this is a forgetting that we have forgotten for over 25 centuries and as a result we are incapable of considering being in any other way than as entity. For us 'that which is' and 'the being the entity is' constitute the real. The notion of being as entity is incontrovertibly self-evident for us. This is because metaphysics considers entities in their entirety so that being is defined as the *common trait of all entities*. By virtue of this common property everything becomes fundamentally identical.

Being in its entitative form creates a unity, that is a togetherness of all beings taken, not as beings in themselves, but as representations. Metaphysics names that which has been reduced to the same in a movement away from being and into existence. All things participating in this flight from the concretion of being take on a similar character since being in its difference and uniqueness gets concealed beneath entities. Being lies at the base of (*sub-jectum*) or stands under (*sub-stans*) all of our everyday representations. This homologizing tendency reduces the rich variety of heterogeneous difference into something bland and instantly recognizable. This levelling or flattening or reduction of being is the desecration metaphysics names. It comes to be as a phenomenon

---

[9] M. Heidegger, *Einleitung zu: 'Was Ist Metaphysik?'* in *Wegmarken* (GA9), p. 371 and p. 381. '. . . bleibt die Frage "Was ist Metaphysik?" . . . vielleicht das Notwendigste alles Notwendigen für das Denken.' '. . . zur Veranlassung des Übergangs vom vorstellenden in das andenkende Denken nichts nötiger sein als die Frage: "Was Ist Metaphysik?"'

when the fulsome plenitude of transcending difference dissolves into uniform transcendent entities. In the compression of the ontic and the ontological, in which the basic ontic-ontological difference gets forgotten, metaphysics identifies the 'being-ness' of being as entities.

In presenting the entity, instead of the 'stuff' of the *sub-jectum, sub-stans,* as being, metaphysics makes the ambitious profession to have explained being. Really though, all it has done is to have ontically reduced unsettled being to an emaciated pale representation. Conveniently, it utterly forgets that although a thing appears to *be* in its existence, in fact and disconcertingly, it *is* not. Being, in other words, is not to be conflated simply with existence. The pretensions of metaphysics are mere posturings which, in addition to arousing general confusion, serve to keep hidden and covered up that which really matters: being as it is in itself with all its possibilities, unrepresented entitatively and without teleological resolution.[10]

The cancellation of the difference between the ontological and the ontical, which metaphysical reductionism effectuates, so that the rich colourful diversity of life collapses into the general and the ontic, results, as we have just said, in the installation of the same: all beings become henceforth entities or representations of being. This move, Chauvet contends, allows metaphysics to be governed by a logic of foundations, requiring a foundational being. Ontical existence presumes a first entity which becomes the base of all entities. This first entity, to which being refers itself, has been given different names: – the Good or the One (Plato); the divine (Aristotle); God in God's very self, absolute entity, 'uncreated being' (*ens increatum*) (Aquinas); both 'first cause' (*causa prima*) and 'ultimate reason' (*ultima ratio*) (Leibniz); 'beginning' and 'end' (*arche* and *telos*) and therefore 'its own cause' (*causa sui*).

Metaphysics has become, from its first beginnings with Plato, a logic of being founded on God or onto-theology. God as the *causa prima*, the *ultima ratio*, has become the ground of all (metaphysical) existence. As the *étant premier* (first entity), God is the principle of causality, the very reason that entities (in the metaphysical scheme of things) come into existence in the first place. In other words, in metaphysics the name for God is the One who Causes Himself, the *causa sui.*

---

[10] S. F. Parsons, reflecting on Aristotle's *phronesis*, calls non-teleological thinking 'being mindful' or 'attunement to what is coming to be'. It is the way in which the essence of the ethical, likewise forgotten since the dawn of Western civilization, comes uniquely to be characterized after metaphysics in a postmodern setting [S. F. Parsons, *How Theological Ethics is Theological*, Unpublished paper, 2011, pp. 4–5].

If God is the foundation upon which all being rests, that is the ground of metaphysical ontology, theology necessarily precedes metaphysics. This realization allows Heidegger to assert:

the fundamental character of metaphysics is onto-theo-logic.[11]

This 'something', which underwrites entities, subsisting beneath them and lying at their base, is brought to our attention through analogy. Metaphysical good follows from an 'aligning (*ana logon*)' with the Ultimate Good, the 'first reality' or God. For St Thomas, other realities can be called being and good to the extent they participate in or are assimilated by (however deficiently) this first being, which by its essence is being and good.

1.2.1 An alternative reading of Heidegger and the question of metaphysics

Having outlined Chauvet's reading of Heidegger's writings on the subject of metaphysics it is now necessary to ask the question: has Chauvet exhausted all that Heidegger has to say on this theme or are there aspects of Heidegger's thinking on metaphysics that Chauvet has overlooked?

A review of Chauvet's direct citations from Heidegger's various writings is illuminating and provides a clue for answering these questions. In his consideration of Heidegger's thoughts on metaphysics Chauvet naturally relies heavily on *Qu'est-ce que la metaphysique?*,[12] which in the French edition includes the introduction and postscript to the main text. *What is Metaphysics?* was Heidegger's inaugural lecture given in 1929 shortly after his appointment, following the retirement of Edmund Husserl, as Professor of Philosophy at Freiburg University. Heidegger supplemented the text of this lecture in 1943 with a postscript and in 1949 with an introduction. *Qu'est-ce que la metaphysique?* is one of the most frequently cited texts in Chauvet's treatment of Heidegger's thinking on metaphysics. However, *at no point in the discussion does Chauvet refer to the main text (1929) of the lecture.* Instead he restricts his references almost exclusively to the introduction (1949) written 20 years after Heidegger's inauguration.[13]

---

[11] M. Heidegger, *Identität und Difference* (GA11), p. 67. 'Der Grundzug der Metaphysik heißt Onto-Theo-Logik.'

[12] This is found in *Questions I et II*, Éditions Gallimard, 1968, pp. 21–84.

[13] This discovery is alluded to in Vincent J. Miller's review of *Symbole et Sacrament*. Miller states that Chauvet offers a 'purely optimistic reading of the *later* (my emphasis) Heidegger' [Vincent J. Miller, *An Abyss at the Heart of Mediation: Louis-Marie Chauvet's Fundamental Theology of Sacramentality*, Horizons, 24/2 (1997), p. 240].

The significance of this cannot be overemphasized since, as we have seen, an understanding of metaphysics lies at the foundation of Chauvet's thesis: having decided that St Thomas' sacramental theology is conducted within a metaphysical schema Chauvet, we may recall, turns to Heidegger's thinking on metaphysics to develop a new sacramental theology that takes account of contemporary thought. It is not the moment to discuss in great depth the detail of *What is Metaphysics?*[14] The content of the lecture unfolds in the following sequence:[15]

1. A description of science and its totalizing hegemony over the thinking of contemporary man.
2. An investigation into that which nourishes the branches of the various positive sciences.
3. The portrayal of this 'ground' as the nothing which is viewed by the sciences as an outrage and a phantasm which is to be dismissed with a lordly wave of the hand.
4. The nothing is more than a negation brought about by a specific act of the intellect because it is encountered beforehand, that is before any act of reflection/intellection, in a fundamental experience.
5. The nothing provides an apprehension (fundamental experience) of beings as a whole and leads to the complete negation of the totality of beings.
6. This fundamental experience as the founding mode of attunement is also the basic occurrence of our *Dasein*.
7. The founding mode of attunement registers in human existence in the fundamental mood of anxiety which therefore reveals the nothing.
8. Anxiety robs us of speech. Because beings as a whole slip away, so that *das Nichts* alone crowds round, in the face of anxiety all utterance of the 'is' falls silent.
9. The fundamental mood of *Angst* is that from which the nothing must be interrogated.

From this brief outline it is clear the question of the nothing and the mood of anxiety are central themes in Heidegger's understanding of metaphysics but are themes strangely neglected by Chauvet. This failure to recognize the co-relation between Heidegger's not-a-thing (or the no-thing) and Plato's not-being (or *genesis*) means Chauvet misses the opportunity to bring Heidegger's thought to bear in the most fruitful way on the theological questions investigated in *Symbol*

---

[14] See Chapter 3 for a more detailed consideration of this lecture.
[15] The following citations are taken from Heidegger's *Was Ist Metaphysik?* in *Wegmarken* (GA9), pp. 106–21.

et Sacrement. Metaphysics, when it is thought through in terms of the nothing, whose presence reveals itself in the mood of anxiety, has profound ontological consequences occasioning the *Verwandlung* (transformation) of man in his *Dasein*. If being is to open itself up to incursions of infinity, such as love and joy, that disconcertingly do not settle in a fixed or higher *telos*, this engagement, encounter or appropriation will take place, not in the symbolic order as Chauvet contends but, as this book argues (following an authentic reading of Heidegger), within the region of the nothing.

Anxiety, in spite of all that has been said so far, is not a being; it has no recognizable entitative shape that is familiar to us and with which we are at home. Nevertheless, it registers with 'beings as a whole' not as an *ens creatum* but as a non-entity, a non-thing, the nothing, at least among those honest enough with themselves not to cheat on the possibilities that *Dasein* throws up. Anxiety does not annihilate beings; it only offers a sense of the real that cannot be grounded at the level of being;[16] life is more than mere existence. When the nothing appears entities do not dissolve but are placed within a broader perspective, albeit one that is strange and Wholly Other. The nothing cannot set up residence where the ordinary and the habitual prevail because it resists domestication. As a result, when the nothing shows, the familiar and the ordinary slip away. The moment the nothing succumbs to being, the nothing becomes something and is itself negated. Or otherwise put, the possible ceases to be a possibility once it is actualized. In this sense regular, everyday existence or being, since it works against unrestrained human flourishing being negatively correlated to the reality and truth disclosed in the nothing, is a form of nihilism.

The nothing is not manufactured in a negation, for negation requires something, an *ens*, to negate in the first place. Indeed Heidegger asks:

> How could negation produce the not from itself when it can make denials only when something deniable is already granted to it?[17]

---

16 Søren Kierkegaard, who (in Heidegger's estimation) went farthest in analysing the phenomenon of anxiety, speaks of dread as a dangerous matter for the overdelicate. It has a religious significance because it allows the movement of faith to be performed 'in such a way that the things of the world are not lost but entirely regained' [*Fear and Trembling . . . A Dialectical Lyric*, p. 47]. Kierkegaard presents the biblical figure of Abraham as the highest illustration of one who lived within the horizon of anxiety ('Abraham is not Abraham without dread' [*Fear and Trembling . . . A Dialectical Lyric*, p. 34]) for he faced the very real prospect, in faithful obedience to God's call, of losing his beloved son Isaac. By allowing himself to be educated by possibility he received an apprehension of the future and a presentiment of a something which was 'nothing'.

17 M. Heidegger, *Was Ist Metaphysik?* in *Wegmarken* (GA9), p. 116. 'Wie soll auch die Verneinung das Nicht aus ihr selbst aufbringen, wo sie doch nur verneinen kann, wenn ihr ein Verneinbares vorgegegben ist?'

Nothing really is no-thing and is therefore prior to acts of negation. The idea that a negating assertion expresses anything at all remains foreign to anxiety because, quite simply, a negation arrives *after* the event of the nothing's epiphany. A negation is a posterior reflection on the nothing's anterior encounter with us. It follows that if the nothing cannot be negated then the movement of nihilism characteristic of ordinary existence can be resisted the moment being finds itself in the nothing. Our *zurückweichen vor* (shrinking back before) beings in the occurring of anxiety is no cowardly flight from life but is rather a bewildered calm.[18] Life's superficialities that ordinarily draw us away from ourselves, refracting the otherwise brightly focused beam of our existence, are disempowered by the stillness befalling in the eerie silence of the nothing. In short, as the disturbing effects of public life are disabled at the onset of the nothing, we are gathered back from fragmenting entanglements to become bright again. The one educated by infinite possibility resists sinking back into the wretchedness of the finite. The omnipotence of *Dasein*'s possibilities (the nothing) overpowers and outwits all human shrewdness and sagacity.

From the perspective of being-at-home-with-itself, the repelling gesture of the nothing, establishing the ontological difference, is repulsive. It exposes the strangeness of being's exploitative strategies, which strive to instrumentalize all things for utilitarian purposes but which end up negating existence. It is little wonder nothing is viewed with disdain, inspiring disgust in those blissfully unaware of a deeper hidden source of life flowing silently by behind the superficies of ordinary life. But, Heidegger says, nothing, rather than attempting to annihilate the defenses of those ignorant of its agitations and repulsed by its paradoxicality, nevertheless continuously nihilates. *Das Nichten* (nihilation) is not some fortuitous incident. Rather, as a repelling gesture towards the retreating whole of beings, it discloses these beings in their *vollen* (full) but heretofore *verborgenen* (concealed) strangeness as what is *schlechthin Andere* (radically other) – with respect to the nothing. This exposure or lighting up of the strangeness that, from the perspective of the nothing, really characterizes being construed existentially or entitatively, enables the original openness of beings as such (their *genesis* foreclosed in their manifestation as being or substance) to arise. For the first time beings as they really are in their transcending nakedness divested of all metaphysical fig-leaves come into existence. The originally *nichtenden Nichts* (nihilating nothing) essentially makes beings aware that they

---

[18]   Kierkegaard prefigured Heidegger's 'shrinking back before' with his 'infinite resignation'. In this 'there is peace and rest' which 'is better armour than iron or steel' [*Fear and Trembling . . . A Dialectical Lyric*, pp. 60–1].

represent emaciations of a more flourishing and abundant life. Only on the ground of the original revelation of the nothing can human existence approach and penetrate beings in their unrefracted intensity.

Dasein means being held out into *das Nichts*. In holding itself out into the nothing, *Dasein* is beyond beings as a whole. This being beyond beings Heidegger calls *die Transzendenz* (transcendence). If in the ground of its essence *Dasein* were not transcending, which now means, if it were not in advance holding itself out into *das Nichts*, then it could never be related to beings nor even to itself. In *das Nichts* in other words the secret of authentic relating or association is to be found.

This then answers the question of the nothing: because it cannot be as an object or any being at all it cannot survive in the universe of entities standing side-by-side with beings. Precisely because it refuses to be construed metaphysically, it makes possible once more the openness of beings as such. The *Nichten des Nichts* (the nihilation of the nothing) promises a new flourishing and allows beings to partake of their destinies which before the renaissance were unreachable.

The implications of what has been said so far seem to present a problem, namely that since, as *Dasein*, we can relate to beings only by holding ourselves out to the nothing and, given the nothing reveals itself in the mood of anxiety, then it seems we must, in order to exist at all, be in a continual state of anxiety. To live must be to be forever unsettled, never certain of anything, perpetually unsure and incurably anxious.[19] Heidegger shows that this is not the case because we immunize ourselves to the pointings of the nothing as we go about the ordinary routines of everyday superficial existence. Anaesthetized to the *nihil* that shines a penetrating (albeit strange) light onto normative existence, we cling to beings and thereby become immersed in the turbulence that characterizes everyday life. This retreat into the oblivion of the inauthentic and the unreal, in which the unity of our being becomes negated as it scatters into the manifold, happens in proportion to our turning away from the nothing.

This condition of entanglement within the superficies of beings, such that I am estranged from myself, is called by Heidegger *heimatlosigkeit* (homelessness). It is a symptom of the desecration or negation of being whose truth is now forgotten because it is no longer able to be thought. Homelessness consists in

---

[19] Anxiety is not to be confused with the psychological state of anxiousness 'ultimately reducible to fearfulness, which all too readily comes over us' [M. Heidegger, *Was Ist Metaphysik?* in *Wegmarken* (GA9), p. 111, 'die im Grunde der nur allzu leicht sich einstellenden Furchtsamkeit zugehört']. No English word adequately captures the nuances contained in *Angst* which, in addition to indicating the distress of the moment, suggests importantly an apprehension of the future, a presentiment of something that is 'nothing'.

the *Seinsverlassenheit* (abandonment of being) by beings. Whatever ways are devised to protect against anxiety (to cheat on the nothing) it is however always there, perhaps tranquillized though still breathing. As it exhales I quiver in my existence. Its presence can be discerned in the jittery, in the indecision of businessmen, in the hesitation of the reserved. It is most evident though in the adventurous and the *verwegene* (daring). When the nothing eventually breaks out in a disruptive moment, instilling dread and anxiety, it requires the cancellation of all flights, a pulling back from the scattering, a homecoming in which I am reunited with myself from whom I had strayed.[20] Those who are daring preserve the ultimate grandeur of existence and are characterized by cheerfulness and the gentleness of creative longing.

Anxiety then is not a rarefied state of mind to which only the few have privileged access. Whether acknowledged or not, anxiety holds sway in season and out of season. It does not require an extraordinary event for it to be stirred to life and can be roused by the most trivial of occasions. When we release ourselves into the nothing, instead of being repelled by the *nihil* and taking flight to the universal realm of beings, we surpass beings as a whole in a moment of transcendence. We may be shunned by those still gripped by the universal and dispersed in the manifold but this homecoming is the destiny of the daring and the reserved, set free 'from those *Götzen* (idols) everyone has and to which they are wont to go cringing.'[21] Learning to know dread is an adventure all must partake in if they are to be liberated from a partial inauthentic existence. As Kierkegaard concludes *The Concept of Dread*:

> He ... who has learned rightly to be in dread has learned the most important thing.[22]

But what have anxiety and the nothing to do with metaphysics, the initial question that launched this enquiry? Heidegger concludes *What is Metaphysics?* by showing how, in the question concerning the *nihil*, an enquiry about what lies beyond the universal or over and above beings as a whole takes place. Since the

---

[20] Kierkegaard calls this the assertion of the Individual in the face of the universal. In the context of a discussion of Abraham he asks 'what of the man who abandons the universal in order to grasp something still higher, which is not the universal?' [*Fear and Trembling ... A Dialectical Lyric*, p. 85]. This suspension of the teleological allows the Individual to live in contradiction to the universal and opens up a new understanding of ethics (the theme of ethics is examined more fully in Chapter 4). Such people, the daring, the reserved, no longer estranged from themselves, are approached with 'a *horror religious*' [*Fear and Trembling ... A Dialectical Lyric*, p. 86] by those lost in the multiplicity or enmeshed in the universal.

[21] M. Heidegger, *Was Ist Metaphysik?* in *Wegmarken*, (GA9), p. 122, 'von den Götzen, die jeder hat und zu denen er sich wegzuschleichen pflegt'.

[22] S. Kierkegaard, *The Concept of Dread*, p. 140.

word 'metaphysics' is a rendering of the Greek *meta ta physika*, in which the *meta* suggests transcending or reaching out beyond ontical beings to the ontological, it follows that the question of the nothing, which likewise explores being from the vantage point, not of *ousia* or the settled stasis of entiative existence but, from the beyond of infinite possibility, encapsulates the whole of metaphysics. By virtue of the foundational relationship of the nothing with being as such Heidegger, echoing Hegel's *Science of Logic* (Vol. I, *Werke* III, 74) concludes pure Being and pure Nothing are *dasselbe* (the same).

In so doing he dismantles the legitimacy of the rule of logic, in which the principle of causality is sacrosanct. The entire enterprise of science starts to look questionable. It allows Heidegger to conclude that when science does not take *das Nichts* seriously its presumed soberness of mind and superiority become laughable.

1.2.2 Why does Chauvet censor Heidegger?

Although it is tempting to apply this conclusion to the presumed soberness of mind and superiority of Chauvet's sacramental theology for the self-same reason, namely because Chauvet neglects to take the nothing seriously, it is perhaps a premature judgement to make at this stage. It remains for us to develop further our critique of Chauvet's reading of Heidegger by asking ourselves the question: why did Chauvet overlook the idea of the nothing in his consideration of Heidegger's thinking on metaphysics? If, as Heidegger claims, such an oversight is common among those who adopt a scientific methodology in their researches, is it possible that a clue to Chauvet's omission lies in his own unacknowledged commitment to the methods of positivism?

An answer to these questions is to be found towards the end of the first chapter of *Symbole et Sacrament*. Chauvet outlines here his view of the non-positivist tradition as this occurs within the discipline of theology. Influenced by Claude Geffré's *Le christianisme au risque de l'interprétation* Chauvet maintains that in spite of the correction brought by the *via negationis*, the movement of thought inaugurated by Pseudo-Dionysius within Christian theology merely highlights the power of human knowledge and its tendency to conceive the divine through the concept of God as the supreme Entity. It is impossible, Chauvet contends, for the apophatic tradition within theology to rid itself of the logical presuppositions inherent in language. When it comes to speak of God as the unnameable, therefore, it is nevertheless and in spite of itself reducing God to the *ens increatum*: God is the uncreated entity (though an entity nevertheless) and therefore something rather than nothing. Negative theology, even in its most sublime moments, where it transcends, through negation, the notion of being as cause, nonetheless remains viscerally connected to a type of language that is irremediably causal and ontological. Although he admits the influence of the apophatic tradition in theology Chauvet is bound, given his methodological predilections, to restrict its importance. He places theology's critical thrust no longer in the prolongation of a negative onto-theology, stressing the unknowability of God, but rather in the believing subjects themselves.

We can conclude therefore, that Chauvet's suspicion of apophatic theologians resulted in his passing over a theme central in Heidegger's early thinking on metaphysics, namely, the nothing. Chauvet's commitment to the cataphatic tradition in theology and his focus on Heidegger's later thought predisposed him to ignore entirely the content of Heidegger's main essay on metaphysics *What is Metaphysics?* Although Chauvet's concern is principally theological, his predisposition away from the apophatic tradition in theology seems to carry over and influence his reading of philosophy to the extent that he positively screens out from Heidegger's writings any mention of the *nihil*.[23]

Theologians, like John Macquarrie, who recognize the importance of the apophatic read Heidegger in a less censorious way. For example, in an essay entitled *Eckhart and Heidegger*, Macquarrie shows how Heidegger's thoughts concerning the nothing have something in common with the same idea expressed in Eckhart's writings. In his discussion of *What is Metaphysics?* Macquarrie points out that this nothing – *das Nichts* – proves to be an expression used also by Eckhart and to be something more than mere negativity or absence of being. In short, this 'nothing' has more of being or reality than the multitude of finite beings.

Macquarrie contends that Heidegger's view of the *nihil* is high theology in all but name, since a sympathetic reading of Heidegger cannot fail to be aware of a religious spirit in his writings. It is superficial to view Heidegger as an atheist for, as Hans Georg Gadamer in his memorial address at the time of Heidegger's death: 'It was Christianity that provoked and kept alive this man's thought; it was the ancient transcendence and not modern secularity that spoke through him.'[24]

---

[23] For example, throughout *Symbole et Sacrement* Chuauvet shows deep sympathy for Levinas' thought. The Lithuanian-born French-Jewish philosopher and Talmudic commentator brands 'existence without existents' (i.e. *das Nichts*) 'evil' (Levinas, *Ethics and Infinity*, p. 49).

[24] J. Macquarrie, Eckhart and Heidegger, *The Eckhart Society Journal*, Spring 1993, No. 2, p. 63.

Chauvet's omission seems to suggest a misunderstanding of the meaning Heidegger ascribed to the nothing and which he carefully worked out in his inaugural lecture at the University of Freiburg. The ontological difference, if really experienced and grasped, requires the invocation of the nothing. Nothing less will do. This is not nihilism, as perhaps Chauvet believes, but a radical assertion of the difference between the transcendent infinite and the transcending finite, between being and beings. The charge of atheism or even nihilism made against Heidegger rests, as he points out himself, on a misunderstanding of his use of the word 'nothing'. The difference between being and beings – the ontological difference – is so fundamental that being is bound to appear as nothing to those whose attention is absorbed by beings.

Having identified this lacuna in Chauvet's reading of Heidegger on metaphysics, it is appropriate now to consider Chauvet's reading of Heidegger in other areas before asking the question: what shape would Chauvet's sacramental theology have taken had the radicality of the ontological difference, as brought to light in the notion of the nothing, been seriously contemplated?

1.3 Overcoming metaphysics: An unachievable task

To be in a position to question metaphysics our existence must be inserted, strange as it may seem, into the whole range of *Dasein*'s fundamental possibilities. This insertion, that is *Dasein*'s relocation, is the release of being into *das Nichts* the nothing. Relying on Heidegger's later writings Chauvet describes this re-basing of existence as a re-ascension to the otherwise *fondement méconnu* (ignored foundation) of metaphysics: the source of metaphysic's life is to be found in the truth of Being.

In order to move beyond metaphysics, to say something more about the neglected ground of being's truth, Chauvet enters into a discussion of *es gibt Sein* (there is being) and *das Sein ist* (being is). Following Heidegger he identifies a problem with *das Sein ist*: in establishing *Sein* as the subject of the verb *ist*, Being can only 'be' existentially or ontically. In other words, this particular formulation risks presenting *Sein* in impoverished form as mere entity. To counter this reductive tendency Chauvet shows how Heidegger, impelled by the thought of the pre-Socratic philosopher Parmenides, deploys the phrase *es gibt Sein*. Rendered in this way, being is no longer thought of as a possessing subject but, as the object of the 'there', is now something Wholly Other than simple existence. Finding its place 'there', *Sein* is no longer founded here in the metaphysical universe of entities. It cannot therefore be the commanding subject as *das Sein ist* suggests. Rather, being is given freely in a bestowal undirected by human subjectivity. In the granting or giving of being, *Sein* comes to be not as existence but as ek-sistence. The statement *es gibt Sein* ('there is being') is to be understood, not in the sense of something already given but rather, in the sense of unique and unrepeatable gift.

Chauvet speaks of Heidegger's *Kehre* as the way in which metaphysics is to be overcome, or how 'being', presently stationed in the here, is to transmigrate to the there. In Heidegger's *Kehre* 'conversion' means understanding ourselves simply as always already infused with the call of being. The de-centering of self that *Kehre* implies disables the tendency to convoke and measure beings starting from an awareness of self. The call of being, speaking behind the loud noise of everyday life, emphasizes the importance of language in any discussion of metaphysical being and its surpassing. Humans exist only when spoken by language and thus only when summoned and convoked by being. In the meditation of language being attracts them only to withdraw; it comes to register its presence in the very movement that conceals it.

However, the language of being's summoning is strange and unfamiliar. It does not follow the ordinary rules characterizing regular speech. To listen to *l'appel de l'être* requires a fundamental recollection or an existential attunement to the key note sounded by being. Hearing and responding to being's murmur qualitatively determines the shape of being itself. We become the words we hear and act upon. If we run for cover at being's call, ignoring its summons and resisting where it impels us to go, we opt against life in favour of a mediocre existence. It is in this sense that language has profound ontological implications. Chauvet conceives the word as *something already spoken* before we come into existence. Responding to being's call means for him sacrificing the immediacy of our individuality and the full range of its possibilities for the sake an already spoken *a priori* universal.

Following this brief diversion, highlighting the importance of linguistics for ontology and metaphysics, Chauvet returns to his main theme, this time emphasizing the key to the overcoming of metaphysics. It is to be found, paradoxically, in *pondering that very thing metaphysics excludes yet which at the same time makes metaphysics possible*. Taking inspiration from Heidegger's lecture *The Onto-theo-logical Constitution of Metaphysics*,[25] he speaks of the

---

[25] M. Heidegger, *Identität und Difference* (GA11), Verlag Günther Neske, Pfullingen, 1957. Translated by Joan Stambaugh (ed.), as *Identity and Difference*, New York, Harper and Row, 2002 (1969).

ontological difference in terms of the 'event' which uncovers and the 'arrival' which takes cover: the 'event' bestows being in the full range of its possibilities while the 'arrival' casts being as an entity. The interplay of these two movements within the space between the two, is the place of the essential origin of the ontological difference. Essential being is seen, therefore, as emerging from the difference. To be mindful of the lively and incessant interplay between the 'event' and the 'arrival', which takes place, albeit unacknowledged, outside the domain of metaphysics, is to overcome metaphysics. It is precisely from this 'play' of being that metaphysics first arose; but the latter has disowned its playful origin by clinging to its representations: the dance of advance and retreat which being carries out, its movement of presence and absence, has been reduced to the presence of an available foundation; originally ec-static, temporality has been tamed into the solid permanence of a constant 'now'; logical clarity has replaced the blend of light and shadow at the breakthrough of being. To overcome metaphysics, one must perform this 'step backwards', this jump into the difference.

Thinking advances when it goes back into (and thinks from out of) this otherwise unthought essence, the fluctuating and never fixed dance of being's advance and retreat. Chauvet names the journey back to the ignored playful origin, 'conversion'. The test of whether a turn, *Kehre*, has genuinely happened is whether we can consent to depart from the solid, reassuring ground of our represented foundation and the stable, fixed point in order to go out towards this insistent *laisser-être* (letting-be) where we lose our footing in the relinquishing of customary mores. Metaphysics finds its essence, not in the thing ostensibly made present in representation, but rather in the transient passing of being intentionally neglected and passed over in the act of representation. In a paradox, the being that being claims to be is by-passed and left behind in the coming to be of being. In other words, with the extinction of any recollection whatsoever of being the ontological difference reduces to a similitude: being conflates to being so that the one is wholly indistinguishable from the other. In short, the heterogeneous is homologized.

When thinking breaks free however, in a departure from being's representations, and thinks instead from out of ignored and overlooked being, metaphysics is overcome. A thinking which pursues the truth about being does not rest content with metaphysics; still, it does not *oppose* metaphysics. To express it in images, such thinking does not tear out the root of philosophy. Rather, it excavates the foundation and ploughs the soil. Chauvet concludes from this that Heidegger's thought is much more than a 'new' philosophy to add to existing metaphysical systems. Rather, in breaking metaphysic's spell (that has bewitched Western thought since Plato) it is a particular way of living within the metaphysical tradition: recalling its forgotten roots and thinking its unthought essence.

Having guided his reader thus far through Heidegger's reflections on metaphysics Chauvet ends his exposition with the question: why has humankind forgotten the unthought essence or the playful origin if this is where the truth of metaphysics is to be found? He answers by suggesting that forgetfulness, in which being backs away from inadequate representations of itself as being, is an essential characteristic of being. Retreating in this way, being nevertheless survives underground beyond being's power of recall and recollection. This forgetfulness, brought on by being's withdrawing, is how Chauvet understands Heidegger's notion of *Ereignis*.[26] This 'event' (*Ereignis*), he says, proceeds from being itself – or rather from being's withdrawal. Such a forgetfulness, veiled by being, belongs to the very essence of being.

To apprehend that which representative thought conceals, so that metaphysics might be overcome, requires the settlement or placement of thinking outside the certainties of calculative reckoning but within the *Ereignis* of forgetfulness. To serenely acquiescence in the *Ereignis* (as forgetfulness) in a *Gelassenheit* (letting-be) is to resign oneself to the fact that the presencing of being will *never* alight upon a higher *telos* or reach an ultimate foundation. In other words, when metaphysics is overcome a new home is found in the uncomfortable *non-place* of a permanent questioning. The rehabilitation of being, ending its homeless wanderings in metaphysical environs is, on the one hand, so simple because it is merely a question of letting being be itself; on the other hand though, it is inordinately complex because the false evidence on which rests the eidetic representations of being must first be unmasked.

1.3.1 An alternative reading of Heidegger and the overcoming of metaphysics

Does Chauvet's account get to grips fully with what Heidegger has to say regarding the overcoming of metaphysics? His description of the *Kehre*, eventualizing a

---

[26] Chauvet's interpretation of *Ereignis* as forgetfulness of being or *seinvergesseneheit* is not an interpretation shared by all Heidegger commentators. *Ereignis* is more frequently understood as an intensification of being in which the full range of human potentialities asserts itself appropriating the individual. The existential effect of consent to the appropriation is withdrawal from dispersion in the manifold. Heidegger draws attention to the sacrificial connotations of *Ereignis*: '*Das Opfer* (sacrifice) is the departure from beings on the path to preserving the favour of being . . . *Das Opfer ist heimisch im Wesen des Ereignisses* (sacrifice is at home in the essence of the event) whereby being *in den Anspruch nimmt* (lays claim upon) the human being *für die Wahrheit des Seins* (for the truth of being)' [M. Heidegger, *Nachwort zu: 'Was Ist Metaphysik?'* in *Wegmarken* (GA9), pp. 310–11].

turn away from eidetic representations of being in a conversion, is engaging. His suggestion that being must return to its playful origin in order to think its unthought essence opens up new and interesting areas of thought. There is almost a poetic quality to Chauvet's suggestion, following Heidegger, that a thinking that thinks beyond metaphysics is a thinking that thinks the truth of being. But it is here, in his investigations into being's truth, that the limitations of Chauvet's reading of Heidegger begin to become apparent. He comes tantalizingly close to teasing out all Heidegger has to say concerning the truth of being. Frustratingly, though, he stops short of penetrating beneath the surface to the implied and deeply concealed nuances.

The remainder of this chapter examines these nuances and explores how they influence an understanding of what it means to overcome metaphysics. Particular reference will be made to Heidegger's *Parmenides* series of lectures. Here Heidegger returns to those traditions of thought which, predating Plato, provided the context or soil for the germination of Plato's metaphysics. While Plato's thought (and the derived metaphysical tradition) attempts the extinction of the infinite, the pre-Socratics promise its recovery. If, as Chauvet has shown, we must reflect upon what representational thought excludes or forgets in order to reach the truth of being (and so overcome metaphysics), we must consider Heiedgger's actual reflections on the oblivion of being (and not merely observe), as Chauvet does, that such reflections are necessary. What does Heidegger mean when he speaks of learning to attend to the *seinsvergessenheit*?

He begins to trace the outline of an answer in his exposition of the meaning of truth or *aletheia* in Greek thought. This is because the root word *lethe* from *aletheia* means oblivion or *seinsvergessenheit*. In pondering *aletheia*, therefore, the very thing metaphysics excludes sharpens once again into focus. In short, reflections on *aletheia* are the keys unlocking the bolted chamber to the otherwise inaccessible *essence impensée* recalled to our attention by Chauvet but not further scrutinized. Suggestively Heidegger observes *aletheia* could be the word that offers a hitherto unnoticed *Wink* (hint) concerning the unthought essence of *esse*.

In the *Parmenides* lecture series Heidegger devotes much of §5 to a consideration of *lethe* which, he points out, though closely connected is not identical with forgetting. In other words, though *Vergessenheit* is cognate with *Vergessene* the former means 'oblivion', suggestive of place, whereas the latter means 'forgotten', pointing to a psychological event. *Vergessenheit* actually names, Heidegger says, that into which the forgotten sinks.

Metaphysics is overcome, less from standing here within the event of forgetfulness itself (as for Chauvet) and more from settling myself there within oblivion, a submerged region into which the forgotten is drawn. When this resituating occurs the possibility of dwelling within my own essence is removed: I become alienated from myself. *Lethe* is not the opposite of *aletheia* but a vital clue to the meaning of truth taken in a Greek way. Since *lethe* pertains to the essence of *aletheia* un-concealedness itself cannot be the mere *elimination* of concealedness. The *a* in *aletheia* in no way means simply an undetermined universal 'un'- and 'not'. Rather, the saving and conserving of the un-concealed is necessarily in relation to concealment, understood as the withdrawal of what appears in its appearing.

In the early and middle Greek periods Heidegger discovers *lethe* was passed over in silence. However, in later Greek literature he finds the word was once again recalled to mind only this time in a memorable and significant context. In Pindar's *Seventh Olympian Ode*, for example, the essence of *lethe* is clarified in one important respect. The scene is the colonization of the island of Rhodes. The colonizers forgot to bring with them the wherewithal for the gleaming fire. As a result of this omission, they were compelled to establish a sacred place and conduct sacrifices without fire on the high point of the city Lindos. The colonizers ordinarily would have thought ahead and made preparations for their task. However, on this occasion, overawed by the purpose of their mission, they appeared to be arbitrarily negligent if not uncharacteristically forgetful. This is because, as Pindar narrates, *awe sometimes overwhelms with the signless cloud of concealment* which withholds from actions the straightforward way and places them outside what is thoroughly disclosed.

For Heidegger these words provide a very beautiful poetic essential elucidation of *lethe*. They point to the fact that *lethe* occupies the same realm and coexists within the same order as awe. Awe does not denote a 'lived experience' of the human 'subject' but rather overcomes man as that which is *das Bestimmende* (the determining) or *das Stimmende* (the disposing). Awe thrusts something upon humans. It gives a sense of being before it was compelled to find its place within beings as a whole or before individuality was homogenized and reduced to fit the universal. Awe is not a feeling that we possess but rather a disposition that takes possession of us.[27] As the disposing mood it determines our essence in spite of ourselves. Heidegger notes, given this significance, that awe is a fundamental word in Pindar's poetry and thereby for the Greeks themselves.

---

[27] Kierkegaard says 'to be placed outside the universal, either because it is one's nature or because the circumstances of life have led one to it, is the beginning of the daemonic: it is not the fault of the individual' [*Fear and Trembling . . . A Dialectical Lyric*, p. 159]. The way to prove that one does not belong to the company of men is to show 'that one can speak in fear and trembling' [*Fear and Trembling . . . A Dialectical Lyric*, p. 109].

It signifies the emergence and opening up of man and his insertion into being. It is not grounded on man as 'subject' but rather is the making or constituting of him as 'resolute', open, disclosing and disclosed towards beings. Whereas awe thrusts something upon man, *lethe*, occupying the same essential sphere beyond conscious subjectivity, brings about a hiding or concealment more commonly known as a forgetting.

In addition to this reference to *lethe* in Pindar, Heidegger turns his attention next to the appearance of *lethe* in *muthos*. In the myth that brings Plato's dialogue on the *Republic* to a close there is a portrayal of *lethe* as the entire district of the 'there'. In essence the region of the 'there' is a demonic place. *Lethe*, Heidegger concludes, is the most extreme and the ultimate place in this 'demonic' district. This observation inaugurates an exploration into the derivation and meaning of the *daimonion*. Because of the essential connections between *lethe* and *aletheia*, as we progress in our understanding of the 'demonic', we will better grasp what 'truth' meant to the early Greeks. This promises to disclose an understanding of being, open to the infinite, that prevailed before Plato's metaphysics. At the same time, this exploration will suggest how metaphysics may be overcome.

Heidegger renders the Greek *daio* of which the *daimonion* is a cognate, as 'the uncanny'[28] or the astounding, visible in the astonishing. *Daio* obtains its character from what is excessive and simultaneously difficult from the perspective of the ordinary busy person. There always seems to be something remaining behind in the course of ordinary human activity and it is this excess or surplus that is named the uncanny or the astounding. We would not be able to busy ourselves with beings were the backdrop of being not continuously in view, for the normal and ordinary subsist in and emerge from out of Being. The 'uncanny' is that which gets left behind (Chauvet's *essence impensée*) when we deal with, and calculate and organize beings. It is that aspect of being which withdraws when being enacts itself in the everyday. Where being comes into focus, there the extra-ordinary announces itself, the excessive that strays 'beyond' the ordinary, that which is not to be explained by explanations on the basis of beings. This is *das Ungeheure* (the uncanny).

---

[28] In this identification of the *daio* with the uncanny Heidegger seems to be making the same connection as Rudolph Otto, alongside whom he taught at Marburg University from 1923 to 1928. For example, Otto says "'Religious dread' [or "awe"] ("*religiöse Scheu*") . . . first begins to stir in the feeling of "something uncanny", (*das "Umheimliche"*) "eerie", or "weird". It is this feeling which, emerging in the mind of primeval man, forms the starting-point for the entire religious development in history. "Daemons" ("*Dämonen*") and "gods" ("*Gotter*") alike spring from this root, and all the products of "mythological apperception" or "fantasy" are nothing but different modes in which it has been objectified' [R. Otto, *Das Heilige*, p. 16]. Although Heidegger reverses the direction of provenance his thinking concerning the uncanny and the demonic seems to owe much to Otto. I explore Otto's possible influence on Heidegger's thought more extensively in Chapter 3.

By virtue of the fact that the uncanny resides elsewhere than within the domain of the *ratio*, or the onto-theological universe of entities and first causes where value is computed and reckoned, it is neither immense nor tiny. It is incommensurable with any standard. The immeasurable something (though not an *ens*) remaining behind 'there' when being emerges 'here' is taxonomically unnamable and as such is apprehended as threatening if not as positively dangerous. In short the uncanny is the simple, the insignificant, ungraspable by the fangs of the will, withdrawing itself from all artifices of calculation, because it surpasses all planning. It is the beyond over 'there' surrounding the ordinary over 'here' within which everything ordinary is suspended and into which everything ordinary falls back.

But the term *daio*, from which the *daimonion* is derived, has richer connotations and further nuances that so far we have failed to detect. In a final burrowing down into its meaning, Heidegger shows what the uncanny is *in itself*: it is based on the shining into beings, on self-presentation in Greek: *daio*. *Daio* means self-presentation in the sense of pointing and showing. Indeed, the self-showing ones, the pointing ones, are who they are and are the way they are *only* in the essential domain of disclosure where being itself self-discloses. Heidegger uses the image of shining light to suggest how the uncanny is perceived by being when being shows itself. The uncanny is the being that shines into everything, including the ordinary world of beings. Its shining often grazes beings like a silently passing cloud-shadow. The beings we deal with and consider to be ordinary are illumined by the uncanny or the inconspicuous, the simple, the insignificant.

Because being as the uncanny shines into being, it cannot ever be explained on the basis of beings nor constructed out of beings. Pure being, precisely because it does not need beings to invent itself, in this sense has no being. In other words, pure being 'is' (or rather 'nothings as') the nothing. Being clear in the clearing from any entanglement with everyday being (the domain in which things come to be), it is unable to be manipulated by the maneuverings of ordinary thinking. Thinking from out of the uncanny is not really a knowing that follows recognizable epistemological rules. It is more essential than knowing because it is in closer proximity to being in that closeness which is concealed from afar. Demons, which must not be understood as evil spirits fluttering about in the way religious historians understand them,[29] emerge from being into beings thus

---

[29] Earlier Rudlph Otto was cited (Note 28) to show the connections between existential moods of dread and awe and daemons and gods. The latter, being sprung from these affective dispositions, are the mythological outposts objectifying otherwise unpronounceable subjective moods befalling the individual.

pointing into the being. Proper thinking occurs, and metaphysics is overcome, when we do not turn away from the pointing, aborting life by cheating on the possible. Rather, in remaining open and acquiescing in the pointing, we emerge as the appointed. Pointed-out in this way we entertain the full range of human possibility becoming what we were destined to become. Demons are not 'demonic' in the normal sense of the word but, if we were to judge them in terms of our usual hazy representations of the 'demonic', are undemonic (*undämonischen*). While demons may not be as gruesome as they are portrayed in popular folklore nevertheless there is danger and difficulty accompanying the uncanny as the shining of being into being. These undemonic *daimones* are anything but 'harmless' and 'incidental'. They are not casual additions to beings, which man is free to bypass according to whim and fancy. Our disposition towards these undemonic *daimones* has dire and profound ontological consequences. In consequence of this inconspicuous unsurpassability, the undemonic *daimones* are more 'demonic' than 'demons' in the usual sense could ever be. The undemonic *daimones* transpire to be more essential than any being.

The Greek Gods themselves are not beings as personalities but undemonic *daimones*. They are 'being itself as looking into beings'.[30] Their *Ungeheures* (uncanniness) is so pure in measure and in mildness that when they appear awe shines everywhere as a preliminary and foreboding glow. Their etherealness, to speak of them in a Christian way, comes about as a consequence of the excess that is left over when the essence of being has come originarily into the unconcealed. Their spiritual character emerges because being always and everywhere infinitely exceeds all beings and protrudes from beings. If the essence of the goddess *aletheia* is thought primordially then, as Heidegger announces, we will experience the demonic (*das dämonische*) in the sense of the Greek *daimonion*. Overcoming metaphysics comes to mean: surrender or submission to the demonic determinations pointing out from the district of the 'there', the site of oblivion making up the truth of being or occasioning and eventualizing man to be in the full intensity of concentrated and resolute being. Thinking the unthought essence of metaphysics is the departure-from or sacrifice-of being for the sake of the truth of being wherein moves the divine, not metaphysically construed as God (who is now deceased) but as the undemonic *daimones*. This sacrifice, in which being recollects itself from its manifold dispersions, is the one demanded by divinity for in *aletheia* there can be no concealment or refuge sought in the indeterminate totality of beings. Sacrifice promises a way

---

[30] M. Heidegger, *Parmenides* (GA54), p. 164, 'sind sie das in das Seiende hereinblickende Sein selbst'.

into the formerly precluded region of the holy where the relentless pointings of the *daimonion* agitate beneath the veil of ordinary consciousness engendering, because unacknowledged, existential disappointment.

A remedy for existential disenchantment is found in the reappointment of being, now attuned-to or showing-up-in the pointings of the *daimonion*. Overcoming metaphysics requires a sense of the holy and abysmal ground of being wherein divinity uncannily moves and being comes to be in the truth of being. To think being requires in each instance a leap, a leap into the groundless from the habitual ground upon which for us beings always rest.

To conclude, if the *lethe* as the demonic district and the wherein of the self-showing and pointing ones is the clearing, wholly distinct-from and other-than metaphysics, then, when we succumb to and allow ourselves to be appointed and determined by the *daimonion*, in a move or leap from the indeterminate totality of beings metaphysics is overcome in the *Bestimmende* (determining) moment of awe; we are transported into the holy domain where demons stir, about which angels proclaim and wherein being finds its truth. To think from out of the truth of being is to think more primordially than metaphysics can. It is the only way in which the essence of *das Heilige* (the holy) can be thought. Only from the essence of the holy *is* the essence of divinity to be thought. Only in the light of the essence of divinity can it be thought or said what the word 'God' is to signify. To overcome metaphysics then is to think *das Heilige* which is nearer to us than we are to our indeterminate selves. The dimension of the holy indeed remains closed as a dimension if the open region of being is not cleared and in its clearing is near to man. Thinking does not overcome metaphysics by climbing still higher, surmounting it, transcending it somehow or other; thinking overcomes metaphysics by climbing back down into the nearness of the nearest. The descent, particularly where man has strayed into subjectivity, is more arduous and more dangerous than the ascent. The descent leads to the poverty of the ek-sistence of *homo humanus*. In ek-sistence the region of *homo animalis*, of metaphysics, is abandoned.

Thought which provokes the abandonment of metaphysics by thinking from out of the essence of the *Heiligen*, the occluded realm of the *daimonion*, is ethics. That thinking which thinks the truth of being as the primordial element of man as one who ek-sists, is in itself the original ethics. Etiquette and convention are no longer determinative of human behaviour for more essential than instituting rules is that man find the way to his abode in the truth of being. Once established there in a moment of awe, human being and activity receive their determination from the daemonic ones who show and point out the way. Whereas before, being was determined by conventional directives and the protocols of everyday existence, after, when the truth of my being shows up in the saying of the silent word, I am the appointed one. All teleologies are suspended in the solemnity of sacrifice annunciating my appointment. Only so far as man, ek-sisting into the truth of being, belongs to being can there come from being itself the assignment of those directives that must become law and rule for man.

There is no higher or gentler law than this, governing that which comes to be. Ethics finds its origin there. Heidegger's fundamental ontology, in other words, has real practical implications for as I come into my truth, sacrificing my being that I may ek-sist, I am impelled by the assignment of those directives to a more radical and fruitful engagement with others and the world.[31]

1.4 Conclusion

Insight into the proper nature of thinking and saying comes only by holding phenomena in view without prejudice.[32]

We set ourselves the aim of reviewing Chauvet's reading of Heidegger to see whether the subtleties and nuances characteristic of Heidegger's thought had been noticed by Chauvet or whether they lay undetected by him. This was done with a view to evaluating Chauvet's sacramental theology which invokes Heidegger's thought to give it a philosophical foundation. We organized our discussion around two main headings that Chauvet deploys in *Symbole et Sacrement* to structure his account of Heidegger's philosophy as follows:

1. *Thinking Metaphysics: Not as Fall but as an Event*
2. *Overcoming Metaphysics: An Unachievable Task*

Our method was both deductive and inductive. Having charted Chauvet's direct citations from Heidegger's writings, quoted throughout *Symbole et Sacrement*, and having sorted these by text, it was possible to deduce the gaps, which came starkly into view, in Chauvet's reading. This method provided us with an initial clue to Chauvet's possible omissions. It was particularly successful in section 1. *Thinking Metaphysics* where it became obvious that Chauvet, for some reason, had

---

[31] In Chapter 4 I explore in more detail the question of Heidegger's ontology and whether or not it has ethical consequences.

[32] M. Heidegger, *Phänomenologie und Theologie* in *Wegmarken* (GA9), p. 76. 'Das eigene Wesen des Denkens und Sagens läßt sich nur einsehen in einem vorurteilsfreien Erblicken der Phänomene.'

passed by the main content of the lecture *What is Metaphysics?* This observation led to the discovery that two important themes of this lecture, *das Nichts* (the nothing) and *der Angst* (dread/anxiety), were wholly excluded from Chauvet's consideration of Heidegger's thinking on metaphysics.

From re-situating certain of Chauvet's citations and key themes back into the body of Heidegger's writings from which they were taken, it was possible through this inductive approach to highlight further omissions. This method was especially successful in section 2. *Overcoming Metaphysics* where, in the lecture *Introduction to 'What is Metaphysics?'*, Heidegger speaks of the *Überwindung der Metaphysik*. This *Überwindung* is a consequence of first learning to attend to the oblivion (*lethe*) of being. Through a close examination of Heidegger's *Parmenides* lecture series, reflecting on a Greek understanding of αλήθεια, a cognate of *lethe*, we were able to conclude against Chauvet that *Seinsvergessenheit* is less an event in the human psyche to be examined, at the instigation of human initiative, and more a foundational existential happening that befalls us, in a dread-filling moment of awe, when we least expect it. When Chauvet says that in order to overcome metaphysics one must perform a step backwards, jumping into the difference, he speaks within the technical or productionist scheme of thought that presumes the initiative for salvation lies with human agency; a scheme of thought he had hoped to move beyond in his investigations into the overcoming of metaphysics.

Having identified aspects of Heidegger's thinking that Chauvet neglected to consider, we were able to arrive at two conclusions:

1. Reading Heidegger in a selective way prevented Chauvet from gaining a true insight into the proper nature of Heidegger's thinking.
2. Chauvet's sacramental theology, which is predicated upon his interpretation of Heidegger's philosophy, would have assumed a different shape had those undetected aspects of Heidegger's thought been given due consideration.

We found a clue as to where this prejudice might lie in Chauvet's assertion that theology's *critical thrust* is to be found no longer in a prolongation of the negative onto-theology stressing the unknowability of God. This means that the *primordial task* of Christian theology is not to purify through analogy the concepts that we use to express God – so that we can reach 'knowledge under the mode of unknowing' (Dionysius). Although Heidegger would not necessarily articulate himself in these terms, it is possible nevertheless to surmise that he was drawn more naturally towards a 'negative onto-theology' in the sense of a positive evaluation of the *nihil* and states of mind like anxiety.

Hemming's *Heidegger's Atheism* successfully demonstrates that although Heidegger had lively presentiments of the divine, he refused nevertheless to voice these in positive theological terms. In this sense, in a way that Chauvet finds problematic, God, in defiance of all epistemologies, was unknowable for Heidegger. 'Heidegger', Hemming says, 'reeks of God, and yet at no point does he say who or what God is'.[33]

In *Phänomenologie und Theologie* (1927) Heidegger makes clear that the method he deploys in his enquiries is not that of the positive or ontic sciences, including the discipline of theology. Theology is a conceptual knowing of that which we call Christianness pure and simple. It is a conceptual interpretation of Christian existence. In short, theology is reflection on the lived experience of faith. Heidegger, in opening himself to ontology through a phenomenology, is able to examine the pre-Christian content of basic theological concepts and in so doing to stress, against Chauvet, the unknowability of God. It is worth recalling Heidegger's answer to his own question 'What is it that phenomenology is to "let us see?"

> Manifestly it is something that proximally and for the most part does *not* show itself at all: it is something that lies hidden (*verborgen*), in contrast to that which proximally and for the most part does show itself; but at the same time it is something that belongs to what thus shows itself, and it belongs to it so essentially as to constitute its meaning and ground.[34]

Heidegger's method leads to 'knowledge' closer to knowledge under the mode of unknowing (Dionysius), which Chauvet rejects, than it does to the cataphatic affirmations of a more positivistic theology favoured by Chauvet. From these considerations it is fair to conclude that Chauvet's omissions stem in part or in whole from his dismissal of the apophatic and his neglect of the significance of phenomenology in philosophy. It is only by viewing Heidegger's philosophy without preconceptions that a proper insight into his thinking emerges.

Having identified areas of Heidegger's thought glossed over by Chauvet, and having sought to explain why this might have happened, we are now in a position to develop a deeper awareness of some of these neglected themes. Only then will we be in a position to revisit the question ultimately directing Chauvet's

---

[33] L. Hemming, *Heidegger's Atheism* (2002), p. 2.
[34] M. Heidegger, *Sein und Zeit* (GA2), p. 35. 'Offenbar solches, was sich zunächst und zumeist gerade *nicht* zeigt, was gegenüber dem, was sich zunächst und zumeist zeigt, *verborgen* ist, aber zugleich etwas ist, was wesenhaft zu dem, was sich zunächst und zumeist zeigt, gehört, so zwar, daß es seinen Sinn und Grund ausmacht.'

researches: is transubstantiation still the most apt term to speak of that which takes place substantially on the altar during the consecration of the Catholic liturgy?

Having examined the philosophical foundations of Chauvet's sacramental theology in this chapter, Chapter 2 will sketch the trajectory of his thinking. Once this has been done, in subsequent chapters those areas overlooked by Chauvet will be further developed. Chapter 3 will examine *das Nichts* and *der Angst*, in the wider context of a discussion of *das Heilige*, with a view to deploying these terms within a theological framework. Chapter 4 will explore the ethical implications of coming into the truth of being or being's relocation to the daemonic district following the overcoming of metaphysics. In other words, it will inquire into the ontological foundations of ethics. Chapter 5 will look at the sacrificial implications of coming into the truth of being through an examination of *Sein-zum-Tode* (being-towards-death) and the determining *Stimme des Gewissens* (the voice of conscience) which, as the echo of an inexpressible Saying, discourses solely and constantly in the mode of keeping silent.

2

Chauvet and Eucharist

This chapter shows how Chauvet's reading of Heidegger, explored and critiqued comprehensively in Chapter 1, instructs his deconstruction of orthodox sacramental theology. It undertakes to demonstrate how his particular reading of Heidegger forms an essential part of the foundation upon which he constructs his theological edifice. It will be possible to see how Chauvet legitimizes his departure from Catholic doctrinal positions through his appeal to his reading, albeit with the omissions identified in the first chapter, of Heidegger's thought. This departure is no more in evidence than in Chauvet's rejection of the aptness of the doctrine of transubstantiation to express theologically the integral content of the Eucharist presence and in his reinterpretation of the visible, true and proper sacrifice that is the Eucharist as 'anti-sacrifice' or the major teaching moment . . . the great pedagogy. His rejections of the doctrine of transubstantiation and the traditional interpretation of sacrifice are grounded in an exegesis of Jn 6.51–8, a passage in which Jesus is questioned by an incredulous audience: 'how can this man give us his flesh to eat?' The doctrine of transubstantiation, claims Chauvet, was wrong to conceive the 'how' in onto-theological terms because the issue at stake here is of another order far more radical.

The task before us is not a straightforward one for, although Chauvet structured his presentation of Heidegger's philosophy under key headings, nevertheless his writing on the sacraments, in particular the Eucharist, does not unfold systematically in accordance with these in the later chapters of *Symbole et Sacrement*. Rather, for Chauvet, Heidegger's proposed new way of thinking after metaphysics, is present continuously if unobtrusively in the background as Chauvet unfolds his theology. Occasionally, as he develops his view of sacrament, he will refer in a more explicit way to Heidegger bringing him once again into the foreground. However, Chauvet does not on the whole provide a direct and visible trail from his preliminary reading of Heidegger to his eventual sacramental theology. In an attempt to introduce clarity in re-presenting Chauvet's theological arguments therefore, the headings identified in the first chapter have been preserved. In doing this Chauvet's conclusions can be more clearly evaluated in the light of my own reading of Heidegger in subsequent chapters.

In what follows it is important to note what is not intended at this stage: in the main text of this chapter Chauvet's theological conclusions will not be appraised in light of the omissions identified in the first chapter, although in the occasional footnote possible inconsistencies in Chauvet's line of argument may be pointed out. This exercise is reserved for later. Since this chapter's principal concern is to sketch how Chauvet progresses from his interpretation of Heidegger to his own sacramental theology, it is pre-eminently descriptive. Only in the final part, entitled *In the Stay of the Appropriating Fourfold*, will a departure be made from this method. Here Chauvet, having shown earlier how Heidegger's thoughts on metaphysics and its overcoming allow for a broader and more encompassing view of the Body of Christ, as this comes into presence in the Eucharistic moment, re-engages with Heidegger: in a consideration of the latter's writings on the fourfold (*das Geviert*) Chauvet attempts to give additional philosophical credibility to his symbolic approach. It is at this juncture that the chapter, until then a descriptive account, reverts to a critical engagement with Chauvet.

Where Chauvet appropriates arguments from other authors, and where the meanings of such appropriations need to be more fully explicated for the sake of the wider discussion, source texts have been identified and additional supplementary citations provided. This is no more evident than in Chauvet's reading of Henri De Lubac.

In order to situate this chapter within the wider context of the overall argument of the book it will first be necessary in *Recapitulation* to highlight certain key themes explored in Chapter 1. In the ensuing section, under the first rubric[1] used by Chauvet in his discussion of Heidegger, what happens to our understanding of Eucharist (when onto-theological terms prevail) in reflections on *how* Jesus gives us his flesh to eat will be shown. In *Res Significata et non Contenta*[2] . . .

---

[1] *Penser la métaphysique non comme une faute, mais comme un événement* (Thinking Metaphysics: Not as Fall but as Event).
[2] L.-M. Chauvet, *Symbole et Sacrement*, p. 301.

A Fatal Evolution, the effect a metaphysical way of thinking has, according to Chauvet, on our understanding of Eucharistic presence will be described. What precisely gets left behind or remains unthought when Eucharistic presence is conceived onto-theologically? In other words (and in the terminology introduced in Chapter 1) what is the unthought essence (*das ungedachte Wesen* or *l'essence impensée*) of the Eucharist as it is presently understood? In *The Esse and Ad-Esse*[3] *of Christ* it will be shown how the notion of substance, uncritically attributed to Aristotle by Chauvet, came to name this metaphysical approach to Eucharist. In *St Augustine*, the *'dichotomie meurtrière'* ('deadly dichotomy') that represented a serious trauma in the conscience of the Church (introduced with the adoption of an exclusively metaphysical approach to the Blessed Sacrament) will be examined. In *Understanding of Divine Subtlety*, the sacred perspective foreclosed with the adoption of this metaphysical view (the infinite which Plato attempted to wipe out) will be discussed.

Having delineated the implications of thinking Eucharistic presence in a metaphysical way in these preliminary sections it will be possible to show how Chauvet, following Heidegger, claims he is able to deconstruct this approach. This section is arranged under the second rubric used by Chauvet in Chapter 1 *Dépasser la metaphysique: une tâche inachevable* (Overcoming Metaphysics: An Unachievable Task). In *procès de la métaphysique* (suit against metaphysics), it will be shown how Chauvet, through a consideration of Heidegger's thoughts on the fourfold (*das Geviert*), moves from the what he claims is the now-discredited notion of substance to the path of symbolism. Having asked the question whether Heidegger would have agreed with Chauvet's claim that the symbol touches the most real aspect of ourselves and our world once metaphysical *substantia* is negated in its overcoming, the chapter concludes with a consideration of Chauvet's post-metaphysical reworking of Eucharistic presence, within the tri-partite structure of word-sacrament-ethics, as indeed still bread, but now *essential* bread.

In thus showing how Chauvet arrives at his postmodern view of Eucharistic presence through his particular reading of Heidegger it will be possible to present, in a subsequent chapter, an alternative understanding of Eucharist founded this time on my own understanding of Heidegger. This is what I will undertake in Chapter 5.

---

[3]   L.-M. Chauvet, *Symbole et Sacrement*, pp. 399–400.

2.1 Recapitulation

We saw in the last chapter how the onto-theological presuppositions of Greek thought, represented in Chauvet's interpretation of Plato's assertion that the infinite as the enemy must be wiped out if humankind is to survive, make it *impossible*, Chauvet contends, for the Scholastics and in particular St Thomas Aquinas to conceive the sacraments in any other way than in terms of causality. It may be recalled that causality is the very principle of the subordination of genesis to 'ousia' ; because something *is* in a substantial way, the creative swirl of infinite genesis is subverted, passed over if not entirely extinguished. We observed that in Chauvet's reading of Aquinas the being or stasis of '*ousia*' is unthinkable without analogy to God as First Cause and, as the *summum ens*, the guarantor of existence. This *analogia entis* is at the heart of an onto-theological view of the world.

By extension and by virtue of the fact St Thomas conducted his thinking within a framework defined by these presuppositions, the sacraments are held, in Chauvet's understanding of St Thomas' position, to cause grace, if only in an analogous sense. In spite of the ambiguity in St Thomas' writings on the sacraments[4] we saw how Chauvet nevertheless concludes that the scheme of sacramental representation operative in St Thomas' thought is technical or productionist. Having arrived at this understanding of sacraments, which Chauvet designates 'metaphysical', he embarks on a reading of Heidegger's philosophy in search of a non-metaphysical perspective. It is from here and upon this ground, as we shall come to see, that he develops and founds his own sacramental theology. In other words, Chauvet engages with Heidegger's philosophy in the hope of finding a way to think the *essence impensée* of the sacraments by reaching beyond the mental framework determinative of Greek thought (epitomized, he thinks, by Plato). Chauvet is, therefore, seeking to re-appropriate Catholic tradition from the perspective of Heidegger's thought.

For Chauvet Heidegger points to a mindfulness or a way of thinking, extricated from an archaic substructure all the more influential for being unconscious. One must continually *counteract* this objectifying scheme, with its implications of causality, instrumentality and production. The Scholastics,

---

[4] On the one hand, sacraments merely signal/figure what is present and on the other they actually cause/effect the presence they signify.

conscious of the limits of this scheme, tried to purify it by analogy for at that time, it was not possible to think in any other way.

2.2 Thinking Metaphysics: Not as Fall but as an Event

2.2.1 *Res Significata et non Contenta* . . . a fatal evolution[5]

In chapter 10,[6] section II[7] of *Symbole et Sacrement* Chauvet contrasts his non-metaphysical and *symbolic approach* to the question of Eucharist with the metaphysical causality he asserts to be the essence of St Thomas' thinking. Through the adoption of symbols the tendency to provide final 'reasons' for things is resisted. By re-placing ourselves on the ground of the symbolic order we begin to think in another way in our departure from the stable platform provided by traditional metaphysics to another ground – one always shifting.

Chauvet contends that once the principle of causality is called into question by thinking outside a framework of Greek thought (biased against the infinite), the inadequacies of scholastic transubstantiation come into view. Although, in canon 1, the Council of Trent had emphasized that not all sacraments are to be understood in the same way and that the Eucharist is the *Blessed* Sacrament or an *admirabile sacramentum*, since the whole Christ is truly, really and substantially contained, nevertheless the Tridentine view, for Chauvet, seems dangerous to us.[8] The reason adduced for this concern is that, whereas the effect of other sacraments like baptism is *'in suscipiente'* ('in the one who receives it'), in the case of the Eucharist the first effect is *'in ipsa materia'* ('in the matter itself'). The claim is that *to prioritize 'sacred physics'[9] over the effect the sacrament has upon the communicant, endangers a central aspect of the mystery.* The Christ of the Eucharist is the *Christus totus* so that the 'head' cannot be isolated from

---

5   Cardinal Henri de Lubac, *Corpus Mysticum: L'Eucharistie et L'Église au Moyen Age* (1948), p. 277, 'une évolution fatale'.

6   L.-M. Chauvet, *Symbole et Sacrement*, p. 387. 'L'Institué Sacramentel' (The Sacraments as Instituted).

7   L.-M. Chauvet, *Symbole et Sacrement*, p. 392. 'Le Corps Eucharistique du Seigneur: *Une figure exemplaire de la résistance de l'institué sacramentel.*' (The Eucharistic Body of the Lord: *an Exemplary Figure of the Resistance of the Sacraments as Instituted.*)

8   This line of argument was advanced in the sixteenth century by English Protestant reformers as part of the justification for the official discrediting and the practical dismantling of the Catholic church. The reformers maintained that the Council of Trent marked the beginning of extreme corruption in the Roman Church.

9   Laurence Paul Hemming, *Transubstantiating Ourselves*, Heythrop Journal, Vol. 44 [October 2003], p. 419.

the 'body', the Church which still remains completely distinct from it. Can one conceive the *esse* of Christ in the Eucharist without the relation of his *ad-esse* to the Church, to the celebrating community, to the believing subjects for whom it is destined?

This fracturing of the *Christus totus*, Chauvet believes following Henri De Lubac, leads inevitably to an 'expulsion' *outside* the intrinsic symbolism of the sacrament of what the Church Fathers considered to be its ultimate reality: the Church as the *truth* of the Eucharistic *'corpus mysticum'*. In other words, when Eucharist is reduced metaphysically to a sacred physics, so that its effect is withheld from the communicant and confined exclusively to the species of bread and wine, the *ecclesia* (Church) gets forgotten; the *ecclesia* is now no more than the *res significata et non contenta* (reality signified but not contained). When the Eucharist is articulated in onto-theological terms the Church sinks into oblivion (*Seinsvergessenheit*) surviving only as the *das ungedachte Wesen* or *l'essence impensée* of the Blessed Sacrament. From the moment when it became the *mystical body*, says De Lubac, the ecclesial body was already detaching itself from the Eucharist. At the same time that it was being thrown out of the *true Body*, the Church was beginning to be thrown out of the *mystery of faith*.

It is the preoccupation with transubstantiation which consigns to oblivion the first scandal of the mystery of faith, namely, that the grace of Christ present in the Eucharist does not suddenly fall 'from heaven'; rather Christ as head *and* body emerges from the *assembly*. In other words, when the Eucharist comes into its truth for Chauvet, it presences as the *crystallization* of Christ's presence in the *assembly* (ecclesia): it is gathered in his name, presided over by him and in the *Scriptures* proclaimed as his living word.

2.2.2 Berengar and the deadly dichotomy

How did it come about the Church settled for this impoverished understanding of Eucharist? Why was the Church content for the real essence of the Eucharist, the *ecclesia*, to remain unthought . . . to be merely signified by the Eucharistic species but not contained within it?

Chauvet, following De Lubac, maintains the West became imprisoned within this *'dichotomie meurtrière'* – *corpus mysticum/corpus verum*, in reaction to the Berengarian controversy of the eleventh century. This reached its culmination in the thirteenth century with a conception of the Church as *corpus mysticum* without any connection to the Eucharist. The Berengarian trauma had the effect of creating a substantial displacement in the traditional approach concerning the threefold Body of Christ: the Church is no longer perceived as the *veritas* of the body that it receives in mystery.[10]

The Augustinian position, which stressed the Eucharistic 'co-corporality' and 'co-sacramentality' of Christ *and* the Church, had supporters, like Alger of Liège, at the time of the controversy. However, in the response of ecclesial authorities to the 'dangerous' views promulgated by Berengar and his followers, this was pushed to one side and ignored. From that day forwards the *veritas* is contained in the Eucharist itself, which is the *corpus verum*, the Church becoming after that the *corpus mysticum* in an absolute way, that is, without any relation to the Eucharistic mystery. According to Chauvet it was recourse to the very subtle Aristotelian concept of 'substance' which enabled the Church to think outside of Berengar's 'physicalism'. It helped secure the Church's defeat of Berengar,[11] through offering an alternative to the sensual ultra-realism of his teaching. Before the application of Aristotle's category of 'substance' to the phenomenon of Eucharistic presence there was a tendency to conceive presence in such a 'sensualist' way that the Body of Christ (following the consecration) had extension, division, locomotion, corruption, taste, colour and so on. After, as St Thomas points out, presence was no longer thought of as something engaging the senses: 'substance' offers no footing to any organ of sense or to the imagination; the essence of things, being no longer grounded in the senses, henceforth was to be found, following Aristotle, in the objects of intelligence.

De Lubac, given the impoverishment suffered by the doctrine of real presence as a result of Berengar's challenges, asserts the introduction of the Aristotelian term 'substance' represents success for Berengar, in spite of fact it appeared to be a positive result for ecclesial authorities. It could be said that the ultra-orthodox party fell into the trap that had been set for them by the heretic, or again that they allied with him in mutilating the traditional teaching. Could Eucharistic realism not have been safeguarded without the almost total abandonment of symbolism? In desperation De Lubac laments:

---

[10]   While Chauvet is concerned with the theological implications of this inversion, in particular with its effect on our understanding of Eucharistic presence, others are concerned with the sociopolitical impact. William T. Cavanaugh, for instance, claims 'the confinement of the Body of Christ to the altar allows for the invention of "modern" politics based on the privatisation of the organic-charitable body and the public assertion of the sovereign territorial state' [Cavanaugh, Eucharistic Sacrifice and the Social Imagination in Early Modern Europe, *Journal of Medieval and Early Modern Studies*, 31:3 [Fall 2001], p. 594].

   It would be interesting to examine the sociopolitical implications of being mindful once more of *ecclesia* in our understanding of the Body of Christ.

[11]   In spite of the controversy (and perhaps as a consequence of it) Berengar publicly retracted his views before his death.

What ruination heresy accomplishes here, even when it is vanquished![12]

The dialectic of substance and accidents,[13] although protecting persistent faith in a real presence of Christ in the sacrament, had nevertheless un-desirous and unanticipated side effects. The beautiful considerations of the past, the symbols flowing with doctrinal richness, were relegated to second place. Though they were never formally repudiated nevertheless they became the forgotten essence, *das ungedachte Wesen* or *l'essence impensée*, of the Eucharist.

It follows therefore that when Chauvet says recourse to the concept of 'substance' is not the only path possible to express theologically the integral content of the Eucharistic presence, he is opening up the possibility once more of affirming the relationship between Eucharist and the Church, as St Augustine had done, if not of rescuing from oblivion the empirically mediated and symbolic dimension of the event of Christ's presence in the consecrated species. If the official response to the Berengarian controversy had the unintended effect of making people forget the ecclesial symbolism altogether, when Chauvet questions the concept that ostensibly diffused the threat posed by Berengar, the once forgotten ecclesial symbolism is once again recalled. Indeed Chauvet cites Augustine to bring home his point:

> ... If then you are the body of Christ and his members, it is your own mystery that is placed on the Lord's table; it is your own mystery that you receive ...
> Be what you see and receive what you are.[14]

2.2.3 St Augustine – *Esse, Ad-Esse* and the symbolic conjunction of the two

For Augustine the Blessed Sacrament was endowed with a richness of incomparable depths: Christ's presence on the altar appropriates those gathered together as *ecclesia* into himself in ways both mysterious and life-transforming. There can be no head without a body: the two mutually necessitate and support

---

[12] Cardinal Henri de Lubac, *Corpus Mysticum: L'Eucharistie et L'Église au Moyen Age* (1948), p. 291. 'Quel ravage accomplit ici l'hérésie, même vaincue!'

[13] Chauvet points out, against Schillebeeckx's claim that the Fathers of the Council of Trent interpreted the dogma of transubstantiation in Aristotelian terms, that 'by deliberately choosing the pair "substance-species," instead of the Aristotelian "substance-accidents," the council deliberately avoided linking the expression of its faith to one philosophy, the Aristotelian' [L.-M. Chauvet, *Symbole et Sacrement*, p. 393. 'comme le montre notamment le choix délibéré du couple "substance-espèces" au lieu de celui, aristotélicien, de "substance-accidents", le concile n'a pas voulu lier l'expression de sa foi à une philosophie, la philosophie aristotélicienne'].

[14] L.-M. Chauvet, *Symbole et Sacrement*, p. 399. '"Si donc vous êtes le corps du Christ et ses membres, c'est votre propre mystère qui repose sur la table du Seigneur, c'est votre propre mystère que vous recevez."'

each other to the extent that it is meaningless to speak of one in isolation from the other. Both Eucharistic realism and ecclesial realism mutually reinforce, support and guarantee one another. Just as ecclesial realism safeguards Eucharistic realism so the obverse is true. Augustine demonstrates the full implications of what is at stake in the *sacramentum*: the indissoluble marriage of Christ and the Church, the impossibility of saying the one, as a simple object ('something facing'), without saying the other. The *sacramentum* illustrates precisely the symbolic conjunction of the two.

For Chauvet, following St Augustine, one cannot conceive the *esse* of Christ in the Eucharist without the relation of his *ad-esse* to the Church. *L'esse du Christ* is not hermetically sealed off from life, being exclusively confined to the Eucharistic species but, instead, is destined for the celebrating community, for the believing subjects. The problem with a notion of substance which speaks of the 'full realization' (*perfectio*) of the Eucharist in the consecration of the matter is that it runs the risk of conflating into one two essential elements that are linked together. In other words, when the final reality of entities is identified with their ontological substance the sensualist dimension of matter, along with the ecclesial symbolism of the Eucharist, gets left behind if not altogether forgotten. On the one hand, one does not take into account the *human* destination that is implied by the *materia* in question, the bread and wine. On the other, one loses sight of a fundamental aspect of the mystery: the Christ of the Eucharist is the *Christus totus*; the 'head' cannot be isolated from the 'body', the Church which still remains completely distinct from it.

2.2.4 Understanding of divine subtlety

For Chauvet, Heidegger's philosophy opens up the possibility of re-uniting these two distinct spheres that came to be dissociated from one another following the Berengarian controversy. It is essential to Chauvet's thesis, where the Aristotelian category 'substance' precludes from consideration all but the substantial presence of Christ (the *esse*) in the Eucharistic species, that these two elements can only properly be grasped on the plane of thought of metaphysical substance.[15] When

---

[15] It is worth pointing out here an apparent inconsistency in Chauvet's understanding of Heidegger and the overcoming of metaphysics. In Chapter 1 Chauvet upholds that overcoming metaphysics indicates *un certain mode d'habiter la tradition métaphysique* (a certain manner of living within the metaphysical tradition) of *recalling* it, this time, however, *en pensant son essence impensée* (by thinking its unthought essence). However here, in the instance of metaphysical *substantia*, he is not suggesting the unthought essence of *substantia* be recalled, but that *substantia* be altogether negated. Given this, it is possible to assert a hidden nihilism (in the sense of 'the mere devaluing of

Heidegger's *procès de la métaphysique* (suit against metaphysics) is invoked, Chauvet contends, the semantic richness of bread and wine, excluded when the onto-thelogical term 'substance' was relied upon, emerges from out of concealment. De Lubac speaks of the raptures that await those who enter more fully and more perfectly into the mysteries seeking to obtain from them ever-greater understanding. In an unconstrained moment he delights:

> What wonderful vistas open up in this way before our understanding! What vast landscapes will it not be given us to travel through, in search of these mystical reasons! And what honing of our thought, what flights, what leaps of our whole being, launching itself up from the springboard of our faith *to an understanding of divine subtlety!* What ingenuity used to scrutinise so many reasons hidden beneath signs and figures! What richness in their discovery! What enchantment in establishing oneself '*in the system of mystical correspondences*'! What a delicious foretaste of the joys of eternity![16]

The question directing the remainder of our enquiry therefore is whether it is necessary to discard altogether the term 'substance' and the associated doctrine of transubstantiation. Is it possible to conceive 'substance' in such a way that it engages the *ecclesia* instead of existing in detached isolation from it? Is substance an anti-Augustinian and metaphysical construal or does it have non-metaphysical Augustinian connotations which have become obscured since the Berengarian affair?[17] If it can be demonstrated that the latter is the case, doubt may be cast over Chauvet's claim that recourse to the concept 'substance' is not the only path possible to express theologically the integral content of the

---

the highest values' [M. Heidegger, *Nietzsches Wort 'Gott ist tot'* in *Holzwege* (GA5), p. 224. 'die bloße Entwertung der bisherigen obersten Werte bezeichnet']) in Chauvet's work.

If overcoming is taken as sublation, as Heidegger recommends, it is clear that it does not mean 'done away with, but raised up, kept, and preserved in the new creation' [M. Heidegger, *Phänomenologie und Theologie* in *Wegmarken* (GA9), p. 76, 'beseitigt, sondern in die neue Schöpfung hinaufgehoben, in ihr erhalten und verwahrt']. In a later chapter we will see how Heidegger's writing on *das Ding* allows for a post-Aristotelian and phenomenological understanding of *substantia*.

[16] Cardinal Henri de Lubac, *Corpus Mysticum: L'Eucharistie et L'Église au Moyen Age* (1948), p. 262. 'Quelles merveilleuses perspectives s'ouvrent ainsi devant l'intelligence! Quelle vaste carrière ne va-t-il pas lui être donné de parcourir à la recherche de ces raisons mystiques! Quel affinement aussi de la pensée, quel envol, quel sursaut de tout l'être s'élevant, à partir de la foi, *ad divinae subtilitatis intelligentiam!* Quelle ingéniosité déployée à scruter tant de raisons cachées sous les signes et les figures! Quelle fécondité dans leur découverte! Quel enchantement à s'établir "in consonantiarum mysticarum ordine"! Quel délicieux avant-goût des joies de l'éternité!'

[17] Chauvet intimates that such may be possible (though he does not pursue this line of enquiry) when he says that the language of 'substance' may 'not be linked to Aristotelianism as such because the second profession of faith imposed on Berengar in 1079 already contains the expression *substantialiter converti* and the term *transsubstantiatio* itself seems to have appeared before 1153' [L.-M. Chauvet, *Symbole et Sacrement*, p. 396, 'non liée à l'aristotélisme comme tel, puisque la seconde profession de foi imposée à Bérenger en 1079 comporte déjà l'expression *substantialiter converti* et que le terme lui-même *transsubstantiatio* semble être apparu dès avant 1153'].

Eucharistic presence. In so doing Pope Paul VI's observation will be shown to have a continuing relevance:

> it cannot be tolerated that any individual should on his own authority take something away from the formulas which were used by the Council of Trent to propose the Eucharistic mystery for our belief.[18]

2.3 Overcoming Metaphysics: An unachievable task

So how does Heidegger's *procès de la métaphysique* (suit against metaphysics), as this has been interpreted by Chauvet and which was discussed and critiqued at length in Chapter 1, enable a post-Berengarian and neo-Augustinian view of Eucharist to emerge? Is it necessary, in order to rethink sacramental presence in a postmodern context, to de-emphasize the contemporary significance of the formulas which were used by the Council of Trent to propose the Eucharistic mystery for our belief? Alternatively, is it possible to arrive at Chauvet's conclusion concerning the true nature of sacraments [19] without compromising or relinquishing language which the Church has established through the long labour of the centuries, a language that is not tied to a certain specific form of human culture, or to a certain level of scientific progress or to one or another theological school?

2.3.1 Heidegger's suit against metaphysics

In Chapter 1 it was noted how the asking of the question *What is Metaphysics?* opens up the possibility of a way of thinking which moves beyond representational thinking to *das andenkende Denken* (a thinking that recalls). It enables a recovery of the ontological difference which is forgotten when metaphysics identifies being with the type of being of entities (their 'being-ness'). Thinking can overcome

---

[18] Paul VI, Encyclical Letter *Mysterium Fidei*, promulgated 3 September 1965, paragraph 24, 'ferendus non est quisquis formulis, quibus Concilium Tridentinum Mysterium Eucharisticum ad credendum proposuit, suo marte derogare velit'.
    Chauvet is not simply rejecting a single word. In jettisoning 'substance' in this way he is calling into question the entire *corpus* of Catholic tradition which refers to it and to which it is assigned. In other words, transubstantiation interlocks with other doctrines such as the Church's teaching on sacrifice. It is of no surprise therefore that Chauvet, having disinherited himself of substance should express reservations with the traditional view of sacrifice.

[19] Namely, that they present the world to us as not reducible to a simple object at our disposal which may be exploited in a purely utilitarian way.

the constraints placed upon it when it reasons and reckons metaphysically, it was seen, by taking a step back from the eidetic representations of being that ordinarily construct reality or that which is real. The step back is a retreat from the same or the 'arrival which takes cover', into the region of difference where the 'event which uncovers' occurs. Slipping the net of its eidetic representations being re-ascends to the very source of its life, that is to the truth of being which is its *ignored* 'foundation'. Following the *Kehre* in the overcoming of metaphysics, that which before was unthought in the forgetfulness of metaphysical thinking, is thought through into the open of unconcealment in recollective thinking. Thinking the unthought essence of metaphysical existence is a recalling of what has become obscured in the the history of the increasing forgetfulness of being, which for Chauvet, it may be recalled, is the *Ereignis*. Overcoming metaphysics, Chauvet says, is like a test of conversion and can be finally summed up in the following question: Can we consent to leave the solid, reassuring ground of our represented foundation and the stable, fixed point in order to let ourselves go towards this demanding letting-be (*Gelassenheit*) in which we find ourselves out of our depth?

In the context of a discussion of the Eucharist the question *What is Metaphysics?* facilitates a consideration of the *l'essence impensée* of the bread/ Body of Christ that is the unintended consequence of conceiving Eucharistic presence in a metaphysical way. The overcoming of metaphysics offers the prospect of recovering the truth of substance or the *verum* (*res*) of the Blessed Sacrament. It was the response of 'ultra-orthodoxy' to the threat of Berengar in the eleventh century which, as was shown, switched the *verum* of Eucharist from the assembly (*ecclesia*) to the Eucharistic species. Chauvet is in no doubt about how Heidegger can assist with the recovery of what has been lost and the task that lies before thinking after metaphysics: his task is *to meditate on what this tradition excludes, which is nevertheless what makes it possible*, as it itself shows by taking backward steps. That every true advance in thought takes place by moving backward, is the deepest lesson Chauvet has learned from Heidegger.

To step-back or turn-away from a metaphysical view of substance is to recall mindfully the traditional teaching concerning the presence of Christ in the Eucharist that had become obfuscated. It is to undo the ruination heresy accomplished even when vanquished. It is to refresh an understanding of the sacraments through a *resourcement* reaching back to the neglected Augustinian tradition.

2.3.2 *Ecclesia* . . . the *Essence Impensée* of Eucharist

When we turn from a metaphysical view of substance, Chauvet says, the *res* or *verum* of the Blessed Sacrament is no longer identified exclusively with the substance of Christ present in the consecrated species (accidents) of the bread and wine. Rather, when substance is exchanged for symbol, the *res* or *verum* of the Sacrament is to be found as much in the *ecclesia* as in the consecrated species. Following Aquinas and De Lubac it could be said *carnis ac sanguinis veritatem, ipsam eorumdem efficientiam* (the truth of the flesh and blood is found in what they effectuate), that is, in the forgiveness of sins. Since the effect of forgiveness is felt as a rejoicing in the soul of the sinner, it follows that the *verum* of Eucharistic presence is less *in ipsa materia* ('in the matter itself') and more, like baptism and the other sacraments, *in suscipiente* ('in the one who receives it') or, in terms of the body corporate assembled in worship, in the *ecclesia*.

Chauvet defines the *ecclesia* as the fundamental sacrament that gives body to Christ making him present to those living between his first coming, over 2,000 years ago, and his second coming in the *parousia*. To balance the 'already', the 'not-yet' inevitably opened up space for a theology of the sacramentality of the Church, which was the only one that could be adapted to an in-between time. Chauvet, thinking anew the *l'essence impensée* of Eucharist, turns from Augustinian tradition to scripture. He underpins his entire theology of the 'sacramentality' of the Church with three Lucan stories: the road to Emmaus (Lk. 24. 13–35), the baptism of the Ethiopian eunuch (Acts 8. 26–40) and the first account of the conversion of Saul (Acts 9. 1–20). Each of these requires an intervention that escorts its protagonist[s] from a position/positions of non-faith to faith: the first at the moment of the breaking of bread in Emmaus, the second at a rereading and interpretation of scripture and the third at the moment of the imposition of hands upon Saul. These interventions, Chauvet says, will later be called the *sacraments* of the Church. They will become the wonder-filled witnesses of a God who 'is' not here except by mode of passage.

God presences in the in-between time through the fundamental sacramental mediation of the Church which exhorts the giving up of all desire to see, touch, find, that is, finally to prove, Jesus. Henceforth his real body can be touched only as *the body symbolized* through the testimony the Church gives about him, through the *Scriptures* reread as his own word, the *sacraments* performed as his own gestures, the *ethical witness* of the communion between brothers and sisters.

It is the last, the return-gift of ethical witness, the concrete practice of the brotherly and sisterly *koinonia*, that demonstrates whether the gift of the good news of the resurrection, offered in word and acceded to in sacrament, have been received in good faith. In other words, the resurrection of Jesus does not in truth take place without provoking the re-surrection of the disciples into witnesses. In short, the *koinonia* is a testimony rendered to the risen Christ. It is by the return-gift of an *ethical* practice that the subject 'verifies' what it has received in the sacrament. Included in the 'element' ethics is, for Chauvet, every kind of *action* not only interpersonal 'moral *praxis*' but also collective 'social *praxis*'. Ethics can, in addition, be expressed as a 'categorical *imperative*' of life and action.

Chauvet turns next to anthropology to legitimize the structure he believes comes into view with the stepping back from metaphysics into *das ungedachte Wesen* or *l'essence impensée*. His structure Scripture-Sacrament-Ethics appears as homologous to a more fundamental *anthropological structure*: cognition-recognition-praxis.

This structure of Christian identity turns out to be the restatement, albeit in an original way, of this fundamental anthropological structure. Within this structure the discursive logic of the *sign*, the identifying challenge of the *symbol* and the world-transforming *praxis* unite into one. Sign, symbol and praxis function, for Chauvet, in the exact same way as the anthropological process of symbolic exchange.[20] Until recently, owing to the deficiencies of metaphysical thinking, the process of gift – reception – return-gift which structures every meaningful relationship has remained unthought: the gift of the always-already written word of scripture, having been received in the sacrament, obliges the recipient to return the gift in the form of ethical witness (a thanksgiving).

2.3.3 *Ecclesia* . . . oblation, sacrifice and *l'Agapê Fraternelle*

In order to become the Body of Christ received in the Eucharist, a reception effected by means of *oblation*, the subject is committed, like Christ, to live out

---

[20] In the Introduction we pointed out Heidegger's own challenge to social anthropology when he says: 'anthropology . . . fail[s] to give an unequivocal and ontologically adequate answer to the question about the *kind of Being* which belongs to those entities which we ourselves are' [M. Heidegger, *Sein und Zeit* (GA2) (1962), p. 50. 'Mit dem Hinweis auf das Fehlen einer eindeutigen, ontologisch zureichend begründeten Antwort auf die Frage nach der *Seinsart* dieses Seienden, das wir selbst sind, in der Anthropologie'].

Heidegger says the same thing in a conversation with Ernst Cassirer during a colloquium on Kant at Davos in Switzerland in March of 1929: 'the question, what man is, doesn't have to be answered so much in the sense of an anthropological system' [Guido Schneeberger, *Beilage IV: Arbeitsgemeinschaft Cassirer-Heidegger* in *Ergänzungen zu einer Heidegger-Bibliographie* (1960), p. 22, 'die Frage, was der Mensch sei, nicht so sehr beantwortet werden muß im Sinne eines anthropologischen Systems'].

In *Expérience et absolu* Lacoste, unlike Chauvet, resists the French convention of reading Heidegger as philosophical anthropology (p. 1).

their own oblation of themselves in this self-giving to others. Chauvet calls this self-giving l'*agapê fraternelle* (agape between brothers and sisters). In the Eucharistic adaptation of this fundamental mechanism of symbolic exchange, found in both New and Old Testaments, sacrifice, as the giving of self to others, is enabled by the grace of the Word from the past being received in the present. In short, without accession to the Word, the true knife of sacrifice, there can be no ethics. Ethics, for Chauvet, is inscription/scripted action or the performance of the always-already word that precedes us. Under the psychic pattern of filiation ethics manifests historically in the present as, not only interpersonal 'moral *praxis*' but also as, the collective 'social *praxis*'.

This is not Rene Girard's idea of sacrifice understood as: a process by which a group unburdens itself onto a scapegoat of both its internal violence, the result of 'mimetic rivalry' which threatens its existence, and the guilt inspired by this violence. Such a model of sacrifice, in which the reconciliation of a group is facilitated by use of a sacralized victim is defective because it dispenses human beings from assuming their responsibility in history. For Chauvet, since Girard's understanding of sacrifice results in a process of *nonrecognition of responsibility* or an abdication of ethics, and since accession to the word, in Chauvet's model, impels the one acceding, to ethical action, the language of sacrifice is no longer to be accorded any particular privilege in Chauvet's sacramental theology. For Chauvet the oblation at the heart of the Eucharistic process that institutes the *ecclesia*, is not sacrifice but *anti-sacrifice*.[21] Girard's thesis, which determines Chauvet's understanding of sacrifice, reveals a tension characteristic of the relation between cult and ethics: there is either a sacrificial regimen with ethical abdication, or a ethical regimen of responsibility. Since it is impossible to do away with the language of sacrifice altogether because of the sacrificial pattern that dwells in all of us Chauvet concedes *anti-sacrifice* as a third term between sacrifice and non-sacrifice. It names this ethical regimen of responsibility. The anti-sacrificial regimen to which the Gospel calls us *rests* upon the sacrificial, but it does so to *turn it around* and thereby to redirect ritual practice, the symbolic point of passage that structures Christian identity, back towards ethical practice, the place where the ritual practice is verified.

[21] Since the publication of *Symbole et Sacrement* in 1987 Girard has changed his mind on the question of sacrifice. Kirwin concludes 'his position now is that the term can only be understood in its transformative history: what . . . corresponds to the third position designated by Chauvet as "anti-sacrifice"' [M. Kirwin, *Eucharist and Sacrifice*, New Blackfriars, Vol. 88, (2007), p. 21].

2.3.4 *Ecclesia* . . . symbolic mediation vs immediate contact with God

This symbolic view of the *ecclesia* has the advantage, claims Chauvet, of denouncing as illusory an *individualism* by which we would believe ourselves to be more Christian the more we achieve immediate contact with God in the silent conversation of meditation. Chauvet is clear that we cannot live in an imaginary direct contact with Jesus that presupposes his 'full' presence. He repeats, delineating the strict boundaries within which a thinking beyond metaphysics must remain, that the recognition of Jesus as Christ and Lord does not happen through direct contact with him. On the contrary, such recognition requires assent to the mediation of his symbolic body, the Church. Accession to the symbolic implies consenting to the presence of the absence, to the presence of a original beatitude or complete fullness of meaning within the subject. For Chauvet, a sacrament is akin to language: rather than bringing me into the fullness of being, instead it breaks forever the imaginary coincidence of the self with itself. Sacraments achieve this break by putting the real at a distance.[22] The coming to truth of the subject that the sacrament effects becomes a mourning for the imaginary coincidence between the (I) of the enunciation and the 'I' of the statement.[23] Instead of taking flight from the melancholy induced by *deuil* (mourning), symbols locate us in the presence of the unthought at the deepest level of thought.

---

[22] Chauvet's mistrust of the real, against which the symbolic realm guards us, is symptomatic of a wider suspicion of nature in general. Nietzsche argues against this suspicion for it blocks access to the realization of humanity's noble destiny. For instance, he says: 'There are enough people who could well entrust themselves to their inclinations with grace and without care, but who do not for fear of the imagined "evil essence" of nature! *That* is why there is so little nobility among human beings; its distinguishing feature has always been to have no fear of oneself, to expect nothing contemptible from oneself, to fly without misgivings wherever we're inclined – we free-born birds! And wherever we arrive, there will always be freedom and sunlight around us' [F. Nietzsche, *Die Fröhliche Wissenschaft* (1986), p. 195. 'Es gibt genug Menschen, die sich ihren Trieben mit Anmut und Sorglosigkeit überlassen dürfen: aber sie tun es nicht, aus Angst vor jenem eingebildeten "bösen Wesen" der Natur! Daher ist es gekommen, daß so wenig Vornehmheit unter den Menschen zu finden ist: deren Kennzeichen es immer sein wird, vor sich keine Furcht zu haben, von sich nichts Schmähliches zu erwarten, ohne Bedenken zu fliegen, wohin es uns treibt – uns freigeborene Vögel! Wohin wir auch nur kommen, immer wird es frei und sonnenlicht um uns sein'].

[23] It is difficult to see how sacraments, as mediations blocking access to being in the fullness of an original beatitude, can be seen as events of human salvation. Instead and insofar as symbols subjugate individualism in Chauvet's theology they actively work against human freedom. If Eucharist is a mourning for the loss of our original beatitude then Mass, instead of being a rejoicing in our salvation becomes a mourning for lost innocence, a melancholic funeral service, albeit my own. These are not moods ordinarily associated with deliverance or salvation. Our souls rejoice *For the LORD our God is bringing us into a good land – a land with streams and pools of water, with springs flowing in the valleys and hills* (Deut. 8.7).

They act as *la butée primordiale* (the primordial stumbling block) against which every fantasy desire for self-possession, for sweeping away all mediation and all contingency, for advancing to immediate and transparent presence of the self to the self[24] must break up. With fatalistic resignation Chauvet, prompted by Lacan's psychology, believes we must accept the death of the illusion *everything in us desperately wants to believe, that is, the illusion that we can somehow pull ourselves out of the necessary mediation of symbols* to apprehend reality directly.

Symbols, instead of enabling the abundant life, represent rather its abortion. In a chilling, unguarded moment, Chauvet announces that 'there is for each of us, always, a child to kill off, the mourning to go through again and again for this representation of plenitude.'[25] Chauvet concludes against life that to reject this death is to forfeit one's life. To be *ecclesia*, therefore, is inseparable from the very process of killing our primary narcissism or, in other words, our imaginary omnipotence and right-to-enjoy-everything. In brief, to reassign the subject to the symbolic order is to renounce to win back its lost paradise, its own origin and the ultimate foundation which would explain its existence.

To encounter Christ in the in-between time requires a person to accede to the symbolic order proper to the Church and to its rules of procedure, especially to the pattern formed by its interpretation of scripture, its liturgical celebrations and its ethical engagement. It is through accession to scripture, sacrament and ethics, the tripartite constituents of Christian identity making up the Church as fundamental sacrament, that one renounces a direct line, one could say a gnostic

---

[24]   What Chauvet believes to be a positive attribute of his method is however something not to be countenanced by Heidegger whose radical ontology aspires precisely for this 'immediate and transparent presence of the self to the self' [L.-M. Chauvet, *Symbole et Sacrement*, p. 149, 'de présence immédiate et transparente de soi à soi']. Heidegger's thought uncovers the self in its authenticity as 'self-actuating' or as 'the Self which has been taken hold of in its own way' [M. Heidegger, *Sein und Zeit* (GA2), p. 129, 'eigens ergriffenen *Selbst*'], that is, as not mediated or dispersed. The latter, the self that for Chauvet coalesces through symbolic mediation, is for Heidegger the self of everyday existence, *das Man*, that is to be surpassed. In Chapter 5 I explore an interpretation of Eucharist as a leaping forth from mediated existence (rather than accession to symbolic mediation) into the resoluteness of self in its ownmost, self-actuating and un-dispersed (recollected) authenticity. In other words my reading of Heidegger proceeds in the opposite direction to that of Chauvet.

    Whereas for Heidegger the object of his phenomenological approach is 'to abandon . . . representations and concepts in order to give linguistic expression to the self-manifest as it shows itself' in the hope that 'a word emerges that is foreign to common usage' [Bernhard Welte, *God in Heidegger's Thought* in *Philosophy Today*, Vol. XXVI, No. ¼, Spring 1982, p. 87] for Chauvet any 'word which seeks to be expressed in a kind of transparent purity is an illusion' [L.-M. Chauvet, *Symbole et Sacrement*, p. 158. 'parole qui voudrait se dire dans une sorte de pureté transparente est illusoire'].

[25]   L.-M. Chauvet, *Symbole et Sacrement*, p. 102, 'il y a pour chacun toujours, un enfant à tuer, le deuil à faire et à refaire d'une représentation de plénitude.'

line, to Jesus Christ.[26] The symbolic order is an *unavoidable stumbling block* which forms a barrier to every imaginary claim to a direct connection, individual and interior, with Christ or a gnostic-like, illuminist contact with him.[27] After the crucifixion, Chauvet reasserts the *Absent One* is present in his 'sacrament' which is the Church: the Church rereading the scriptures with him in mind, the Church repeating his gestures in memory of him, the Church living the sharing between brothers and sisters in his name. It is these forms of witness by the Church that Jesus takes on a body and allows himself to be encountered.

Having arrived thus far, it is pertinent to ask one final question: does Heidegger explicitly discuss symbolism anywhere in his writings? Chauvet believes he does in his lectures *Das Ding* and *Bauen Wohnen Denken*[28] where Heidegger explains what he means by *Das Geviert*. 'With regard to this gathering of the *Fourfold*', Chauvet says, 'the word that comes immediately to mind is *symbol*.'[29] Before concluding this chapter, therefore, we will consider Heidegger's *Fourfold* and its influence upon Chauvet's sacramental theology and his symbolic approach to Eucharist.

2.3.5 *Eucharistia* . . . in the stay of the appropriating fourfold

Having followed Heidegger through his thinking concerning the overcoming of metaphysics in order to think the Eucharist's unthought essence and to call into question a metaphysical view of substance that, following the Berengarian controversy, came to name and define Eucharistic presence, Chauvet asks: what is reality on this *other terrain*? If we are now displaced from the terrain of classical metaphysics, from whose standpoint the real presence has been viewed, what does the Body of Christ look like on the path of symbolism?

Until now the *ad-esse* of the Eucharist has been considered to show how, for Chauvet, going beyond metaphysics opens up an understanding of *ecclesia* as the fundamental sacrament or symbolic mode of Christ's presence in an

---

26 Chauvet interprets resentment of the Church and resistance to its claim to be the fundamental sacrament of Christ's presence in the time in-between Jesus' First and Second Coming as a 'symptom of this "gnostic" desire for the immediate contact with Jesus Christ' [L.-M. Chauvet, *Symbole et Sacrement*, p. 192, 'symptôme de ce désir, "gnostique", de branchement direct sur Jésus-Christ'].

27 If the commentaries on Heidegger's work by his students Karl Löwith and Hans Jonas are correct to interpret his philosophy 'as crypto-Christianity or crypto-Gnosticism' [Benjamin D. Crowe, *Heidegger's Religious Origins* (2006), p. 17] then there is here a tension between Heidegger authentically construed and Chauvet's reading of him.

28 M. Heidegger, *Das Ding* and *Bauen Wohnen Denken* in *Vorträge und Aufsätze* (GA7).

29 L.-M. Chauvet, *Symbole et Sacrement*, p. 406. 'Le mot qui nous vient immédiatement à l'esprit à propos de ce rassemblement du *Quadriparti* est celui de *symbole*.'

in-between time. Before metaphysics' overcoming, the *ecclesia*, Chauvet claims, is excluded from the Eucharist; after metaphysics, when the *ad-* (the for whom) of the *esse* is taken into consideration, the Eucharist comes into its own when it radically engages the Church. By a process, homologous to the system of symbolic exchange identified by anthropologists working in traditional societies, the Eucharist instaurates the unprocessed individual into an embracing body of signifiers. These transform, by inscription, an otherwise meaningless world into one bursting with significance; the 'narcissistic' tendencies of the individual are sublimated by the universal symbols of the Church. The self, by forgoing the pretension of going back to its origin, comes to participate in the Body of Christ, whose corporality in this in-between time is found within a symbolic universe always-already extant and spoken into a unity before my arrival. 'Our existence', says Chauvet, 'is Christian insofar as it is *always-already inscribed in the order of the sacramental*'.[30]

The truth of the Eucharistic is found in its effect: the incorporation of the individual within this wider encompassing totality. In short, for Chauvet, the Body of Christ is experienced in sacrament by the individual when an anterior body of symbols appropriates, a process by which the group's system of values are transmitted. To come into Christ's presence in the in-between time is, for Chauvet, to be plunged into the body of signifiers – material, institutional, cultural and traditional – of the Church. This subjection, in which the institution stamps its 'trademark', its 'character', on one's body, engenders my identity as Christian, albeit an identity takes place through mourning.[31] At the same time as coming into presence in this way, the individual receives a commission to relate to others under the psychic scheme of filiation, as brother and sister. In the sacramental rite the self is put at the disposal of the Other whom it can let act in the Church's mediation. The self lets the Other act by performing a gesture which is not from itself, by saying words which are not its own,[32] by receiving elements which it has not chosen. For Chauvet, it is precisely in this act of disappropriation that the self is given back to itself.

---

[30] L.-M. Chauvet, *Symbole et Sacrement*, p. 162, 'l'existence ne peut être chrétienne que comme toujours-déjà traversée de sacramentalité'.

[31] The truth of being is a consenting to the presence of the absence or accepting *le manque-à-être* (the lack-in-being) which is necessarily implied by reassigning *de l'homme dans l'ordre symbolique* (humans to the symbolic order).

[32] This performance of gestures that are not from the self's self and this saying of words which are not the self's own are characterized by Heidegger as inauthenticity. In Chapter 5 I show how Heidegger's thought could lead to an understanding of Eucharist as that which releases the self from totalizing regimes of subjection. Sacramental theology, after Heidegger and contrary to Chauvet, speaks of human salvation in the sense of deliverance, from schemes of mediated and transcendental existence that nullify, into the realm of being in its ownmost where authentic life is to be found. This realm, I show in Chapter 3, is depicted by Heidegger through *das Nichts* as the Holy.

Having clarified what the *ad-esse* or *ecclesia* means for Chauvet it is now appropriate to consider the *esse*, or the Body and Blood of Jesus in the species of bread and wine. Using a pitcher (jug) as his focus, Heidegger's reflections on substance or thingness can be summarized, Chauvet maintains, in four points:

1. The essence of the pitcher cannot be approached by science itself owing to the kind of knowledge that characterizes scientific thinking. Because it applies the form of a pre-existing ideal to the thing present-at-hand, any qualities or characteristics of the pitcher that fall outside the boundaries of the ideal, are negated or excluded from consideration. Science annihilates this thing which is the pitcher to the extent that it does not admit things as being determinative of what is real. Scientific knowledge had destroyed things as such as things long before the atom bomb explosion. The thingly-ness of the thing, ordinarily unthinkable, is made available to thought once again in meditative thought.

2. When the pitcher is approached meditatively it becomes clear that *la choséité* (the 'thingness') of the pitcher is not found in the matter constituting it but rather in the emptiness that holds. The emptiness 'holds' by *taking* what is poured out and *retaining* it within itself. Pouring out is the possibility for which the essence of the pitcher is shaped.

3. Given the double meaning attributable to the German word *schenken* (to offer and to pour), something is simultaneously *offered* as it is poured from the pitcher. The gift of the pouring is more than drink for mortals: offering suggests gift-giving in the sense of religious libation. This pouring of the libation as a drink offered to the immortal gods is the authentic pouring. In the pouring of the consecrated drink, the pouring pitcher unfolds its being as the pouring which offers. Heidegger elaborates:

> 'The consecrated libation is what our word for a strong outpouring flow, "gush," really designates: gifts and sacrifice. "Gush," Middle English *guschen, gosshen* – cf. German *Guss, giessen* – is the Greek *cheein*, the Indoeuropean *ghu*. It means to offer in sacrifice. To pour a gush, when it is achieved in its essence, thought through with sufficient generosity, and genuinely uttered, is to donate, to offer in sacrifice, and hence to give.'[33]

In what is poured the spring 'lingers'. In the spring, the rocks remain present in the water from the spring; and in the rocks, the heavy sleep of the earth

---

[33] M. Heidegger, *Das Ding* in *Vorträge und Aufsätze* (GA7), p. 174. 'Der geweite Trank ist das, was das Wort "Guß" eigentlich nennt: Spende und Opfer. "Guß", "gießen" lautet griechisch: xeein indogermanisch: ghu. Das bedeutet: opfern. Gießen ist, wo es wesentlich vollbracht, zureichend gedacht und echt gesagt wird: spenden, opfern und deshalb schenken.'

which receives rain and dew from heaven. The wedding of heaven and earth is present in the water from the spring. Insofar as heaven and earth remain 'lingering' in what one pours out they belong to the thingness of the pitcher. The thingness of the thing is therefore to be found in the earth, sky, gods and mortals. In the staying of the fourfold the simple oneness of the four comes to be. Its thingness is not found in one or other of the fourfold but comes to presence from out of the mutual appropriating, expropriating and belonging of each to the other. Heidegger says this manifold simple gathering is the jug's presencing. The jug's presencing is the pure, giving gathering of the onefold fourfold into a single time-space, a single stay. To underscore how he thinks the unthought essence of metaphysical being, Heidegger asks the question how does the thing presence? He responds: *Das Ding dingt* (The thing things). *Das Dingen versammelt* (Thinging gathers). Appropriating *das Geviert*, it gathers the fourfold's stay, its *Weile* (while), into something that *Weiliges* (whiles): into this thing, into that thing. The Eucharist, we could say, things something for the while of its lingering within the gathering of the appropriating fourfold.[34]

4. In this rendering of the thingness of substance as the gathering of the fourfold into a simple oneness that does not permanently perdure but rather stays a while, the word that comes to Chauvet's mind is 'symbol'. In an ingenious move he reads Heidegger's reflection on the essence of a bridge in *Bauen Wohnen Denken* to support his equation of the fourfold with symbol:

> 'Inasmuch as it is this thing, it gathers the *Fourfold*' and it is symbol. '*It is never first a simple bridge and later a symbol*': its 'thingness', we would say, happens in no other way than in its symbolic expression.[35]

Chauvet's conclusion that the thingness of substance is *of a completely different order* from that of the metaphysical 'substance' and is even unthinkable in terms of classical metaphysics, whose internal logic it defies, is unproblematic in

[34] M. Heidegger, *Das Ding* in *Vorträge und Aufsätze* (GA7), pp. 165–88.
[35] L.-M. Chauvet, *Symbole et Sacrement*, "'En tant qu'il est cette chose, il rassemble le *Quadriparti*", et il est symbole. "*Il n'est jamais d'abord un simple pont et ensuite un symbole*": sa "choséité", dirons-nous, n'advient pas ailleurs que dans son expression symbolique.'
  There is an apparent inconsistency here in Chauvet's thought. In the context of the existence of the human being Chauvet applauds the symbolic order (and the sacraments that are part of it) for being 'the primordial stumbling block' [L.-M. Chauvet, *Symbole et Sacrement*, p. 149. 'la *butée primordiale*'] to immediate access to things as they are in themselves. For Chauvet the virtue of a symbol lies in its ability to rescue the real 'from its natural state by placing it at a distance' [L.-M. Chauvet, *Symbole et Sacrement*, p. 128, 'en l'arrachant, par mise à distance, à son état brut']. But distance from what if symbols confer reality in the first place so that 'the ontological' opens 'through the symbolic'? [L.-M. Chauvet, *Symbole et Sacrement*, p. 560. 'l'ontologique ... par le symbolique'].

itself. However, in his conflation or identification of thingness with symbolic expression, Chauvet bends Heidegger's words to fit a predetermined purpose already present in his mind before he approaches Heidegger's text. He sets out in search of a justification for his symbolic approach which has emerged following his enquiries into psychology, linguistic semiology and anthropology. Heidegger is made-use-of to corroborate an already existing position rather than to inform Chauvet's position itself. In other words, Chauvet makes use of Heidegger to baptize or to give a philosophical credibility to his own symbolic approach initially conceived altogether independently of Heidegger's thought. In reading Heidegger with his mind already made up as to where Heidegger's thinking might lead, Chauvet shields himself from the possibilities latent in Heidegger's phenomenology.

Let us be clear: in *Bauen Wohnen Denken* Heidegger's view on symbols is the exact opposite of what Chauvet claims it to be: Heidegger does *not* reduce the thingness of a thing to the symbolic order. When the bridge is viewed phenomenologically it is not *expressive* of its thingness but rather is itself, 'in the very way in which it shows itself from itself'.[36] To get to the thingness of the thing, or the *essence impensée* (unthought essence) of substance, representations and concepts must be abandoned in order that the self-manifest shows itself. This manifesting or showing is not expressing (in the sense of pressing unprocessed non-being through an always-already pre-existing *a priori* thing that it may become something) but is rather the immediacy of thingness-in-itself presencing prior to mediation. If it is inherent to the nature of mediating structures that, in ascribing significance, meaning and purpose to being, in the process they nullify at the same time, how else can one be mindful of the thingliness of the thing other than by stepping out from mediating structures and participating directly in the thing as it is in itself? In *Bauen Wohnen Denken* Heidegger is adamant:

> if we take the bridge strictly as such, it never appears as an expression. The bridge is *ein Ding* (a thing) and *only that*.[37]

Substance or presence cannot be mediated symbolically for symbols are expressions that block access to the real. Symbols are *la butée primordiale* (the primordial stumbling block) to immediate and transparent presence. The thingness of a thing as it is in and of itself can only be encountered

---

[36] M. Heidegger, *Sein und Zeit* (GA2), p. 34, 'von ihm selbst her zeigt, von ihm selbst her sehen'.

[37] M. Heidegger, *Bauen Wohnen Denken* in *Vorträge und Aufsätze* (GA7), p. 155. 'Wenn wir die Brücke streng nehmen, zeigt sie nich nie. Die Brücke ist ein Ding und *nur dies*.'

phenomenologically. For Heidegger symbols are expressions (i.e. mediations of thingness) which, in the process of mediating, cast into shadow the thing they purport to disclose. In other words, as Hemming observes, when thought metaphysically, 'at the very moment where things become things they occur as nullified'.[38] As such symbols cannot reach the unthought essence of being, the thingness of the thing as it really and truly is substantially in itself. Although Chauvet recognizes the inadequacies of his symbolic approach for expressing the significance of the Eucharistic presence, which is the scandal of the mystery of faith, he believes nevertheless it offers major advantages. We will now see how, in spite of these reservations, Chauvet applies his symbolic approach to an understanding of the *esse* of sacramental presence.

2.3.6 *Eucharistia* . . . now essential bread

When the metaphysical view of the substance of bread is overcome, so that metaphysics' false dichotomies are unmasked, and its unthought essence is thought through symbolically, by stepping back from eidetic representations into the stay of the appropriating fourfold, the reality of bread is transformed. Whereas the metaphysical route of substance is merely a preparation for one decisive response, Chauvet says, *the symbolic path* of connection between earth, sky, gods and mortals, as constitutive of the reality of the bread, *belongs to the response itself*: there is a possible 'cor-respondance' between the strange mystery of Christ giving himself as the bread of life and the singular strangeness of humankind coming to its truth when it shares its life as one shares bread.

When the isolated Eucharist, as bread of value and socially instituted food, is restored to its place within a coherent whole in the ritual act, it is taken outside the realm of commercial or utilitarian value and comes forth into a 'world' of meaning. The restoration of the isolated bread to an encompassing totality, so that it comes into its truth now as something to be shared, ritually enacts the reassignment of the individual to the symbolic order: coming into singular strangeness of his truth, previously 'narcissistic' life, being now distributed in the manifold, is shared out for others. Innocence dies, a *child* is killed, intensified life is diluted in the dispersal required for the establishment of *ecclesia*.

The transformation the bread undergoes in the passage from the 'metaphysical' scheme of cause and effect to the symbolic scheme of communication through

---

[38] L. P. Hemming, *Postmodernity's Transcending . . . Devaluing God* (2005), p. 3.

language does not mean for Chauvet that it becomes literally the Body of Christ: one must no longer say *'Ce pain n'est plus du pain* ('This bread is no longer bread'). Instead *it remains bread; though bread as it is in its truth.* Emplaced within a symbolic realm and endowed with symbolic richness it is made heavy with a traditional semantic burden which would not have been unfamiliar, says Chauvet, to Jesus. The bread is socially instituted as a symbol for what one shares (precisely during a meal), a sharing that concerns the fellowship of subjects in their communal destiny as brothers and sisters in life and death and their communal belonging to one culture. It is essential, for Chauvet, that *bread be shared with others in a meal.*[39]

Whereas for centuries the bread at the consecration was understood to transubstantiate really and truly into the Body of Christ so that the eventuated reality was identified with its ontological substance that excluded this semantic richness of bread, now, on the basis of Chauvet's rereading of the Eucharist in the light of modern philosophers like Heidegger, social anthropologists like Lévi-Strauss and Turner, psychologists like Lacan and language theorists including Vergote and Bourdieu, Chauvet 'advances' our understanding of Eucharistic theology with his symbolic understanding of bread which, following the act of consecration, becomes the *mediation of fellowship.*

In the same way that the essence of bread in the symbolic act of religious oblation is never so much bread as when it gathers within itself heaven and earth, and believers who hold fellowship, there is a corresponding effect in the subject participating in the ritual: just as the bread emerges into a world of meaning in its restitution within a coherent whole, being made heavy under the weight of a traditional semantic burden, so too does the participating individual come into its truth through setting up a new relation between subjects or between subjects and their sociocultural 'world' or both.[40] Sacramental grace understood from the perspective of symbolic efficacy leads to the instauration of a new relation between persons. This, the making effective of our own filiation and condition

---

[39] It is in the ritual breaking of the bread *'that its ultimate reality is manifested,* its true essence revealed' as 'the *ad-esse* of Christ giving his life' [L.-M. Chauvet, *Symbole et Sacrement,* p. 417. *'qu'on en manifeste la réalité dernière,* qu'on en déploie l'essence . . . *l'ad-esse* du Christ donnant sa vie']. The ultimate effect of the sacrament is 'the *Christus totus,* Head *and* members' [L.-M. Chauvet, *Symbole et Sacrement,* p. 418, 'le *Christus totus,* Tête *et* members'].

[40] Chauvet's understanding of the effect of the sacrament of the Eucharist could not contrast more starkly with Kierkegaard's (many of whose thoughts were appropriated by Heidegger). For example, he says 'the one who goes there seeks stillness; the one who sits there is in stillness; even if there is speaking, the stillness only intensifies. How still! *There is no fellowship – each one is by himself; there is no call for united effort – each one is called to individual responsibility; there is no invitation to community – each one is alone'* (S. Kierkegaard, *Three Discourses on Imagined Occasions,* New Jersey, Princeton University Press, pp. 9–10 (my emphasis)).

as brothers and sisters in the passage from the status of 'slaves' to that of '*sons and daughters*' is the ultimate effect of the sacrament for Chauvet. Sacramental efficacy is found not in the physical particles, '*in ipsa materia*' ('in the matter itself'), but like baptism, its *effet premier* (first effect) is located now '*in suscipiente*' ('in the one who receives it'). Indeed, as already shown, the Eucharist is verified not by a 'sacred physics',[41] in which one substance changes into another, but by the *praxis* of ethics in which the one who receives moves beyond utilitarian master/ slave relationships in the passage to *brotherly and sisterly union*. This restoration of *social relationship* between members of the group, or transition to a new filial status, is effected in the name of the absent Third Party that gathers them – the Ancestor, the God, the Law.

This 'Third Party' is the sacrament instituted over 2,000 years ago in the early stages of Christianity[42] and as such, like the always-already of linguistic forms, is a radical given which precedes each of us. Through assignment to this something instituted, which always-already precedes me and over which, as an *impregnable place*, I have no dominion, my concentrated being is dispersed enabling filial relations with others and revealing the truth of who I am. In exactly the same way that language is the *instituting* mediation of subjects inasmuch as it is *always-already instituted* for Chauvet nothing is *more instituting* of the Church in its identity as Church-of-Christ than this *most instituted* namely the sacraments instituted through our Lord Jesus Christ. The reality of a sacrament as a *donné programmé* (programmed given), or the body of the glorified Christ as *antecedent* to its reception by us in Communion, is that it acts as an insurmountable resistance to any imaginary flight towards a God disconnected from our corporality[43] and historicity.[44] It also prohibits idolatry understood by

---

41 L. P. Hemming, *Transubstantiating Ourselves, Heythrop Journal*, Vol. 44 [October 2003], p. 419.
42 We saw earlier how Chauvet maintains that an 'entire theology of the "sacramentality" of the Church' [L.-M. Chauvet, *Symbole et Sacrement*, p. 176, 'toute une théologie de la "sacramentalité" de l'Église'] can be distilled from key Lucan texts that portray the passage from non-faith to faith.
43 Corporality for Chauvet is the body that comes into being when unprocessed human subjectivity is subjugated to (processed by) symbolic forms or 'structured by a culture' L.-M. [Chauvet, *Symbole et Sacrement*, p. 157, 'habité par une culture']. As such it is a concept that 'seeks to express this symbolic order' [L.-M. Chauvet, *Symbole et Sacrement*, p. 156, 'veut exprimer cet ordre symbolique'].
44 Chauvet here alludes to the scholastic tendency to portray the sacramental relationship between God and man in terms of a disembodied and a-historical hypostatic union. His symbolic approach, that presents this relationship in term of the Pasch of Christ, embodies this relationship in concrete history. The transcendental domain of the programmed given operates with a different sense of temporality than the unmediated domain of immediate and transparent presence. If time is understood in a fundamental way as the occurrence of destiny unfolding in the region of immediacy and if the sacraments put this region of *le réel* (the real) at a distance, then it is questionable how impactful Chauvet's approach actually is in real time.

Chauvet as 'the reduction of God to the conditions of what we think, say, or experience about God'.[45]

Had the Fathers of the Council of Trent been able to make these distinctions, Chauvet believes, they would not have had to insist in the change of bread into the Body of Christ. Chauvet elaborates:

> ... On the altogether different terrain of symbolism and *due to* the fact it is so different that the verb *'be' no longer has the same status it had at its origin* because the *Sein* is inseparable from the human *Da-Sein* and thus from language, from which it nevertheless remains distinct, to say that 'this bread is the body of Christ' requires that one emphasise all the more it is indeed still bread, but now *essential* bread, bread which is never so much bread as it is in this mystery.[46]

Transubstantiation signifies, for Chauvet, a change in the meaning of the substance of bread. It does not indicate the displacement of the substance of bread, whether construed metaphysically or symbolically, by another substance altogether, namely the Body of Christ. In other words, *le corps eucharistique du Christ est le pain par excellence* (the Eucharistic Body of Christ is indeed bread par excellence). When Chauvet claims the *vere, realiter ac substantialiter* ('truly, really and substantially') of the Council of Trent is understood in an altogether different way from that of classic onto-theology he is taking something away from *formulis, quibus Concilium Tridentinum Mysterium Eucharisticum ad credendum proposuit* (the formulas which were used by the Council of Trent to propose the Eucharistic mystery for our belief). The Eucharist may find its truth after metaphysics in the *for-whom* of its essence (the *ad-esse*, the *ecclesia*) but it is not to be found exclusively there. Quite apart from issuing a challenge to any

[45] L.-M. Chauvet, *Symbole et Sacrement*, p. 413, 'la réduction de Dieu aux conditions de ce que nous pensons, disons ou expérimentons de lui.'

It could be argued that the reduction of God to an always-already given that mirrors the antecedent structure of language is a belittlement of God and therefore a form of idolatry. Far from being 'the great symbol of the prohibition against idolatry' [L.-M. Chauvet, *Symbole et Sacrement*, p. 413, 'le grand symbole de l'interdit d'idolâtrie'] the Eucharist, as Chauvet understands it symbolically, becomes a form of idolatry itself.

Heidegger understands the gratuity of existence not in terms of something existing beforehand but in terms of the irruption of an *ereignis*. Gratuitousness is more a being grasped by the things we can not see (the phenomenal content of phenomena lost sight of in the act of mediation) than by things that are anterior, in the sense of always-already given or seen. I develop this theme further in Chapter 4.

[46] L.-M. Chauvet, *Symbole et Sacrement*, p. 410. 'Sur le terrain tout autre du symbolique, et *parce qu*'il est autre au point que le verbe *'être' n'a originairement plus le même statut* du fait que le *Sein* est inséparable du *Da-Sein* humain et donc du langage dont il demeure pourtant distinct, dire que "ce pain est le corps du Christ" requiert que l'on souligne d'autant mieux qu'il s'agit bien là toujours de pain, mais de pain *essentiel*, de pain qui n'est jamais autant pain que dans ce mystère.'

contemporary understanding of orthodoxy through questioning the 'formulas' deployed by the Church to define the same, Chauvet calls into question the Catholic resonances detectable in Heidegger's philosophy.[47]

The remainder of this research will examine Chauvet's assertion in greater depth and seek to answer the question: had Chauvet read Heidegger without the mis-interpretations thus far identified would he have arrived at a different understanding of substance and the associated doctrine of transubstantiation? In other words, had Chauvet understood Heidegger differently, would it have been necessary for him to challenge Catholic orthodoxy as this is set down in the formulas of the Council of Trent?

2.4 Conclusion

Chauvet's reading of Heidegger and the overcoming of metaphysics, I have shown, allows him to think Eucharistic presence outside the delimitations of an onto-theological universe that construes substance metaphysically. To 'overcome' the metaphysical view of the world (characterized by instrumentality and causality) is to move, for Chauvet, into the symbolic characterized by mediation through language and symbol. Because it is by his *word* that God creates, when being is unhinged from its entitative representations in the overcoming of metaphysics, the ontological, closed off in the hinging, re-opens this time in a verbal modality through the symbolic. It is this verbal modality that from the outset locates the divine work in the symbolic order. In short, when immediate and transparent being accedes to the always-already spoken word, transcending the human individual, the child of innocence dies as it is marked with the stamp of the Other. Insofar as the world is now impressed by the word it is confessed in mourning as creation.

It is in becoming other than myself, to assume an identity that is Christian, that the difference between God and man, for Chauvet, asserts itself. This difference registers in man as the presence of an absence which is metaphorically inscribed as a lack, lack-in-being. Through the gift of the antecedent word, a giving that constitutes grace, the world, confessed now as creation, comes forth as an offer. Chauvet emphasizes:

---

[47] Heidegger, alluding to his own Catholic origins, says: 'only someone thus rooted in a really vital Catholic world could have an inkling of the necessities that exerted an effect on the path of my questioning up to this point like subterranean earthquakes' [M. Heidegger, *Besinnung*, (GA66), p. 415].

this gift is *gratuitous*, necessitated by nothing, preceding all existence, forbidding humanity under pain of 'sin' the pretension of going back to its origin, of establishing itself in existence, or of founding its world by itself.[48]

The self-actuating self is abhorrent to Chauvet and is precisely what the sacraments block access to and cause to stumble. In fact the irreducible positive precedence of the always-already word, bespoken in the act of creation, erects a reassuring barrier against every exacerbation of subjectivity which would pretend to reduce creation to human creativity. The positivity of an unavoidable precedence actually manifests to the human subject as a calling to assume this reality in a creative way so that all may find their place and live in this universe organized as a 'world'. To access the 'hereness' of the anterior donated word requires relinquishing scientific thought in the adoption of meditative thinking.[49] The reception of word or the world as creation implies, in the act of relinquishing, an offering or oblation. In other words, the confession of creation is itself charged with sacramentality. It is in the 'sacrament-mystery' of the oblation, Chauvet stresses, that the 'mystery' of creation finds its 'expression'.

In order to participate in creation human beings must allow the sacrificial pattern that dwells in all of us to structure our existence. The gesture of disappropriation becomes the concrete mediation of the appropriation of the world as 'given'. To be fractured by the word (in the same way as one opens the dense wholeness of a loaf of bread in order to share it) is to be responsible for creation. The reception of the gifted word refracts the intensive bright beam of individuality into a multiplicity of colours impelling the 'return-gift' of the offering.

Ethics and sacrifice (though as anti-sacrifice) are therefore inextricably bound together to such degree that *ecclesia*, as the interplay in the symbolic exchange of word-given (scripture) in ritual (sacrament) and gift-returned (ethics), comes to its truth in the latter, that is, in social and moral praxis. Ethics, says Chauvet, is is the place of veri-fication, the *veritas* . . . of the Eucharist. Eucharist plunges us into the universe of the always-already spoken word which refers us back

---

[48] L.-M. Chauvet, *Symbole et Sacrement*, p. 560, 'don *gratuit*, nécessité par rien, précédant toute existence, interdisant à l'homme comme "péché" toute prétention à remonter à l'origine pour s'autoposer dans l'existence ou pour fonder, par soi-même, son monde.'

[49] In English recusant theology this transition from one mode of thought to another is referred to as 'denominational conversion' (Michael Questier, *Conversion, Indoctrination . . . in Late Elizabethan and Jacobean England*, in *The Reckoned Expense*, ed. Thomas McCoog, Bibliotheca Instituti Historici S.I., Rome, 2007, p. 357). This contrasts with 'evangelical conversion' which relies on an active rousing of the individual will 'towards resolution' (ibid., p. 359) or, in Chauvet's terminology, on an *exacerbation de la subjectivité* (an exacerbation of subjectivity). Chauvet's symbolic approach does not allow for evangelical conversion.

to creation in the exigency of a counter-gift. The implication of recognizing creation in the Eucharistic moment is pre-eminently ethical, so that the world, confessed as creation, becomes likewise the locus of salvation history, a 'house' open to brothers and sisters.

2.5 Postscript . . . a critical re-engagement

He who pretends to go beyond a metaphysic must produce thereby another thought. And he who pretends to go beyond all metaphysics most often risks taking up again, without being conscious of it, its basic characteristic . . . The principal weakness of reductionist interpretations stems precisely from their exclusively anthropological, hence metaphysical, treatment of the Eucharist.[50]

In Chapter 1 it was argued that for Heidegger thinking the unthought essence of metaphysics is the departure from, or sacrifice of, being for the sake of the truth of being wherein moves the divine, not metaphysically construed as God (who is now deceased) but in the 'undemonic *daimones*'[51] of the nothing. In other words, coming into the truth of being, whether this be the being of the Eucharistic species, bread and wine, or the being of the communicant, is a leap, not into an always-already world of symbolic forms in an instauration fracturing individuality, as we have seen it is for Chauvet, but a total disengagement from anterior transcendental mediations which disperse the concentrated flow of being, into the holy and abysmal ground of nothingness wherein divinity uncannily moves hovering over the void of the nothing and breathing life into the lungs of intensified wholesome being. Chauvet's passage from metaphysics to symbolism blocks access, it has been shown, to the thinghood of substance as it is from and in itself, whether this be the being of bread and wine in the immediacy of unprocessed presence or the being of man in his ownmost, self-actuating and un-dispersed (resolute) authenticity. Chauvet is not thinking from out of the domain of unmediated pure being, from the immediate and transparent presence of the self to the self which, it was shown in Chapter 1, is but another name for the nothing, *das Nichts: Das reine Sein und das reine*

---

[50] J.-L. Marion, *Dieu Sans L'Être*, pp. 230–1 and p. 242. 'Celui qui prétend dépasser une métaphysique doit en produire une autre *pensée*. Et celui qui prétend dépasser toute métaphysique risque le plus souvent d'en reprendre, sans en avoir nulle conscience, la caractéristique de fond . . . La principale défaillance des interprétations réductionnistes tient précisément à leur traitement exclusivement anthropologique, donc métaphysique, de l'Eucharistie.'
[51] M. Heidegger, *Parmenides* (GA54), p. 157.

Nichts ist . . . dasselbe (pure being and pure nothing is . . . the same). A truly radical ontology would find in *das Nichts*, the basic occurrence of our *Dasein*.

This omission can be attributed to Chauvet's neglect of the importance of *das Nichts* in Heidegger's understanding of what metaphysics is, a neglect that was uncovered in our review of Chauvet's reading of Heidegger in Chapter 1. We have seen that Chauvet, in interpreting the overcoming of metaphysics to mean a jump from the transcendental realm of metaphysics to the transcendental realm of symbolic forms, refuses Heidegger's invitation to explore a more radical, albeit dangerous, ontology.[52] In doing so he confirms Jean-Luc Marion's observation that 'eucharistic presence never finds itself so much submitted to metaphysics as in the conception that criticizes the theology of transubstantiation as metaphysical'.[53] The consequences of this, as we have shown, are far reaching for Chauvet's sacramental theology: not only does the being of bread, in spite of becoming the mediation of fellowship, nevertheless remain unchanged in its essential substance after the fraction, but the being of the communicant, although coming to its truth in its instauration within an always-already symbolic universe, nevertheless continues substantially unchanged in its everyday existence. Heidegger forewarns against this mis-interpretation of the step back from metaphysics in his lecture on substantiality or thinghood:

> The step back from one thinking to the other is no mere shift in attitude . . . all attitudes . . . remain committed to the precincts of representational thinking. The step back does, indeed, depart from the sphere of mere attitudes. A mere shift in attitude is powerless to bring about the advent of the thing as thing.[54]

Overcoming does not signal, as Chauvet implies, an annihilation of metaphysical *substantia* altogether. It does not sanction nihilism. This is because the *essence* of

---

[52] Heidegger reserves harsh words for people who fall into this trap: 'One can scarcely exaggerate the grotesque way in which people proclaim my attempts at thinking to be a demolishment of metaphysics and at the same time, with the aid of those attempts, keep to the paths of thought and ideas that have been taken from – I do not say, are thanks to – that alleged demolition' [M. Heidegger, *Zur Seinsfrage* in *Wegmarken* (GA9), p. 416. 'Das Groteske ist kaum mehr zu überbieten, daß man meine Denkversuche als Zertrümmerung der Metaphysik ausruft und sich gleichzeitig mit Hilfe jener Versuche auf Denkwegen und in Vorstellungen aufhält, die man jener angeblichen Zertrümmerung entnommen – ich sage nicht, zu verdanken – hat'].

[53] J.-L. Marion, *Dieu Sans L'Être*, p. 240, 'jamais la présence eucharistique ne se trouve autant soumise à la métaphysique que dans la conception qui critique comme métaphysique la théologie de la transsubstantiation.'

[54] M. Heidegger, *Das Ding* in *Vorträge und Aufsätze* (GA7), p. 183. 'Der Schritt zurück von einem Denken in das andere ist freilich kein bloßer Wechsel der Einstellung . . . alle Einstellungen . . . in den Bezirk des vorstellenden Denkens verhaftet bleiben. Der Schritt zurück verläßt allerdings den Bezirk des bloßen Sicheinstellens . . . Für die Ankunft des Dinges als Ding vermag ein bloßer Wechsel der Einstellung nichts.'

the nothing (that from out of which *substantia* emerges), does not draw us into itself but pushes us away. This is the *Nichtung* (*action* of the nothing) generative of being and spawning the universe.

In short, to overcome does not mean to dispose of, but to have at one's disposition in a new way. As a departure from the sphere of attitudes, overcoming metaphysics has a sacrificial, as distinct from Chauvet's oblationary and fracturing, structure: sacrifice is the departure from beings on the path to preserving the favour of being.

Heidegger's philosophy calls for something more radical than Chauvet is willing or prepared to allow. Chauvet, in presenting the Eucharist as an *unavoidable stumbling block* forecloses access to the realm of immediacy, the site where (as we will see in Chapter 3) *das Heilige* (the Holy) or divinity presences for Heidegger.

To further demonstrate Heidegger's objection to the symbolic approach espoused by Chauvet, it is illustrative, by way of conclusion, to consider Heidegger's critique of Ernst Cassirer's *Mythical Consciousnes*, the second volume in a series entitled *The Philosophy of Symbolic Forms*.

Cassirer claims the meaning of the world opens up to us only when we rise to a standpoint from which we view all being and change as rational and symbolic at once.[55] To this Heidegger responds that 'the interpretation of the essence of myth [or the order of symbolic forms] as a possibility of human *Dasein* remains accidental and directionless as long as it is not founded on a radical ontology of *Dasein*.[56] In a written transcription (stenographic report) of a conversation between Cassirer and Heidegger at a colloquium on Kant at Davos in Switzerland in 1929, Heidegger explains in what a radical ontology of *Dasein* might consist: 'Only if I understand nothing or dread do I have the possibility of understanding being.'[57] Heidegger is recorded as saying, in response to Cassirer's claim that philosophy frees man radically, to be sure, from dread as a pure state of feeling:

> the central problematic of philosophy itself . . . must lead man back beyond himself into the whole of 'that-which-is', in order to make manifest to him,

[55] E. Cassirer, *Mythical Thought*, p. 259.

[56] Heidegger's review of Cassirer's *Philosophie der symbolischen Formen, 2. Teil: Das mythische Denken* (Berlin, Bruno Cassirer, 1925) appeared originally in *Deutsche Literaturzeitung*, 21 (1928), pp. 1000–12. It has been republished in the third volume of Heidegger's *Gesamtausgabe* (GA3). An English translation of the same is contained in *The Piety of Thinking* (Bloomington and London, Indiana University Press (1976), pp. 32–45).

[57] Guido Schneeberger, *Beilage IV: Arbeitsgemeinschaft Cassirer-Heidegger* in *Ergänzungen zu einer Heidegger-Bibliographie*, (1960), p. 21. 'Nur wenn ich das Nichts verstehe oder Angst, habe ich die Möglichkeit, Sein zu verstehen.'

for all his freedom, the nothingness of his *Dasein*. This nothingness is not an inducement to pessimism and dejection . . . Philosophy has the task of throwing man back into the hardness of his fate from out of the softness of one who merely lives off the work of the spirit.[58]

In more poetic vein Heidegger describes the space that philosophy ought to occupy:

The situation is not a safe harbor, but rather the leap into a moving boat, and it all depends on getting the line for the sail in hand and looking to the wind.[59]

In the context of sacramental theology we could say that sacraments, after Heidegger and in the light of his thought, can now be conceived, not as mediations blocking access to being in the fullness of an original beatitude but, as events leading man back beyond himself into the whole of 'that-which-is', in order to make manifest to him, for all his freedom, the nothingness of his *Dasein*. They effect, through unhinging being from the transcendental order, man's descent into the nothingness and dread, that swirling chaotic vortex, constitutive of being's radical depths, that he may emerge (following immersion in the turbulence) in his pureness. Sacraments after Heidegger, it will be shown, cannot be taken as the primordial stumbling block to being's relocation to the abysmal and otherwise unreachable roots of being. Salvation will not allow itself to be thereby postponed and pushed back into an eschatological beyond: it is available here and now. Sacraments, it will be shown, block access to inauthentic transcendental constructions of being that efface original beatitude. In so doing they make available being in its authenticity, a making-available that rescues being from an emasculated life cut off from the roots of being wherein God, after metaphysics, moves.

To read Heidegger without the kind of preconceptions and prejudices we have identified in Chauvet has far-reaching implications for sacramental

---

[58] Guido Schneeberger, *Beilage IV: Arbeitsgemeinschaft Cassirer-Heidegger* in *Ergänzungen zu einer Heidegger-Bibliographie* (1960), p. 22, 'der zentralen Problematik der Philosophie selbst, die den Menschen über sich selbst hinaus in das Ganze des Seienden zurückzuführen hat, um ihm bei all seiner Freiheit die Nichtigkeit seines Daseins offenbar zu machen. Diese Nichtigkeit ist nicht Veranlassung zu Pessimismus und Trübsinn . . . die Philosophie die Aufgabe hat, aus dem faulen Aspekt eines Menschen, der bloß die Werke des Geistes benutzt, den Menschen zurückzuwerfen in die Härte seines Schicksals.'

[59] M. Heidegger, *Phänomenologische Interpretationen zu Aristoteles. Einführung in die phänomenologische Forschung* (GA61), p. 37. 'Diese Situation ist nicht die rettende Küste sondern der Sprung ins treibende Boot, und es hängt nun daran, das Tau für die Segel in die Hand zu bekommen und nach dem Wind zu sehen.'

theology, more especially in the field of ethics (discussed in Chapter 4) and in the domain of cult or the Mass (examined in Chapter 5). Before exploring these implications though it is necessary first to examine in greater detail the region of *das Nichts* (Chapter 3) completely overlooked by Chauvet in his reading of Heidegger (Chapter 1) and therefore neglected in his symbolic approach to sacraments.

3

Heidegger and *Das Nichts*

This chapter examines the notion of *das Nichts* and the referent that it indicates since, as demonstrated in Chapter 1, Chauvet does not take it into consideration in his reading of Heidegger on metaphysics. In Chapter 2 the implications of this omission for Chauvet's sacramental theology were identified: it enabled him first to dismiss humanity's pretension of going back to its origin and secondly to caricature as 'megalomaniacal' the fantasy desire for self-possession, for sweeping away all mediation and contingency, for advancing to immediate and transparent presence of the self to the self. If a sacramental theology is to be situated within a domain that Chauvet treats with deep suspicion because of his imagined 'evil essence' of nature, it is first necessary to rehabilitate, or portray in a more positive light, the discredited task of going back to origins where existence comes to its truth and self can be encountered in its full immediacy. This chapter will demonstrate how *das Nichts*, understood as the original nothing (*nihil originarium*), evokes not something arbitrary and purposeless to be protected against but rather the holy itself whose suffusions remedy existential disillusionment.

This chapter shows, against Chauvet, that Heidegger's thought (following the basic experience of primitive Christianity outlined by Friedrich Schleiermacher[1] and Rudolph Otto) represents a counter-movement or a total inversion of life's usual tendency. Anthropological research, which examines the habitual routines of ordinary social life (and upon which Chauvet relied), are of no assistance here.

---

[1] Along with Augustine, Bernard of Clairvaux, Luther and the Spanish mystics of the Counter-Reformation period Heidegger counts Schleiermacher (who as we show in this chapter influenced Otto's thought) as one in whose writings the basic life experience of primitive Christianity is expressed. As Crowe goes on to show it was 'the "basic experience" of religious life [that] had the most profound and long-lived effect on his [Heidegger's] intellectual development' [B. Crowe, *Heidegger's Religious Origins*, p. 33].

Chapter 1 suggested the possibility that Heidegger was influenced to some extent or other by Rudolph Otto, a teacher colleague during his years at Marburg University (1923–7). While the connections between the two authors are not necessarily easy to make, especially because Otto taught within the theological tradition[2] and Heidegger within the philosophical,[3] nevertheless, when it comes to the theme of *das Nichts* that persistently surfaces throughout Heidegger's writings, resonances between the two writers are detectable.

Before launching into this enquiry we will look at some of the discussions by other authors that suggest evidence of Otto's alleged influence on Heidegger. Having established this to be at least a possibility, sanctioning to some degree what follows, certain essential and defining themes from Otto's most influential text *The Idea of the Holy*[4] will be discussed with a view to answering the question: what are the distinctive characteristics of religious life and the holy? It will be shown how Otto, starting with the everyday view of the holy as a moral category, develops within a theological framework defined by Schleiermacher, an understanding of the holy as the numinous. It will be demonstrated how *das Heilige* (newly defined) shows within the human subject as nothingness that engenders less a sense of dependence on a remote metaphysical God and more a creaturely feeling in the face of the unfamiliar and uncanny. Next, Heidegger's writings will be reviewed for traces, if not possible reworkings of these characteristics. His inaugural lecture *Was Ist Metaphysik?*, where Heidegger explicitly discusses *das Nichts*, and certain of his later works, where he adopts the term *das Heilige* (e.g. in *Elucidations of Hölderlin's Poetry*) will be considered in close detail. Finally, a discussion of the nothing in the light of our findings will be resumed. It will be demonstrated that when Heidegger says *das Nichts*

---

[2] Otto's translator, John W. Harvey, remarks in his preface that Otto 'was much more a religious philosopher than a dogmatic theologian' (*The Idea of the Holy: An Inquiry into the Non-rational Factor in the Idea of the Divine and its Relation to the Rational*, p. xi). Although Otto introduced certain philosophical ideas into his analysis of the holy, itself taken to be the schematization of an '*a priori*' principle understood in a Kantian sense (*The Idea of the Holy*, p. 45), nevertheless in *The Idea of the Holy*, his 'most central and important work', the emphasis is more upon comparative religions. Otto's aim is 'to realize at first hand what in the religious experience which they [religions] enshrine is specific and unique and what on the other hand is common to all genuine religions, however diversely expressed in sacred writings, ritual or art' (p. x).

[3] In Heidegger's last public paper prepared for a theological conference at New Jersey's Drew University in early 1964, and read out to the delegates on Heidegger's behalf, he repeats his early thoughts from 1927 on the relationship between theology and philosophy. He says: 'theology [might] once and for all get clear about the requisite of its major task not to borrow the categories of its thinking and the form of its speech from philosophy or the sciences, but to think and speak out of faith for faith with fidelity to its subject-matter' (cited in Macquarrie's *Heidegger and Christianity*, p. 102).

[4] Rudolf Otto, *Das Heilige*, 9th German Edition. Translated by John W. Harvey as *The Idea of the Holy . . . An Inquiry into the Non-rational Factor in the Idea of the Divine and its Relation to the Rational*, London, Oxford University Press, 1950 (1923).

he can be thought to be speaking of the holy (understood phenomenologically, in its originary sense). *Das Nichts*, it will be shown, enables the hidden fullness (*vorborgenen Fülle*) to be gathered in a holy presencing. It will be seen to bear an identifiable resemblance (sketched more fully in Chapter 5) to the primeval void from out of which determinate being arises from primordial indeterminacy.

This conclusion will provide the impetus for Chapters 4 and 5 where an attempt will be made to show that, when ethics (Chapter 4) and cult (Chapter 5) are examined in the light of a reading of Heidegger that takes seriously the significance of *das Nichts*, something surprising occurs: instead of requiring a departure from the traditions of Catholic orthodoxy, as Chauvet suggests, a more balanced reading of Heidegger's philosophy leads rather to an endorsement of Catholic tradition. This, we will come to see, is no more evident than in the frequently challenged doctrine of transubstantiation.

3.1 Literature review

In *The Phenomenology of Religious Life* Heidegger himself approvingly cites Wilhelm Windelband when the latter names the transcendent *das Heilige*: the holy is *experienced as transcendent reality*. Insofar as the domain of transcendence is brought to disclosure in and is closely allied with Heidegger's talk of the nothing and the holy[5] it is particularly pertinent that Macquarrie says:

> What cannot be denied is that enshrined in Heidegger's thought is a holy reality.[6]

This observation follows an earlier one in Macquarrie's *Heidegger and Christianity* where importantly and interestingly the author speculates whether Heidegger owes something to Rudolph Otto, one of his colleagues at Marburg with whom he sometimes had discussions.

Ben Vedder in *Heidegger's Philosophy of Religion: From God to the Gods*[7] points out that in a letter to Rudolph Otto dated March of 1919, Husserl

---

[5] A connection between Eckhart's use of *das Nichts*, to portray the fecund matrix from which life springs in superfluous abundance, and Heidegger's use, to indicate a holy realm wherein Being dwells, was noted in Chapter 1. Following Caputo, we saw how thinking or uniting with the nothing, as 'that which surpasses and transcends everything . . . is the "mystical union" of the soul with God which forms the center of focus of every mystical teaching and does so no less in Meister Eckhart' (J. D. Caputo, *The Mystical Element in Heidegger's Thought*, p. 17).

[6] J. Macquarrie, *Heidegger and Christianity*, p. 100.

[7] B. Vedder, *Heidegger's Philosophy of Religion: From God to the Gods*, p. 20.

mentions Heidegger in connection with Otto's work on the holy. Husserl writes that Heidegger inclined strongly towards problems of religion. Sheehan is more emphatic: it was Heidegger in fact, along with another student, who brought Otto's *Das Heilige* to Husserl's attention in the first place. Husserl, in an extract from his letter to Otto says:

> Through Heidegger and Oxner (I no longer know who took precedence in the matter) I became aware last summer of your book on the holy, and it has had a strong effect on me as hardly no other book in years.[8]

In spite of certain reservations with the text, which perhaps Heidegger himself shared with Husserl given their mutual influence, Husserl ends his letter with 'the most beautiful' compliment that a phenomenologist could offer: the work, he says, is a return to *origins*. *Das Heilige* will, in Husserl's estimation, hold an *abiding* place in the history of genuine philosophy of religion or phenomenology of religion for it is a beginning. Its significance is that it goes back to the 'beginnings', the 'origins', and thus is genuinely 'original'.

Sheehan goes so far as to suggest that Heidegger's lecture series *The Phenomenology of Religious Life* follows Husserl's 'programme' for further research in the emerging field of the phenomenology of religion. Crucially, this 'programme' was drawn up by Husserl following his reading of *Das Heilige* and was sketched out in his letter to Otto.[9] Highlighting and drawing into the open the influence of *Das Heilige* on Heidegger's thought, Sheehan asks us to compare this programmatic delineation of a phenomenology of religion with what we have just seen in Heidegger's course. Sheehan invites his reader to compare Husserl's theory of religious consciousness and its correlates on the one hand, and Heidegger's hermeneutic of factical life-experience and correlative worlds on the other; to contrast Husserl's systematic eidetic typification of the levels of

---

[8] T. Sheehan, 'Heidegger's *Introduction to the Phenomenology of Religion*, 1920–21', p. 59.

[9] Husserl writes to Otto: 'It would seem to me that a great deal more progress must be made in the study of the phenomena and their eidetic analysis before a theory of religious consciousness as a philosophical theory could arise. Above all, *one would need to carry out a radical distinction: between accidental* factum *and the* eidos. *One would need to study the eidetic possibilities and its correlate. One would need a systematic eidetic typification of the levels of religious data, indeed in their eidetically necessary development*.' (Italics have been used here to highlight the 'programme' that Sheehan shows Heidegger follows.) This has far-reaching consequences in terms of Otto's influence over Heidegger since Sheehan also indicates how in the lecture series *The Phenomenology of Religious Life* Heidegger worked out certain key themes that were to resurface later in *Being and Time* [T. Sheehan, Heidegger's *Introduction to the Phenomenology of Religion*, 1920–1, p. 59]. In other words Otto's account of the basic experience of primitive Christianity may have influenced, to some degree, Heidegger's later writings, including *Sein und Zeit*. Crowe seemingly endorses this view when he says 'primitive Christianity provided . . . the kind of "basic experience" that was needed for a radical re-envisioning of philosophy by providing an initial purchase on the phenomenon of life' [B. Crowe, *Heidegger's Religious Origins: Destruction and Authenticity*, p. 32].

religious givens on the one hand, and Heidegger's historically enacted situation structured by primordial temporality on the other.[10]

An attempt will be made to substantiate further the proposition that the phenomenon laying claim to Heidegger, which he thematizes as the nothing, is not essentially different from the extra-ordinary reality gripping Otto, who deploys the schema of the 'holy' or, more precisely, the 'numinous' to give voice, however inadequately, to that which is Wholly Other than regular things and objects.[11] In other words, it is claimed that Heidegger's *das Nichts* and Otto's numinous beckon, in spite of appearances, from out of a single and common region.[12] Indeed Otto, when speaking of the numinous object (the numen) as the Wholly Other,[13] comments that mysticism calls this 'that which is nothing'. By this 'nothing' is meant not only that of which nothing can be predicated, but that which is absolutely and intrinsically other than and opposite to everything that is and can be thought. The 'nothing' of the Western mystic is, Otto says, 'a numinous ideogram of the "wholly other"'.[14]

3.2 *Das Heilige*

There are three main stages to Otto's argument. He begins with a brief survey of current notions of the holy as these are understood within the various religious traditions (though with especial emphasis on Christianity). He moves next to the radicalization or purification of this term, stripping it of the accretions that have gathered over the centuries and which have come to conceal the true being of the

---

[10] T. Sheehan, Heidegger's *Introduction to the Phenomenology of Religion*, 1920–1, p. 60.

[11] Otto's writings on the 'Wholly Other' invoke a deep sense of the ontological difference. Kovacs believes Heidegger is attempting something similar for through the Holy he is trying to unwrap the nature of the ontological difference [G. Kovac, *The Question of God in Heidegger's Phenomenology*, p. 167].

[12] The point of making this connection in the wider argument of this book is to demonstrate that the success of attempts to make the sacraments intelligible to a postmodern audience, by interpreting them through Heidegger's thought, will be compromised to the extent they altogether neglect the phenomenon of *das Nichts*.

[13] On account of Harvey's close personal friendship with Otto ('a great well-wisher and understander of England' [*The Idea of the Holy*, pp. xiii–xiv]), Otto was closely involved in Harvey's translation from the original German. Indeed, in the foreword to the first English edition of 1923 Otto writes 'this foreword gives me a very welcome opportunity to express my thanks to the translator for his care, his remarkable delicacy of interpretation, and for the valuable supplementary pages he has added. An English critic has said that "the translation is much better than the original"; and to this I have nothing to object' [*The Idea of the Holy*, Foreword by the Author]. Given this, I will only provide the German for the English citations when it is necessary for my argument to do so. Page numbers from Harvey's English translation will be provided in brackets in the main body of the text.

[14] Unless otherwise stated all citations are taken from John Harvey's translation of *Das Heilige*, (9th German Edition) *The Idea of the Holy: An Inquiry into the Non-rational Factor in the Idea of the Divine and its Relation to the Rational*, pp. 1–40.

holy. Insofar as phenomenology (and philosophy) is concerned with a return to origins, so that phenomena are encountered, not at the superficial level of eidetic representations that conceal the originary, but rather primordially as they are in and of themselves, Otto's quest for the truth of the holy is a phenomenological undertaking. Finally Otto presents what the holy is in its authentic piety and quintessence. He sets out his 'analysis' of the phenomenon of the holy under the following headings:

1. Creature feeling
2. '*Mysterium tremendum*'
    a. *Tremendum* – Awfulness
    b. *Tremendum* – Overpowering-ness
    c. *Tremendum* – Energy or Urgency
    d. *Mysterium* – The 'Wholly Other'
    e. *Mysterium* – Fascination

3.2.1 Present notions of the holy

Before he launches into his investigation of the holy, Otto prefaces his thoughts with a warning against prevalent misconceptions about the meaning of God and religion which he says are wrongly, though nevertheless habitually, conceptualized in exclusively rational terms. The term *rational* is reserved by Otto for instances where an object is or can be thought conceptually. 'We must guard against an error,' he says, which claims 'that the essence of deity can be given completely and exhaustively in ... "rational" attributions'. God proves to be something more than the ideas and concepts used in religious discourse. These 'rational attributes', that otherwise are seriously misleading, in fact 'imply a non-rational or supra-rational Subject of which they are the predicates'. This 'Subject' cannot be comprehended in its deeper essence by means of the synthetic essential attributes used for its de-nomination.[15]

As the ineffable (the supra-rational Subject) utterly slips the grasp of conceptual ways of understanding. If human subjectivity is understood to be simply and no more than a rational entity[16] it might be thought, this being the

---

[15]   The French philosopher, Henri Bergson, speaking generally about metaphysics makes a similar point when he says 'concepts never actually give us more than an artificial reconstructon of the object, of which they can only symbolize certain general, and in a way, impersonal aspects; it is therefor useless to believe that with them we can seize a reality of which they present to us the shadow alone' (Bergson, Henri, *An Introduction to Metaphysics*, p. 20).

[16]   In the sense of the Cartesian *cogito*, as a *res cogitans*.

case, that there can be no human awareness or apprehension of the ineffable; it merely and of necessity passes us by. Otto's thesis challenges this presumption by proposing a facility within the human subject that detects and registers the non-rational and ineffable in its variant and often surprising epiphanies. Although it eludes the conceptual way of understanding, he says, it must, in some way or other, be within our grasp, else absolutely nothing could be asserted about it. Not even mysticism, in speaking of it as the ineffable, means to imply that absolutely nothing can be asserted of the object of religious consciousness; otherwise, mysticism could exist only in unbroken silence, whereas what has generally been a characteristic of the mystics is 'their copious eloquence'.

Nourishing this deeper notion of human subjectivity and corresponding to it, there is, Otto asserts, a deeper and more profound religion that subsists in contrast to religion rationally construed. The latter posits and presumes a rational human subject. Orthodoxy, Otto observes, does not find in the construction of dogma and doctrine a way to do justice to the non-rational aspect of its subject. Instead of keeping the non-rational element in religion alive in the heart of the religious experience, orthodox Christianity manifestly failed to recognize its value. By this failure it sought to interpret God in a one-dimensional intellectualist and rationalistic way.

A consequence of bringing the ineffable within reach of human thought through restrictive rational conceptions and attributes is that men shut their eyes to that which is quite unique in the religious experience.[17] In other words, vital aspects of the experience of God are negated. Any sense of the emotional content of the religious life[18] and of human subjectivity is lost.

Properly understood, religious life opens up a domain of human experience that presents us with something unmistakably specific and unique, peculiar to itself. From this Otto concludes that religion is not exclusively contained in any series of 'rational assertions'. Rather it becomes important, for a true understanding, to bring the relation of the different 'moments' of religion to one another clearly before the mind so that its nature may become more manifest. The quite distinctive category of the holy or sacred attempts such a gathering of these different religious 'moments'. Although the 'holy' is a concept like any other it nevertheless points beyond itself to that which eludes conceptualization.

---

[17] Depicting God conceptually is 'like children trying to catch smoke by closing their hands' (Henri Bergson, *An Introduction to Metaphysics*, 1916, p. 55).

[18] It may be recalled in Chapter 2 how Chauvet spoke disparagingly about *de l''indicible' et du 'touchant'* (the 'unutterable' and 'touching') which he portrayed as *les sables mouvants* (quicksands). For him, the virtue of reducing the sacraments to the symbolic order is that they block access to the *'touchant'* protecting the individual from the danger of being swallowed up by *les sables mouvants*.

However, over time 'holiness' and 'the holy' have become inextricably bound up with ethics and the moral good to such a degree that the quite specific element or 'moment', which sets it apart from 'the rational' has become overlaid if not completely obscured. We have come to use the words 'holy', 'sacred' (*heilig*), Otto suggests, in an entirely derivative sense, quite different from that which they originally bore. We generally take 'holy' as meaning 'completely good'; it is the absolute moral attribute, denoting the consummation of moral goodness.

3.2.2 The De-Kanting of *das Heilige* – isolating the overplus

This construal of the 'holy' in the Kantian sense, as unwavering obedience to the moral law, could not be further from its authentic meaning. Otto's *Das Heilige* sets out to excavate the originary feeling[19] that the 'holy' in fact names. There is a surfeit of meaning over-spilling those definitions of the sacred which attempt to reduce it, in an unholy desecration, to the moral good. This common usage of the term, Otto says, is inaccurate. It is true that all this moral significance is contained in the word 'holy', but it includes in addition a clear overplus of meaning which though incomprehensible can nevertheless be felt.

Otto coins the term the 'numinous' to give voice to this excess or something extra in the meaning of 'holy' over and above the meaning of goodness. *Omen* has given us 'ominous', and so there is no reason why 'numinous' should not be formed, says Otto, from *numen*. His aim is simply to suggest this unnamed Something to the reader so that he may himself feel it. In the process Otto hopes to recall to life within his reader the forgotten and ancient 'object' of the word *das heilige*, which is not a thing in the ordinary sense of the word but is preeminently a living force. This unique original feeling-response was the intended *res* of the Hebrew *qadosh*, to which the Greek *hagios* and the Latin *sanctus*, and, more accurately still, *sacer*, are the 'corresponding terms'. The central aim of *Das Heilige* then is to conjure up (insofar as this could ever be possible) through

---

[19] Heidegger attributes the recovery of the importance of *des Affektiven* (the affective life) of feelings, which 'has been able to make scarcely one *Schritt vorwärts* (forward step) worthy of mention since Aristotle', to the 'merits of *der phänomenologischen Forschung* (phenomenological research)'. Phenomenology, he says, 'has again brought *diese Phänomene* (these phenomena) more unrestrictedly into our sight' [M. Heidegger, *Sein und Zeit* (GA2), p. 139]. In a footnote he cites Pascal as one who was aware of the significance of the 'affective life'... And thence it comes about that in the case where we are speaking of human things, it is said *il faut les connaître avant que de les aimer* (to be necessary to know them before we love them), and this has become a proverb; but the saints, on the contrary, when they speak of divine things, say that *il faut les aimer pour les connaître* (we must love them before we know them), and that *on n'entre dans la vérité que par la charité* (we enter into truth only by charity); they have made of this one of their most useful maxims' [M. Heidegger, *Sein und Zeit* (GA2), p. 139, footnote 1].

a unique 'numinous' category of value, a definitely 'numinous' state of mind which is always found wherever the category is applied. In terms of the previous chapter, Otto's aim is to move out from a metaphysical understanding of the holy by recalling to mind the *essence impensée* (unthought essence) of *das Heilige*.

3.2.3 The truth of the holy

Otto's entry point into what Husserl named his 'original' contribution to a phenomenology of one's consciousness of God is through the special features of the quite 'unique and incomparable' experience of solemn worship. The main content of *Das Heilige*, 'bold and full of promise',[20] can be seen as an answer to the question: in what does the content of religious worship consist? Otto expressly avoids focusing in on the sense of moral duty aroused in scriptural reflection and directs his attention instead to the rapture often experienced at the high point of worship. To be *rapt* in worship is one thing; to be morally *uplifted* by the contemplation of a good deed is another; and it is not to their common features, but to *those elements of emotional content peculiar to the first* that Otto would draw attention as precisely as possible.

3.2.4 *Kreaturgefühl* – creature feeling

To get to the emotional content of religious rapture Otto turns, in the first instance, to Schleiermacher's *Abhängigkeits-gefühls* feeling of dependence which is of primary importance in the experience of solemn worship. Although Otto credits Schleiermacher with making this important discovery, he nevertheless offers a critique of the phrase feeling of dependence for two reasons: first, since the 'feeling of dependence' can be aroused by non-religious stimuli, for instance a sense of personal insufficiency and impotence or a consciousness of being determined by circumstances and environment, it is at best only analogous to the religious event that occasions the feeling of rapture in worship and at worst a concealment of so primary a datum in our psychical life that is really, truly and substantially only definable through itself.

Otto therefore proposes to re-name this special feature in the experience of solemn worship, creature-consciousness. He is quick to stress however that it is not the '*conceptual* explanation of the matter' that is of concern in

---

[20] Direct citation from a letter dated 10 September 1918 from Husserl to Heidegger made available to me by Thomas Sheehan.

'creature-consciousness' but rather the thing the concept points towards (the thing signified) which though signalled can never be fully and adequately reached conceptually. Creature-consciousness is the emotion of a creature, submerged and overwhelmed by its own nothingness in contrast to that which is supreme above all creatures. All that this new term, creature-consciousness, can express, is the moment of submergence into nothingness before an overpowering, absolute might of some kind.

Secondly, for Otto, Schleiermacher's feeling of dependence is merely a category deployed by the self to define itself in a self-depreciating way. To feel dependent on something other than my self, requires a self (however depreciated and lacking in independence) to be the subject of the feeling. A feeling of dependence can only come about and be evaluated as such from a particular stand-point, which in this case is the 'I' of the subject whose independence is threatened and brought into relief in the feeling of dependence. Without a measuring self there can be no sense of dependence on another. The religious emotion would be directly and primarily a sort of *self*-consciousness, a feeling concerning oneself in a special, determined relation of dependence. In other words, if the holy could only be experienced through the mediation of the human psyche, being confined to a finite self, we would never come to an awareness of ourselves as infinite beings or of the holy as the numinous.

From this Otto shows that God, for Schleiermacher, can only be inferred by reasoning to a cause beyond myself to account for my feeling of dependence. The notion of God as an inferred First Cause is anathema to Otto who, citing William James (though reservedly), construes divinity as a primary immediate datum of consciousness. For Otto the creature-consciousness, instead of implying God as a Supreme Entity, casts the divine as the numinous. The creature-feeling is itself a first subjective concomitant and effect of another feeling-element, namely 'awe', which casts it like a shadow, but which in itself indubitably has immediate and primary reference to an object outside the self. This object is the 'numinous'.

Using the terms *Geschaffenheit* (createdness) and *Geschöpflichkeit* (creaturehood) Otto shows how the feeling of dependence, in presupposing a God as First Cause as all causing and all-conditioning, is responsible for the *createdness* of beings. The inadequacy of feeling of dependence to give voice to the rapture of worship lies in the fact that it does not enter at all into that immediate and first-hand religious emotion which we have in the moment of worship. It belongs rather to the *rational* side of the idea of God. On the other hand creaturehood, instead of suggesting the creature is the work of God's creative act, rather proposes impotence and general nothingness against over-powering might, dust and ashes as against 'majesty'. Otto observes that when the self is thought through in terms of *creaturehood* new horizons in human thinking open up. As soon as speculative thought has come to concern itself with creaturehood – as soon as it has come to analyse this 'majesty' – we are introduced to a set of ideas quite different from those of creation or preservation.

The realm of created being is not identified exclusively with static eidetic forms in the moment of religious rapture but is seen in the fullness of its abundant, unsettled and quivering life. The insight into being thus afforded enables a comportment towards others that does not desecrate the wholeness of creaturely being but allows instead for full engagement and authentic encounter. In such moments, the narrow preoccupations of created being are silenced. When the finite limitations of ordinary existence are exposed in the lightning flash of religious rapture, as the creaturehood of the creature irresistibly asserts itself in the face of the created, life is taken out of the self that formerly prevailed, in a holy mortification. In the rapture of worship we come upon ideas, first, of the annihilation of self,[21] and then, as its compliment, of the transcendent as the sole and entire reality.

Mysticism, as a mode of rapture, celebrates this self-depreciation, the estimation of the self, of the personal 'I', as something not perfectly or essentially real, or even as nullity, a self-depreciation which comes to demand its own fulfilment in practice in rejecting the delusion of selfhood and so makes for the annihilation of the self. No sooner has the self dissolved than the fullness of life, until now bypassed and neglected, comes rushing in. The rapture of worship is the intoxification of being flooded and overwhelmed by the irrepressible urgency of an abundant life. Mysticism leads to a valuation of the transcendent object of its reference as that which through *Seinsfülle* (plenitude of being) stands supreme and absolute, so that the finite self contrasted with it becomes conscious even in its nullity that *Ich nichts, Du alles!* (I am naught. Thou art all).

There can be no consciousness of absolute dependence since the entity that consciously reflects is swept aside by a feeling of the absolute superiority and supremacy of a power other than myself who ushers in a new sense of human consciousness as the 'plenitude of being'. This moment is not confined necessarily to religious space but, as Otto illustrates, can happen wherever nature, in primordial and uncorrupted beauty, steals away the breath that ordinarily

---

[21] Chapter V discusses Heidegger's reworking of the same idea in his discussion of being-towards-death.

sustains the self. Citing an English journal the *Inquirer*, Otto quotes a South African Boer interviewed for an article entitled *Thoughts on South Africa* . . .

> . . . When you are alone in the veld like this and the sun shines so on the bushes, does is ever seem to you that something speaks? It is not anything you hear with ear, but it is as though you grew *so small, so small,* and the other *so great.* Then the little things in the world seem all *nothing.*[22]

The sense of nothingness that befalls the one in the grip of the religious moment of rapture is the common strand uniting creature feeling, the term Otto designates to replace Schleiermacher's feeling of dependence, with the self-depreciation or annihilation of self that happens when fulsome being in all its creaturehood overpowers and breaks into the otherwise closed world of finite created being. Otto's unique and originary contribution to a phenomenology of religion lies, it will now be shown, in the way in which he develops this sense of self-obliteration and nothingness that accompanies and is the prerequisite for the numinous moment.

3.2.5 *Mysterium Tremendum – Unsagbaren Geheimnis* (Mystery inexpressible)

A term key to unlocking Otto's contribution and which enables him to speak of 'that determinative affective state', which though gripping and stirring the human mind nevertheless remains unthinkable, is *mysterium tremendum.* Having arrived at the one appropriate expression to come to terms with the moment that deeply stirs our affections and occupies our mind with a well nigh bewildering strength Otto nevertheless cautions that our attempted formulation by means of a concept is once more a merely negative one. This having been said though, *mysterium tremendum* is better able to illuminate the positive quality of the 'object' of the affective state even if, as with all concepts, it fails to exhaustively grasp that which it denominates. It points beyond itself to the affective state that engendered it. Conceptually *mysterium* denotes merely that which is hidden and esoteric or that which because extraordinary and unfamiliar is beyond conception or understanding, The term does not define the object more positively in its qualitative character. However, even though what is enunciated in the word is negative, what is meant is something absolutely and intensely positive.

---

[22] R. Otto, *Das Heilige,* p. 27. Otto's citation from James in *Das Heilige* is in the original English.

Having issued this qualification Otto sets out to define '*mysterium tremendum*'.

The feeling of it may at times come sweeping like a gentle tide, pervading the mind with a tranquil mood of deepest worship. It may pass over into a more set and lasting attitude of the soul, continuing, as it were, thrillingly vibrant and resonant, until at last it dies away and the soul resumes its 'profane', non-religious mood of everyday experience. It may burst in sudden eruptions up from the depths of the soul with spasms and convulsions, or lead to the strangest excitements, to intoxicated frenzy, to transport, and to ecstasy. It has its wild and demonic forms and can sink to an almost grisly horror and shuddering. It has its crude, barbaric antecedents and early manifestations, and again it may be developed into something beautiful and pure and glorious. It may become the hushed, trembling and speechless humility of the creature in the presence of . . . whom or what? In the presence of that which is a *mystery* inexpressible and above all creatures.

Otto dedicates the remainder of the opening seven chapters to a rigorous analysis of '*mysterium tremendum*' offering reflections on three moments characteristic of the *tremendum* – *Schauervollen* (Awfulness), *Übermächtigen* (Overpoweringness) ('*majestas*') and *Energischen* (Energy or Urgency), and two moments definitive of *mysterium* – *das 'Ganz Andere'* (the 'Wholly Other') and *das Fascinans* (Fascination). We shall discuss these before returning to consider the main concern of this chapter, namely to enquire into the influence of Otto's phenomenology on Heidegger's thought.

a. *Tremendum* – *Schauervollen* (Awfulness)
b. *Tremendum* – *Übermächtigen* (Overpowering-ness)
c. *Tremendum* – *Energischen* (Energy or Urgency)
d. *Mysterium* – *Das Ganz Andere'* (The 'Wholly Other')
e. *Mysterium* – *Das Fascinans* (Fascination)

3.2.5a *Tremendum* – *Schauervollen* (Awfulness)

Tremor, the root noun in the adjective *Tremendum*, conjures to mind the perfectly familiar and 'natural' emotion of *fear* which, Otto tells us, is a pale imitation and analogy for a quite specific kind of affective response. That having been said though, fear (understood in an analogous sense) may be used to elicit and bring to disclosure a sense of *tremor*. Fear, as an eidetic form, may be insufficient as a concept to exhaustively grasp its term of reference but, at the very least, it directs us to the neighborhood wherein the '*quale*' towards which it points, abides. Otto's phenomenological approach permits an appreciation of *tremor* that recalls to life those aspects of the phenomena (its *essence impensée*) bypassed and thereby concealed in ordinary discourse. The full phenomenal content of *tremor* comes mysteriously into view during Otto's enquiry.

He notes particular expressions in other linguistic traditions that attempt to recall to mind the content of *tremor* in its fullness, that is, its *Seinsfülle*: in Hebrew *hiqdish* (hallow) means to keep a thing holy in the heart, to distinguish it by a feeling of peculiar dread. The *'emah* of Yahweh, the fear of God, is dispatched or poured forth by Yahweh almost like a daemon so that it seizes upon a man with paralysing effect. It is closely related to the *deîma panikón* (panic-stricken dread) of the Greeks. It manifests in the Old Testament as a terror fraught with an inward shuddering such as not even the most menacing and overpowering created thing can instill. It has something spectral about it.[23]

In Greek the term *sebastos* (augustus) was convoked as a name proper only to the *numen* so that it could not fittingly be given to any creature, not even to an emperor. To attempt such a denomination was almost idolatrous for the early Christians. From the range of modern languages, English is particularly well endowed with suitable concepts and phrases that closely approximate Otto's meaning, for example 'awe', and 'he stood aghast'.

German, however, and contrary to expectations perhaps, lacks native-grown expressions to convey the fully ripened feeling or emotion that Otto is attempting to bring to light through his phenomenological investigation into the 'holy'. The word *erschauern*, especially in its more inferior and basic phases in such words as *grausen* and *Schauer*, and the more common and evocative *gruseln* ('grue'), *gräsen*, and *grässlich* ('grisly')' do succeed however to some extent in designating the numinous moment. *Scheu*, when positioned between inverted commas, succeeds where these other terms fail for it changes its meaning from ordinary 'dread' to the word most indicative of the numinous, namely, 'awe' as '*religiöse Scheu*' ('religious dread'). Even before this moment of '*Scheu*' irrupts or befalls, it has its antecedent stage in, tellingly and most importantly, '*dämonische Scheu*' ('daemonic dread') or *panischer Schrecken* (the horror of Pan) with its queer perversion, a sort of abortive offshoot, the '*gespenstischen Scheu*' (dread of ghosts'). It first begins to stir in the feeling of *das 'Unheimliche'* ('something uncanny') eerie or weird. It is this feeling which, emerging in the mind of

---

[23] Heidegger speaks of *Angst*, which owes much to Kierkegaard's 'dread', in similar ways.

primeval man, forms the starting-point for the entire religious development in history. 'Daemons' and 'gods' alike spring from this root, and all the products of 'mythological apperception' or 'fantasy' are nothing but different modes in which it has been objectified.

Religion finds its origin in this constituent of our nature, primary, unique, underivable from anything else. The moment of the uncanny and daemonic is the *Grundfaktor* (basic factor) and the *Grundtrieb* (basic impulse) underlying the entire process of religious evolution. To be paralysed in horror and to shudder in a ghostly shiver are the physical bodily consequences when the uncanny shows. Being something more than ordinary fear, it lights up an arena beyond being that is closed to natural man. The distinguishing moment, that separates religious dread and awe from merely being afraid and terrified in a natural sense, is found in the feelings of '*Unheimlichen*' ('uncanniness'). The physical reaction to which this unique *Scheu vor dem 'Unheimlichen'* ('dread' of the uncanny) gives rise is also unique, and is not found in the case of any 'natural' fear or terror. We say: 'my blood ran icy cold,' and 'my flesh crept.' The distinction between such a 'dread' and natural fear is not simply one of degree and intensity. The awe or 'dread' *may* indeed be so overwhelmingly great that it seems to penetrate to the very marrow, making man's hair bristle and his limbs quake. But it may also steal upon him almost unobserved as the gentlest of agitations, a mere fleeting shadow passing across his mood.

The onset of religious dread has ontological consequences for the subject undergoing the 'experience': a new and non-natural mental disposition, unique in kind and different in a definite way from any 'natural' faculty' awakens. Instead of natural man and the everyday natural world of ordinary experience being the measure of existence this newly revealed capacity belonging to the spirit of man testifies to a completely new function of experience and standard of valuation. Religious dread and awe, as man comes to be in his authenticity, give rise in other words to a devaluation of the customary and familiar. They allow for a non-natural estimation and appraisal of life itself. This devaluation reduces what before the epiphany was some 'thing', into no thing; as the feeling of *eigener Nichtigkeit* (personal nothingness) and *Versinkens* (submergence) before *der 'Scheu' objektiv* (the awe-inspiring object) directly experienced steals itself, the world I formerly inhabited collapses into ruins.

As religions evolve, Otto maintains, this crudely naïve and primordial emotional disturbance, the experience of religious awe and the devastation of nothingness that accompanies 'daemonic dread', gets overlaid if not thoroughly sanitized and domesticated.[24] But even as man constructs devices to shield himself from the nothing of 'the *unsagbar* (ineffable) something', even when the numinous moment has long attained its higher and purer mode of expression, that is, in its conceptualization as a God or a demon, nevertheless, it is possible for the primitive types of excitation that were formerly part of the numinous to break out in the soul in all their original naïveté and so be experienced afresh. Without this breaking-down in order to break-through, the *Seinsfülle* (plenitude of being) announced by the *tremor*, that is, its *essence impensée*, would remain unthought. Though the numinous emotion in its completest development shows a world of difference from the mere *dämonischen Scheu* (daemonic dread), yet not even at the highest level does it belie its pedigree or kindred. Even when the worship of 'daemons' has long since reached the higher level of worship of 'gods', these gods still retain as *numina* something of the 'ghost' in the impression they make on the feelings of the worshipper, namely, the peculiar quality of the 'uncanny' and 'aweful', which survives with the quality of exaltedness and sublimity or is symbolized by means of it. This moment, softened though it is, does not disappear even on the highest level of all, where the worship of God is at its purest. Its disappearance would be indeed an essential loss.

For those who see in God or the divine nature nothing but goodness, gentleness, love and a sort of confidential intimacy, in a word, only those aspects of God which turn towards the world of men, the overwhelming of awe and daemonic dread is gravely disturbing. Those accustomed to think of deity only by its rational attributes must see mere caprice and wilful passion in these daemonic exhibitions.[25] Nonetheless, as Otto shows, these lie at the heart of the Old and

---

[24] Odo Casel in *The Mystery of Christian Worship* attempts an interpretation of the Roman Catholic liturgy in the light of the *mysterium*. Over time, he says, the mystery itself disappeared beneath a mass of more or less personal devotional exercises. However, after the ebb and failure of what he calls this 'anthropocentricism', once more the tide of 'a deeper divine life begins, a striving for God as he really is, for the dreadful majesty revealing itself in the New Testament, not merely as terror as it did in the Old, but as the deepest, incomprehensible love: the abyss of love which would plunge us into itself' (pp. 36–7). Faced with the mystery, 'the inconceivable, the power of God's action which surpasses all thinking', at the heart of worship man can only tremble 'not in reverence and terror only, but in love' (p. 37). That mystery should be definitive of Eucharist is not surprising for Casel for as he points out the words *sacramentum* and *mysterion* have been interchangeable terms from the earliest times. He says: 'Christians, even in the oldest translation of the Scripture, used the word *sacramentum* where *mysterion* could not be translated. So *sacramentum* took on the whole range of meaning *mysterion* had had' (p. 56). In the realm of religious consciousness the mystery belongs more to *eros* 'the soul of the individual striving upwards to God' (p. 55) than to *agape*.

[25] Chauvet, it was shown in Chapter 2, is sufficiently suspicious of human individuality to portray it in its purity, undistributed in the fracturing manifold of a symbolic universe, as narcissistic. The virtue of sacraments construed as symbols (for him) lies in their ability to instaurate the individual within a transcendent realm of existence thereby rescuing him from himself. For Heidegger this represents an emasculation of being, the poisoning of life.

New Testament experience of God. The Wrath of Yahweh, *orgé theon* (Greek), has no concern with moral qualities but is instead like a hidden force of nature, like stored-up electricity, discharging itself on anyone who comes too near. The Wrath of God, so far from being a diminution of His Godhead, appears then as a natural expression of it, a moment of 'holiness' itself, and a quite indispensable one. This *orgé* (Greek) is nothing but the *tremendum* itself. Something supra-rational throbs and gleams, palpable and visible in the 'wrath of God', prompting a sense of 'terror' that no 'natural' anger can arouse.

3.2.5b *Tremendum – Übermächtigen* (Overpowering-ness)

Having dealt with the first 'moment' characterizing the *quale* signalled by the word form *tremendum*, which can be now summarized as absolute unapproachability, Otto defines a second essential quality of the *tremor* (awe or religious dread) as the moment *des Übermächtigen* (of overpoweringness) or *majestas*. This second element of majesty may continue to be vividly preserved, where the first, that of unapproachability, recedes and dies away.

In the instant of the numinous moment a sense of a might or power that overwhelms and breaks down any resistances offered by a recalcitrant self, gives rise to a feeling of absolute overpoweringness. In this moment, the onset of the Holy Other, the self becomes aware of its nothingness or its *Kreatur-gefühl* in a feeling of humility. It is especially in relation to this element of absolute overpoweringness or majesty that the *Kreatur-gefühl* (creature-consciousness) comes upon the scene, as a sort of *Schatten* (shadow) or subjective reflection of it. This in contrast to the overpowering of which we are conscious as an object over against the self, there is the feeling of one's own submergence, of being but dust and ashes and nothingness. And this forms the numinous raw material for the feeling of religious humility.

The no-thing comes to be in proportion to the dawning of a consciousness of the absolute superiority or supremacy of a power other than myself. As power in its plenitude asserts itself so the *Seinsfülle* (plenitude of being), uncontainable and uncreated by any thing, comes to life. The feeling of our creaturehood, in which we see ourselves in humility as nothing, is contrasted and distinct from the feeling of our createdness where-in we consider ourselves to be something. The *tremenda majestas* of the holy arouses an awareness of the insignificance and littleness of every creature in the encounter with that which is above creatures. This 'awful majesty', as an essential ingredient of the *tremor*, is therefore definitive of *mysterium tremendum* which Otto deploys to bring to light the concealed and forgotten truth[26] of the holy. When we identify with the overwhelmingly and supremely powerful numinous something, we become, in a redemption from existence delimited by rational concepts, in a moment of exhilaration, intoxication and overpowering-ness, the nothing that is the truth of the something.

3.2.5c *Tremendum – Energischen* (Energy or Urgency)

A third and final moment in the adjectival *tremendum* of the *mysterium tremendum*, the 'ideogram' Otto deploys to get access to the phenomenal content of the 'holy' excluded from consideration in everyday usages of this thereby disabused word, is the 'urgency' or 'energy' of the numinous object. As the Holy instils a sense of awful and overpowering majesty in the uncanny moment of its befalling, it simultaneously unleashes in its absolute unapproachability and absolute overpoweringness a surge of raw and unprocessed vitality. It is intimately bound up with the *orgé* (Greek) or Wrath of the divine and everywhere clothes itself in symbolical expressions . . . vitality, passion, emotional temper, will, force, movement (the *mobilitas Dei* of Lactantius), activity, impetus.

This 'urgency' or 'energy' of the numinous object recurs time and again from *des Dämonischen* (the daemonic) level up to the idea of the 'living' God and has, Otto claims, given rise to resistance if not fierce opposition to God defined philosophically through rational speculation. It is offensive to a projection of God as static apathetic constancy to assert that, in fact, he is unconstrained vibrancy perpetually in motion and never settling into a recognizable stasis of presence. Insofar as nothing more is implied beyond and beneath these rational word forms, philosophers are right to have rejected as mere anthropomorphisms these expressions of the energy of the numen. However, where something more was intended, so that these terms stood for a genuine aspect of the divine nature – its non-rational aspect which served to protect religion itself from being 'rationalized' away – they are wrong.

Luther (an influence for Otto) in his controversy with Erasmus defended this union of 'majesty' – in the sense of absolute supremacy – with this 'energy', in the sense of a force that knows no stint nor stay, which is urgent and active, compelling and alive. In the mystical tradition as well, under this 'urgency and pressure', there is a sense of kinship with the *orgé* (Greek) that flowers in the mysticism of love. The experience of wrath or the 'daemonic', since it has the potential to show as love, need not be a negative one as ordinarily it is assumed

[26] Heidegger's *Seinsverlassenheit*.

to be.[27] Goethe, Otto believes, knew this supremely well especially in the meaning he gives to the term. The chief characteristic of the 'daemonic', expounded in Book 20 of Goethe's *Dichtung und Wahrheit*, is that it goes beyond all 'conceiving', surpasses 'understanding' and 'reason', and consequently is 'inapprehensible' and cannot properly be put into statement. Poetry and the rhythms and displays of nature come closest to saying something, even if inadequately, of the daemonic. Following Goethe Otto believes that in Poetry there is, from first to last, something daemonic, especially in its unconscious appeal, for which all intellect and reason is insufficient. It therefore has an efficacy beyond all concepts. In general the daemonic is manifested throughout nature, visible and invisible, in the most diverse ways.

The daemonic is unmediated naked force that manifests itself in a downright positive and active power. In some men, in which it stands out dominatingly and in whom it works, an incredible force goes forth from them and they exercise an incredible power over all creatures, or, perhaps even over the elements. Not being 'devilish' but 'beneficient' it 'intersects' rather than opposes the moral order. As an operative, efficacious force it does not fit comfortably with (and so challenges) ideas of the divine.

3.2.5d *Mysterium – Das 'Ganz Andere'* (The 'Wholly Other')

Having demonstrated that the third characteristic moment in the experience of religious dread and awe, signalled and indicated by the adjective *tremendum* in the phrase *mysterium tremendum*, lies in the dark (because concealed and forgotten) experience of the daemonic, Otto turns his attention next to the substantive idea *mysterium* in order to better apprehend the full implications of the term. It would be a mistake, he says, to think that the analysis of the qualifying adjective 'aweful' (*tremendum*) reveals all there is to say about the *mysterium* since the elements of meaning implied in 'awefulness' and 'mysteriousness' are in themselves definitely different.

Otto settles on the word *stupor* which comes to mind in the experience of the *mysterium*. The Greek *thámbos* and *thambeîsthai*, through the sound *thamb*, for Otto, excellently depict this state of mind of blank, staring wonder plainly different from *tremor*. When that which is completely other than us, whether such an other be named 'spirit' or 'daemon' or 'deva', or be left without any name,

---

[27] There are echoes of Nietzsche here in Otto's positive portrayal of the demonic. For example in *Thus Spake Zarathustra* Nietzsche says 'to him . . . who is possessed of a devil, I would whisper this word in the ear: "Better for thee to rear up thy devil! Even for thee there is still a path to greatness!"' [F. Nietzsche, *Also sprach Zarathustra* (1999), p. 90. 'Dem aber, der vom Teufel besessen ist, sage ich diess Wort in's Ohr: "besser noch, du ziehest deinen Teufel gross! Auch für dich giebt es noch einen Weg der Grösse!"'].

comes to presence in a region beyond ordinary rational consciousness, we experience in a peculiar 'moment' of consciousness (the *stupor* before something 'Wholly Other'), an astonishment that strikes us dumb, absolute amazement. The most striking expression of the mysterious is therefore the 'Wholly Other' or that which is quite beyond the sphere of the usual, the intelligible and the '*Heimlichen*' (familiar) since it falls outside the limits of the 'canny'. Being defined in contrast to the customary, *stupor* fills the mind with blank wonder and astonishment.

Stupor is aroused by virtue of the fact that in the moment of the 'mysterious', everything that once was familiar and ready-to-hand evaporates into nothingness leaving us though groundless, nevertheless supported. The certainties we once knew for sure are reduced to nothing, making us exceptionally vulnerable. In spite of this though, the condition of nakedness in which I stand self-exposed exercises a strange and alluring appeal.[28] Even though the 'Wholly Other' does not exist in the regular sense of the word because it has no place in our scheme of reality, belonging to an absolutely different one, nevertheless, and perhaps because of this, it arouses an irrepressible interest in the mind. The 'numinous object', because it exists in stark contrast to everything familiar to nature in general, becomes the 'supernatural' or the 'supramundane', or simply 'that which is above the whole world-order'.

Mysticism, Otto reports, given the absolute otherness of the numen, names the 'Wholly Other' *das Nichts*. With this denomination, the fundamental ontological difference between ordinary mundane existence (*Seienden*) and uncanny supra-mundane being (*Sein*), comes sharply into focus. Mysticism concludes by contrasting the '*Ganz anderen*' ('Wholly Other') with being itself and all that 'is', and finally actually calls it *das Nichts* (that which is nothing). By this 'nothing' is meant not only that of which nothing can be predicated, but that which is absolutely and intrinsically other than and the opposite of everything that is and can be thought.

While mysticism exaggerates 'to the point of paradox' the *negation* and contrast between being (*Seienden*) and the non-being of *das Nichts*, as the only means open to conceptual thought to apprehend the *mysterium*, it simultaneously retains the *positive quality* of the 'Wholly Other' as a very living factor in its over-brimming religious emotion. This strange 'nothingness' of Western mystics, which is the *res* pointed out by the *mysterium*, finds a parallel, Otto claims, in 'the *suyam* and the *sunyata*, the "void" and "emptiness," of the Buddhist mystics'. The 'void' of the Eastern, like *das 'Nichts'* of the Western, mystic is a numinous ideogram of the 'Wholly Other'.

---

[28]   The moment of fascination, at the onset of the numinous, is discussed more fully in the next
section.

3.2.5e *Mysterium – Das Fascinans* (Fascination)

Given the *nihil* implicit in the first moment of the *mysterium*, about which the only positive statement that can be made is that it is the transcending 'Wholly Other', it might be thought that man would do his utmost to avoid the possibility of experiencing the *stupor* typifying the *mysterium*. However, as counter-intuitive as at first sight it might appear to be, there is nevertheless something uniquely *attractive* about the qualitative *content* of the numinous experience. So much so that for Otto, the second moment that characterizes the *mysterium* is *das fascinans*.

In spite of the fact that man is left speechless and awe-struck before that which defies the artifices of regular discourse, the history of man's religious life reveals his concerted attempts to enter into the dark and mysterious region that opens up in the *mysterium tremendum*. The daemonic-divine object may appear to the mind an object of horror and dread, but at the same time it is no less something that *allures with a potent charm*. The creature, who trembles before it, utterly cowed and cast down, has always at the same time the impulse to turn to it, to somehow make it his own.

The excitement that thrills in the moment of rapture is not merely something to be wondered at but something that entrances him. The sense of bewilderment, confounding that which is most cherished in the ordinary commerce and activity of regular existence, is redeemed by a something that captivates and transports man with a strange ravishment, rising often enough to the pitch of dizzy intoxication. It is, Otto proclaims, the Dionysiac effects of the numen whose strangeness and unfamiliarity enthrals unexpectedly though irresistibly.

The religious life begins with man's attempts to solicit the mysterious and fascinating numen in those 'queer "sacramental" observances and rituals and procedures of communion'. Man has sought, Otto says, to identify his self with the prodigious force of the numen and to remain in these strange and bizarre states of numinous possession. The *vita religiosa* reaches its consummation, he claims, in the sublimest and purest states of the 'life within the Spirit'.

Although it (the numen) bestows a beatitude beyond compare[29] its true nature can neither be proclaimed in speech nor conceived in thought. It may

---

[29] Its worth recalling Chauvet's suspicion of an originary beatitude which he claims, because the subject is confined to the symbolic order, is (like the real) impossible to access. Chauvet's symbolic 'fatalism' requires consent or resignation to a *deuil de toute béatitude originelle a retrouver* (mourning for the hope of ever recovering original beatitude) [L.-M. Chauvet, *Symbole et Sacrement*, p. 103]. In other words, since it is the Otto's numen that bestows a beatitude and since symbols explicitly operate against the recovery of a *béatitude originelle* Chauvet's theology, in this sense, prevents access to the numen.

be known only by direct and living experience. In other words, to be drawn into the nothing of the mysterious numen is to live life in all its urgency and fullness. It is being with an intense authenticity that cannot tolerate the inauthentic and insincere. Life lived in pure and undiluted concentration dissolves the inhibiting protocols of ordinary existence.

In the moment of fascination the mind turns from all images to grasp expressions that are purely negative. The fact that man is enraptured and intoxicated by 'whole chains of such negations' demonstrates that the content of the numinous experience is independent from overt conceptual expressions and can be firmly grasped, thoroughly understood, and profoundly appreciated, purely in, with, and from the feeling itself so that the 'something more' of the *fascinans* is lived. At its highest point of stress the fascinating becomes the 'overabounding', 'exuberant', the 'mystical' moment which exactly corresponds to the *epikeina*.

That which fascinates is like the rapture of Nirvana: it appears to be a cold and negative state of mind but it is in fact felt in consciousness as in the strongest degree positive. Otto concludes his analysis of the constituent words of the *mysterium tremendum* and the first part of *Das Heilige* with a brief discussion of a Greek term that encompasses all of the possible nuances contained in *mysterium tremendum*. *Deimos*, he says, may mean evil or imposing, 'potent and strange, queer and marvellous, horrifying and fascinating, divine and daemonic', and a source of energy but it is able, unlike any other term in any other language, to concentrate in a single word the whole and unreduced numinous impression that phenomena may make on the being of man. In other words, everything that Otto has endeavoured to say concerning the *mysterium tremendum*, as the originary phenomenal content of the phenomenon of the holy, is suggested fully and comprehensively in the reality signalled by the single Greek word *deimos*.[30] The closest the German can get is in the expression *das Ungeheure* which is that which is not *geheuer*, that is approximately, the uncanny – in a word, the numinous. If the fundamental meaning of the 'uncanny', Otto concludes, be really and thoroughly felt in consciousness, then the word could be taken as a fairly exact expression for the numinous in its aspects of mystery, awfulness, majesty, augustness and 'energy'. Even the aspect of fascination is dimly felt in it.

[30]   Kierkegaard upholds it is with the help of the daemonic that a person becomes the Individual whose unlimited possibilities are released once extricated from the delimiting sphere of the Universal. He is confident that 'there is infinitely more good in a daemonical than in more trivial men' [S. Kierkegaard, *Fear and Trembling: A Dialectical Lyric*, p. 144].

Otto arrives at these concluding remarks following an exegesis of the choric song from Sophocles'*Antigone*. The phrase '*polla ta deima konden anthston deimotepon pelei*' (much there is that is uncanny; but nought is more uncanny than man) perfectly illustrates for Otto how Greek writers have deployed the term *Deimos* and its derivations to conjure the feeling of numinous awe. Though there is much in the world that is weird and uncanny, nothing is more uncanny (or we should say holy) than the being of man. This observation, we will shortly come to see, is critical in substantiating our claim that Heidegger's thought was influenced by Otto's phenomenology of religion worked out in his text *Das Heilige*.

3.2.6 Conclusion

At the beginning of his enquiry into the holy and to direct his ensuing researches, Otto formulated the question: in what does the content of religious worship consist? Taking the *mysterium tremendum* as his starting point he is able to answer, at the end of the beginning of *Das Heilige*, with a single word: *Deimos*. His analysis of the adjectival *tremendum* and the nominal *mysterium* allows readers unfamiliar with the nuances inhering in Greek words to appreciate the true *quale* pointed out by *deimos*. For Otto, it is the holy as *deimos* that is the truth of worship and its living substance.

Having completed our discussion of the main themes of Otto's *Das Heilige*, which, as we have shown, are a development of certain of Schleiermacher's key principles, for instance the latter's *Abhängigkeits-gefühls*, we are now in a position to appraise Heidegger's writings to see how Otto's asserted influence manifests itself.

3.3 Heidegger's philosophy

Given the significance for Chauvet's theology of Heidegger's thinking on metaphysics, it is appropriate now to further explore Heidegger's inaugural lecture *Was Ist Metaphysik?* In July 1929, on the occasion of his appointment to the professorial chair vacated by Edmund Husserl at Freiburg University, Heidegger presents in a clear and concise way what he understands metaphysics to be. In this section, aspects of Heidegger's thinking, which may suggest Otto's influence, will be identified. *Being and Time, Elucidations of Hölderlin's Poetry,*

Hölderlin's Hymn 'The Ister' and *Parmenedes* will then be examined to situate these identified aspects within the broader corpus of Heidegger's writings.

3.3.1 *Was Ist Metaphysik?*

In the first chapter the broad content of *Was Ist Metaphysik?* was outlined with the intention of evaluating Chauvet's reading of this lecture. This exercise revealed that Chauvet had overlooked two essential themes: *das Nichts* (the nothing) and *die Angst* (anxiety).[31] An attempt was made to move into the space Heidegger occupied when thinking through his critique of metaphysics to gain a more nuanced appreciation of these themes or phenomena.

Having now considered Rudolph Otto's major work *Das Heilige,* first published in German in 1918 and, as we have just seen, familiar both to Heidegger and Husserl, the symmetries between Heidegger's *Angst* and *das Nichts* and Otto's *Schauervollen* (awefulness) or *anderen Scheuen* (peculiar dread) and the *das ganz Andere* (Wholly Other) or *Kreaturgefühl* (creature feeling), respectively, will now be investigated. This exercise will be approached phenomenologically so that the limitations of rational metaphysical thinking, casting into shadow the *Seinsfülle* of that which is being thought, dissolve in the vortex of a more original inquiry.

3.3.1a *In the vortex of a more original inquiry*

The audience attending Heidegger's inaugural lecture was made up of academics, teachers and students, all too familiar with the positivism of science. Heidegger therefore begins *Was Ist Metaphysik?* from a starting point taken for granted by his audience: a survey of how science questions the phenomenon which it is investigating. Science's metaphysical questioning, he says, has a twofold character: first, each question encompasses the whole problematic of metaphysics and in fact *is* the whole of metaphysics and secondly, any metaphysical question offers an insight into the being of the questioner who must also be present in the question.

---

[31]   In David Farrell Krell's translation of the lecture, *die Angst* is rendered as anxiety. However, in Thomas Sheehan's translation (contained in *The New Yearbook for Phenomenology and Phenomenological Philosophy I*, [2001]) *die Angst* becomes dread. Macquarrie and Robinson, in their translation of *Being and Time*, note that 'while this word (*die Angst*) has generally been translated as "anxiety" in the post-Freudian psychological literature, it appears as "dread" in the translations of Kierkegaard and in a number of discussions of Heidegger'. This having been acknowledged they feel however that 'in some ways "uneasiness" or "*malaise*" would be more appropriate still' [M. Heidegger, *Being and Time* (1968), p. 227 [H:182], footnote 1].

Science, in other words, first implies a totality of beings (within which each thing finds its accommodation and in terms of which it receives its definition) and secondly has ontological implications, in the sense of bringing about a distinct mode of human subjectivity in the one thinking scientifically. So much so that our human existence is determined by science. Heidegger elaborates. When science becomes our passion, something essential occurs with us in the very ground of our existence. But what exactly?

He devotes the first part of *Was Ist Metaphysik?*, *Die Entfaltung eines metaphysischen Fragens* (Unfolding a Metaphysical Question), to saying something more of the 'something essential' that happens to us in the roots of our being when science's hegemony prevails, determining the way we think and how we view others. It affects us in three important ways which Sheehan, in his particular translation, especially highlights:

1. *Weltbezug* (relation-to-the-world)
2. *Haltung* (orientation) and
3. *Einbruch* (in-break).

The manner in which we relate to other beings is determined insofar as science defines who we are. Mathematical knowledge, the epistemological basis of the sciences, may have the character of 'exactness' but it lacks a rigour normally associated with the humanities. What it knows and takes to be knowledge therefore is only an approximation of what a thing is in itself. The relation-to-the-world that governs every science qua science, Heidegger says, lets the sciences pursue beings and make them, in their whatness and howness, an object of research, definition and grounding. The ideal of the sciences is to help us achieve an approximation to the essence of all things.

Science, even though it only ever arrives at an approximation of what a thing is in itself, owing to the fact it exalts exactness over rigour, nevertheless forgets, in a convenient amnesia, the insufficiency of its knowledge, due to its orientation. It privileges or orientates its approximations over anything that might come before or exceed its pronouncements. Even though our pre- and extra-scientific activities are also ways of relating to what-is, science, because of this orientation, gives the subject matter, and it alone, a basic, complete and explicit primacy. Because science is stubbornly beholden to the objects it invents it is able to assume a proper, if limited, role of leadership in the whole of human existence.

Science's *relation-to-the world* and its *orientation* require the human subject to go out in aggressive pursuit of its objects. The human disposition of active and willed pursuit, the blind wilfulness of our self-vaunting reason, sustaining science's hegemony, engenders the *Einbruch* (in-break) of a mode of human existing that, given science's orientation, comes to define (even though inadequately and approximately) human nature. What happens, Heidegger says, in this 'pursuit' is nothing less than the *in-break* of this one being, the human, into the whole of what-is, with the result that this *Einbruch* (in-break) breaks open beings as what and how they are. In its own way, the in-break that breaks-open helps beings become themselves for the first time.

The being or subject that hatches into existence, in the relentless and restless pursuit for *certitudo* (certainty) and exactness, is the *ego cogito*. The trinity of relation-to-the-world, orientation and in-break bring to scientific enquiry and the mode of human subjectivity it spawns, the clarifying simplicity and rigor of human openness. To the extent that, in Heidegger's enigmatic words, all that remains to be said is:

> Our relation-to-the-world relates only to beings (what-is) ... *und sonst nichts* (and nothing else).
>
> Every orientation is guided by beings (what-is) ... *und weiter nichts* (and by nothing besides).
>
> In the break-in, our research activity confronts beings (what-is) ... *und darüber hinaus nichts* (and nothing more).[32]

3.3.1b Das Nichts in the Augenblicke

If the *sonst nichts* (nothing else), the *weiter nichts* (nothing besides) and the *darüber hinaus nichts* (nothing more) are taken at face value then Heidegger's inaugural lecture would have been cut short before it had properly got under way. However, as we shall now explore, the *sonst nichts* (nothing else), the *weiter nichts* (nothing besides) and the *darüber hinaus nichts* (nothing more) of our relation-to-the-world, orientation and break-in provide Heidegger with a vital point of access to the *Wesensgrund* (essential ground) within which the sciences are rooted but about which they have forgotten. *Das Nichts*, in other words, is a signpost pointing us to 'something else' besides, or more literally *einem Anderen* (an other), which proves to be the soil within which science (as metaphysics) is planted and from out of which it draws its sustenance.

---

[32] M. Heidegger, *Was Ist Metaphysik?* (GA9), p. 105. 'Worauf der Weltbezug geht, ist das Seiende selbst – und sonst nichts. Wovon alle Haltung ihre Führung nimmt, ist das Seiende selbst – und weiter nichts. Womit die forschende Auseinandersetzung im Einbruch geschieht, ist das Seiende selbst – und darüber hinaus nichts.'

These designations (the nothing else, besides and more), taken phenomenologically, are the true beginning and starting point of *Was Ist Metaphysik?* When Heidegger asks: what about this 'nothing'? Is it just an accident that we speak this way so naturally? Is it a mere turn of phrase – *und sonst nichts* (and nothing else)? His audience would have heard a rhetorical question that, given its appearance so early on in the lecture, indicated the territory over which the remainder and main content of the lecture would range.

Mischievously (perhaps) he taunts his listeners when he says science must now reassert its hard-headed seriousness and insist that it deals only with beings (what-is). Science views *das Nichts* as an absurdity, a ghost. But, Heidegger wryly observes, in order unceremoniously to dismiss the nothing science must first accept that it (the nothing) exists; such presupposing confers being on the nothing even if, shortly after bringing the nothing to life, it summarily takes it away again. By giving up the nothing in this way, he asks, do we not concede it?

In spite of itself, when science wants to know nothing about the nothing, it is unwittingly acknowledging another order of being about which it wants to know nothing. In other words, when science tries to express its own essence, it appeals to the nothing for help. It makes a claim on what it rejects.

What is being alluded to here and what Heidegger discusses in the remainder of the lecture is this *zwiespältiges* (double valence).[33] Science's reference to the nothing, when it tries to express its own essence, highlights and brings into view the ontological difference:[34] the *Seiende* (what-is) of science is what it is and emanates from the more originary *Sein* (being) of the nothing. Science receives its nourishing juices and strength from the nothing that supports it.

So, having delimited the field of enquiry into the being of metaphysics to the nothing, what then *is* the nothing? Heidegger is appalled that such a question is even contemplated for it betrays a complete lack of understanding of the nothing: if the nothing *is* something in the sense that it has a 'whatness' (quiddity) or an 'isness' then it ceases to be the very no-thing that it is, namely, the nothing. Such questioning merely reduces the nothing to an entity and in so doing says absolutely nothing about that which it is claiming to speak. Heidegger warns therefore that posing the question in terms of what and how the nothing *is* changes what we are asking about into its opposite. The question robs itself of its own object. Thus any answer to this question is utterly impossible because it

---

[33] That is to say, the 'what-is' of science is not the only order of being; it coexists with something (the nothing) beyond science's mere approximations.

[34] In the 3rd edition (1931) Heidegger provides a footnote for *zwiespältiges* explaining the 'double valence' as *ontologische Differenz*.

necessarily takes the form: *das Nichts 'ist' das und das* (The nothing *is* this or that). Both the question and the answer about the nothing are inherently absurd.

If logic were the only method available to approach the question of the nothing then, as we have just seen, there would be nothing further to say on the subject. Since the essence of thought is to always think about *something*, Heidegger observes, thought would contradict its own essence if it thought about nothing. The very best it (logic) can do is to proclaim the nothing as the 'what-is-not' (*Nicht-haften*), that is the negation of what-is, but it is still, lamentably, a 'what-is . . .' and therefore not a nothing but a something. Can there ever be a way out of this impasse where the nothing is merely the negation of a something . . . an 'is' nevertheless?

Hesitatingly Heidegger announces, in defiance of logical thinking and the blind wilfulness of our self-vaunting reason that maybe the occurrence of *das Nichts* does not depend on *das Nicht* ('is-not') and the act of negating (*die Verneinung*). Maybe *die Vereinung* and *das Nicht* can occur only if *das Nichts* first occurs. This point, Heidegger reveals, has never been explicitly raised as a question and much less been decided.

The given-ness of the nothing in its occurrence means that it can appear without reference to the something, a referring that takes away the no-thing-ness of the nothing. Heidegger's argument, which he unfolds in the rest of the lecture, is this:

. . . *das Nichts* is closer to the origin than *das Nicht* and *die Verneinung*.

The nothing requires no vaunting self to wilfully intend its presence or to bring it to life; we are so finite, Heidegger says, that our own wills and decisions cannot effect an original encounter with the nothing. As such, *das Nichts* is other than beings altogether, coming of its own volition in a sudden, fleeting and unexpected augenblicke (moment). It must first be given. We must be able to encounter it. If the nothing disables the ordinary faculty of human reason then the only way to continue investigating it[35] is through a basic experience of the nothing.

Heidegger observes that fleeting human moods, which are non-rational phenomena (in the sense that they are not susceptible to conscious manipulation) offer the possibility of continuing researches into the nothing, all regular channels available to the *ego cogito* now being foreclosed. In *Being and Time*[36] Heidegger points out that the existentially basic character of moods lies in bringing one

---

[35] Though not as *gegenstand* (object) standing over against me as subject.
[36] First published in 1926, three years before *Was Ist Metsphysik?* was delivered.

back to something and that anything which is observed to have the character of turning up and disappearing in a fleeting manner, belongs to the primordial constancy of existence. It is in the domain of what we call a 'feeling', however fleeting, that an answer to the conundrum before us awaits.

But it is important to recognize that a feeling does not have to be merely a component of thinking and willing, for example, in the way that the feeling of boredom can be. Rather a feeling or mood can stand in its own right without reference-to or the need-for human thought or human volition to bring it into being. Feeling or mood can have an absoluteness and independence from rational intentionality that make them potential occasions of nothing's epiphany. An original encounter with the nothing occurs only in a *Stimmung* (mood) whose disclosive essence is dedicated to revealing *das Nichts*. In the *Grundstimmung der Angst* (basic mood of dread) human beings have such a mood that brings them face-to-face with the nothing but only for a fleeting moment and on rare occasions.

3.3.1c *Der Grundstimmung der Angst* – a peculiar kind of calm

The *Grundstimmung der Angst* is unlike, say, the feeling of boredom which requires a something to be bored-of and which reveals what-is in terms of a whole. In *Angst* there is no point of reference; there is no thing or totality in relation to which my dread is aroused. That in the face of which one has *der Angst* is not an entity within-the-world. In *Angst* one does not encounter an actual thing whose threatening nature can be manipulated and neutralized by allocating it a place (or involving it) within a larger universal whole. *Angst* is not like fear or boredom which requires a specific thing to lay hold of us. Rather, it is fundamentally different from fear. What we have fear *of*, Heidegger says, is always a specific thing that threatens us in a specific way. Moreover such fear *of* . . . is always fear *for* something specific. Because fear *of* and fear *for* are defined by specific objects whenever we experience fear we are seized and held by some *thing* that affects us. In trying to save ourselves from that particular thing, we become unsure of our relation to other things and lose our bearings as a whole.

The *Grundstimmung der Angst* is not the panic of confusion that comes with losing our bearings on account of something that grabs our attention. On the contrary, dread is suffused with a peculiar kind of calm. Although there is no thing that arouses the feeling of dread, it is still nonetheless 'dread *of* . . .', though without a determining and defining object. Dread *of* is always dread *for*, but again, not for a specific thing. What we have dread *of* and *for* is indeterminate not because *we* are unable to define it, but because it itself cannot be defined.

The feeling of dread, determined and specified by . . . (the non-object of an indefinite nothing) and un-referred to a familiar totality (whose terms dictate the character of being and the manner in which being comes into presence), is a vacancy (which though vacant nevertheless registers) and an emptiness (which though empty nevertheless makes its presence felt). All that can be said of this basic feeling is that in its presencing it feels *unheimlich* (so strange), unhomely and without lodgings in the whole. Everyday lostness in the 'they' is threatened by the the onset of the uncanny calling us out from the familiar, dislodging us so that we are free to wander down the un-kept pathways of an indefinite unknown. Nothing can be said of that which arouses the feeling of strangeness or of the one who undergoes the feeling. All things, including our subjectivity, sink into indifference. As the region of being, wherein we habitually find our home, recedes at the onset of the nothing, so the mores supporting and sustaining ordinary life untie and slip away. *Das Seiende* (whatever-is) no longer speaks to us. To be alone in the stillness, when all chatter ceases and the fixed forms of being recede into shadowland, is an terrifying prospect but one which *Grundstimmung der Angst* facilitates.

In *Being and Time* Heidegger says the totality of involvements of the ready-to-hand and the present-at-hand discovered within-the-world is, as such, of no consequence. It collapses into itself. The world has the character of completely lacking significance. We are left vulnerable and exposed in the moment of *angst* with no-thing to uphold us. The sense of tranquillized self-assurance or being-at-home that the everyday publicness of the 'they' brings with it, collapses with entry into the existential 'mode' of the '*not-at-home*'. When *das Seienden im Ganzen* (the whole of what-is) recedes we are overwhelmed with anxiety. Oppressed by the moment the air from our lungs exhales and breathing becomes arduous. Without the whole there is no hold. As beings slip away, what remains and overwhelms us is precisely 'no . . .' *Die Angst*, in short, reveals *das Nichts*.

The 'me' that was before, now in the presencing of the nothing, hangs suspended in *Angst*. Angst, Heidegger says in *Being and Time*, takes away from Dasein the possibility of understanding itself, as it falls, in terms of the 'world' and the way things have been publicly interpreted. Subjectivity is transformed into openness, as the fixities of immutable being disintegrate in the perpetual flux of a swirling vortex so that who I was before dissolves into the elusive I, myself in its authenticity, there all along but outside of my reach. I recollect the pieces of my scattered being, reduced to multiple fragments in the explosion launching me into ordinary existence, as I contract, under pressure from an originary movement, into authenticity. The truth of my being, which before the moment of dread was impossibly evasive now, comes resolutely[37] into its own: with the encroachment of the nothing, the whole of whatever-is slips away and in a holy nativity I emerge.[38] 'In the unnerving state of "left-hanging-with-nothing-to-hold-on-to"', Heidegger says, 'all that remains is pure open-ness'.[39] I am liberated *from* possibilities which 'count for nothing' as I become free *for* those that are authentic.

The discovery that the truth of who I am lies beyond what-is as a whole in the original revelation of the nothing is, in other words, the uncovering of transcendence. Our being held out into the nothing, on the grounds of this hidden *Angst*, *is* our surpassing of the whole of what-is. It is transcendence. The sudden encounter with ourselves and beings as we and they are in the indiluted intensity of transcending being, leaves us lost for words. Dread, Heidegger says, strikes us dumb.[40] As the unified whole of what-is slips away and *das Nichts* crowds in on us, all utterance of 'is' falls silent in the face of it. Amidst the strangeness of dread we often try to shatter the empty stillness with a mindless chatter, but that only proves the presence of the nothing.[41]

Having found a way to approach *das Nichts* in the mood or feeling of dread, that comes to a presencing in spite of the fact that it does not rely upon logical categories of thought or scientific ways of thinking, Heidegger is in a position to answer the question he earlier sets himself: *Wie steht es um das Nichts?* (how is it with the nothing?)[42]

It is not an entity for even though the nothing *enthüllt sich in der Angst* (shows up in dread) it does so *nicht als Seiendes* (not as something-that-is) and certainly

---

[37] In *Being and Time* Heidegger says 'anxiety can mount authentically only in a Dasein which is resolute. He who is resolute knows no fear; but he understands the possibility of anxiety as the possibility of the very mood which neither inhibits nor bewilders him' [M. Heidegger, *Sein und Zeit*, (GA2), p. 344. 'Eigentlich . . . kann die Angst nur aufsteigen in einem entschlossenen Dasein. Der Entschlossene kennt keine Furcht, versteht aber gerade die Möglichkeit der Angst als *der* Stimmung, die ihn nicht hemmt und verwirrt'].

[38] 'For unto us a child is born, for unto us a son is given' (*Isaiah* 9.6). Kierkegaard terms the one who 'renounces the universal in order to become the individual', the Knight of Faith to be distinguished from the tragic hero who renounces the individual (*eigentliche*) for the universal (*nichtigen Möglichkeiten*) [*Fear and Trembling . . . A Dialectical Lyric*, p. 109].

[39] M. Heidegger, *Was Ist Metaphysik?* (GA9), p. 112. 'Nur das reine Da-sein in der Durchschütterung dieses Schwebens, darin es sich an nichts halten kann, ist noch da.'

[40] Kierkegaard observes that 'silence is . . . the state in which the Individual becomes conscious of his union with the divinity' [*Fear and Trembling: A Dialectical Lyric*, p. 129]. 'Abraham', he continues, 'is silent – but he *cannot* speak: and therein lies his anxiety and dread'. Since 'speech is a consolation which translated me into the universal' [*Fear and Trembling: A Dialectical Lyric*, p. 171] Abraham's silence guarantees him as a knight of faith, that is, as one who renounces the universal to become the individual.

[41] M. Heidegger, *Was Ist Metaphysik?* (GA9), p. 112.

[42] Heidegger's concern in phrasing the question in this way is not to imply an 'is-ness' to the nothing such as occurs in the question 'what is the nothing?'

not *als Gegenstand* (as an object). Rather, in *der Angst* (dread) we encounter *das Nichts* (the nothing) as *in eins mit dem Seienden im Ganzen* (at one with the whole of what-is). Even though this appears to contradict Heidegger's earlier observation that the nothingness of the nothing is such by virtue of the fact it has no point of reference to beings as a whole, in fact it simply says that when the nothing emerges beings are not annihilated. Rather they are met *in der Unheimlichkeit* (in all their strangeness)[43] in their non-metaphysical mode of existence. He says:

> the nothing appears with and in the beings that are slipping away in terms of a whole. In dread, therefore, there is no annihilation of all-that-is.[44]

Heidegger is not saying that in the moment of dread beings are obliterated and consumed into nothingness;[45] rather he *is* saying that when the nothing shows, a new and transcendent mode of the being comes to life opening up a space within which beings can be seen and encountered in the truth and authenticity of what they are. In the clear night of the nothing experienced in dread there occurs the original revelation of the 'is' of what-is: the fact that things are and *nicht Nichts* (not nothing). In *Being and Time* Heidegger says that anxiety/dread brings Dasein face to face with its ownmost being-thrown and reveals the uncanniness of everyday familiar being-in-the-world. It brings one back to the pure 'that-it-is' of one's ownmost individualized throwness. He continues:

> The present-at-hand must be encountered in just *such* a way that it does *not* have *any* involvement *whatsoever*, but can show itself *in einer leeren Erbarmungslosigkeit* (in an empty mercilessness).[46]

The presencing of *Das Nichts* is not the end and final point of the moment of dread for, once upon us, it (the nothing) persistently impels us back to the world to encounter *it* in *its* truth. The original revelation of the nothing pushes for a radical and authentic engagement with others in the truth of what *they* are, so that the phenomenal content of their being is not overlooked. Such encounters, impelled by the nudgings of *das Nichts*, reach out to authentic potentiality-for-being in

---

43   M. Heidegger, *Was Ist Metaphysik?* (GA9), p. 113. Heidegger adds a footnote in the 5th edition 'Unheimlichkeit und Unverborgenheit' ... 'strangeness and hiddenness'.

44   M. Heidegger, *Was Ist Metaphysik?* (GA9), p. 113. 'Vielmehr bekundet sich das Nicts eigens mit und an dem Seienden als einem entgleitenden im Ganzen. In der Angst geschieht keine Vernichtung des ganzen Seienden an sich.'

45   The ideal of Eastern religions, such as certain strains of Buddhism, and Western mystical traditions to merge being with the empty void of the nothing, so that there is no engagement with the world but absolute withdrawal, is not what Heidegger intends in his thinking on the nothing. It is this pushing back which allows us to speak of ethics in the context of Heidegger's philosophy.

46   M. Heidegger, *Sein und Zeit* (GA2), p. 343. 'Es muß gerade begegnen, damit es *so gar keine* Bewandtnis mit ihm haben und es sich in einer leeren Erbarmungslosigkeit zeigen kann.'

the other inviting them to come into the otherwise neglected regions of their being. Heidegger put it thus:

> the nothing does not draw us into itself; rather, its essence is to push us away. In pushing us back away from itself, it directs us to the receding beings that it lets slip away in terms of their whole. This business of pushing us back and directing us toward beings that are slipping away as a whole, is the way the nothing presses in upon openness during dread: this is the *essence* of the nothing, the *action* of the nothing.[47]

The nothing does not come to presence through the negation of all-that-is for such negation would always arrive too late to produce the nothing and, as we have just seen, we encounter the nothing at one with the whole of what-is. Since annihilation and negation cannot account for *die Nichtung* (the action of the nothing). Heidegger concludes therefore:

> the nothing itself 'nothings'.[48] In its essence the action of the nothing lies at the origin and consists in letting openness encounter[49] for the first time what-is insofar as it *is*.[50]

---

[47]   M. Heidegger, *Was Ist Metaphysik?* (GA9), p.114. 'Dieses zieht nicht auf sich, sondern ist wesenhaft abweisend. Die Abweisung von sich ist aber als solche das entgleitenlassende Verweisen auf das versinkende Seiende im Ganzen. Diese im Ganzen abweisende Verweisung auf das entgleitende Seiende im Ganzen, als welche das Nichts in der Angst das Dasein umdrängt, ist das Wesen des Nichts: die Nichtung.'

[48]   In the 5th edition Heidegger provides clarification by way of a footnote: 'that is: occurs as the action-of-the-nothing; holds forth; grants the nothing' [M. Heidegger, *Was Ist Metaphysik?*, (GA9), p. 114. '... als Nichten west, währt, gewährt das Nichts'].

[49]   In the 5th edition Heidegger includes a footnote that reads: 'Properly speaking, it lets openness encounter the *being* of what-is, i.e., the difference' [M. Heidegger, *Was Ist Metaphysik?*, (GA9), p. 114. '... eigens vor Sein des Seienden, vor den Unterschied'].

[50]   M. Heidegger, *Was Ist Metaphysik?* (GA9), p. 114. 'Das Nichts selbst nichtet . . . Das Wesen des ursprünglich nichtenden Nichts liegt in dem: es bringt das Da-sein allererst vor das Seiende als ein solches.'

This 'business of pushing us back and directing us toward beings that are slipping away as a whole' [M. Heidegger, *Was Ist Metaphysik?* (GA9), p. 114, 'diese im Ganzen abweisende Verweisung auf das entgleitende Seiende im Ganzen'] so that in our openness we encounter 'for the first time what-is insofar as it is' [M. Heidegger, *Was Ist Metaphysik?* (GA9), p. 114, 'allererst vor das Seiende als ein solches'] is the action of the nothing that results, if not resisted, in 'right' human conduct.

This is not a praxis driven by rational categorical imperatives, as in the case of an ethics construed as etiquette, but is where the source lies for understanding of human behaviour informed by Heidegger's thought. In his *Letter on Humanism* Heidegger is more pronounced. There comes from the action of the nothing, that is, 'man ek-sisting into the truth of Being', [M. Heidegger, *Brief über den Humanismus (1946)* in *Wegmarken*, (GA9), p. 360, 'der Mensch, ich die Wahrheit des Seins ek-sistierend'] 'the assignment of those directives that must become law and rule for man' [M. Heidegger, *Brief über den Humanismus (1946)* in *Wegmarken*, (GA9), pp. 360–1, 'die Zuweisung derjenigen Weisungen kommen, die für den Menschen Gesetz und Regel werden müssen']. The action of the nothing, that is 'the truth of Being, . . . offers a hold for all conduct' [M. Heidegger, *Brief über den Humanismus (1946)* in *Wegmarken*, (GA9), p. 361, 'die Wahrheit des Seins . . . den Halt für alles Verhalten verschenkt']. The deed that result from the action of the nothing, in 'the humbleness of its inconsequential accomplishment', 'surpasses all "*praxis*"' being 'more essential than instituting rules' [M. Heidegger, *Brief über den Humanismus (1946)* in *Wegmarken* (GA9), p. 361, 'das Geringe seines erfolglosen Vollbringens . . . alle Praxis übertrifft . . . wesentlicher als alle Aufstellung von Regeln'].

3.3.2 Otto's influence

Having completed our discussion of Heidegger's inaugural lecture the symmetries between its key themes and those contained in Rudolph Otto's *das Heilige* will now be drawn out. The results of this exercise will assist with the search for a more nuanced understanding of Heidegger's *das Nichts*, a theme key to *Was Ist Metaphysik?* but one wholly overlooked by Chauvet in his reading of this lecture.

We may recall that Otto began his exegesis of the word 'holy' with a survey of current understandings of the term. He concluded that by and large it had, over the centuries, come to be associated with ethics and the moral good construed in a Kantian and rational way. In a similar fashion, Heidegger launched into his investigation of metaphysics observing how the term, in a modern context, was taken most often to refer to scientific procedures that reduce phenomena, in a levelling off, to something that can be calculated and reckoned. Both authors display from the outset therefore a disdain (if not contempt) for the reductionisms characteristic of transcendental thought, one Kantian and the other scientific.

Otto, following Schleiermacher, turned to the domain of feeling, in particular the *Abhängigkeits-gefühls* (feeling of dependence), to uncover a more originary understanding of the holy. It was in feeling rather than in moral reckoning that he sought to gain access to the true phenomenal content of the holy otherwise closed off to human experience. Likewise, Heidegger found in what we call a 'feeling' a way to transcend the rational consciousness of the *ego cogito*, the mode of human subjectivity that 'in-breaks' and which is the prerequisite for any scientific enquiry. Feeling, for Heidegger, provides a new way to conceive metaphysics which otherwise is inextricably bound up with the positivist traditions of science.

Although the realm of feeling was important for Otto, he nevertheless set out to refine Schleiermacher's feeling of dependence. This was because the term presupposes a self/psyche capable of feeling a sense of dependency. It was in danger therefore of reducing religious experience to psychology. His coining

---

Francis Volpi in *Heidegger and the 'Homelessness' of Modern Man* underscores this observation when he says 'the thought of Being [i.e. the action of the nothing] is in itself already an "ethics" in the sense that, through the "insight into what is," it grasps the phenomena of the technologically determined world by the roots and attempts to correspond to them' [Burt Hopkins and Steven Crowell (eds) *The New Yearbook for Phenomenology and Phenomenological Philosophy*, Seattle, Noesis Press, Ltd, 2003, p. 283]. The next Chapter (4) investigates how Heidegger's thought can assist in the development of a phenomenology of ethics.

of the term *Kreaturgefühl* (creature-consciousness) was an attempt to suggest that human awareness is not confined exclusively to the categories of rational thought. Existential states of being convey meaning as much if not more than psychological events and uttered words. To *know* and to *understand* are two different things.[51] The truth of the holy comes into view when the self is submerged and overwhelmed by its own nothingness. Nothingness then is the hallmark of the '*Kreaturgefühl*'.

Likewise, we saw that not all feelings for Heidegger were appropriate for obtaining access to the truth of metaphysics. Fear, for example, because it is aroused by a specific *gegenstand* (object) keeps me imprisoned within a metaphysical world. Because *das Nichts* (the nothing) is not an object standing over there inventing me as a subject here, it offers the prospect of leading beyond Cartesian subjectivity to a more fundamental awareness of myself as an individual un-scattered in the manifold and untranslatable into the universal. In the feeling or fleeting mood[52] of dread (*angst*), that accompanies *das Nichts'* epiphany, the real meaning of metaphysics is found. Although there is no thing here, in the sense there is an absence, nevertheless some thing presences within the being of man. This is succinctly expressed as 'the event of pres-ab-sence'.[53]

Being recoils from any involvement in the universal totality of beings, as one's own unfathomable possibility asserts itself in transcendence. There seems to be an audible resonance between Heidegger's notion of coming to be beyond what-is in pure openness, in the unnerving state of 'left-hanging-with-nothing-to-hold-on-to', and Otto's '*Kreaturgefühl*': when Otto writes 'creature-feeling' is the moment of submergence into nothingness Heidegger says that what remains and overwhelms us – as beings slip away – is precisely 'no . . .'.

---

[51] For example, 'Revelation' does not mean 'a *mere* passing over into the intelligible and comprehensible. Something may be profoundly and intimately known in feeling for the bliss it brings or the agitation it produces, and yet the understanding may find no concept for it' [R. Otto, *The Idea Holy*, p. 135].

[52] We saw earlier in *The De-kanting of* 'das Heilige' – *A Purification* how phenomenology opens access to the affective life of feelings ordinarily closed off in scientific enquiry. Phenomenology, Heidegger says, 'has again brought these phenomena more unrestrictedly into our sight' [M. Heidegger, *Sein und Zeit* (GA2), p. 139.'. . . wieder eine freiere Sicht auf diese Phänomene geschaffen zu haben']. Although Heidegger does not elaborate the distinction between 'feeling' and 'mood', except in the sense that the mood of dread has no thing as its object in contradistinction to feelings which are determined and specified by a recognizable object, Schleiermacher observes that feelings and intuitions 'are only dissolutions of religious sensibility' [F. Schleiermacher, *Über die Religion*, p. 52.'. . . nur Zersetzungen des religiösen Sinnes sind . . .']. It is this 'first mysterious moment . . . before intuition and feeling have separated' that, I believe, Heidegger names when he uses 'mood' as a refinement of 'feeling'. For him, in 'the silvery flash' [*Über die Religion*, p. 63.'. . . der Silberblick'] of mood, the most originary and primordial affective state that the method of phenomenology opens up for consideration, is found.

[53] T. Sheehan, Heidegger's *Introduction* . . ., p. 47. Heidegger is following Kierkegaard here who, says: 'anxiety's nothing is an actual something' [S. Kierkegaard, *The Concept of Anxiety*, p. 111].

Another area where resonances are detectable in Otto and Heidegger's writings is in the phenomenon of dread.[54] We saw how for Otto the moment of awfulness was key to unlocking the meaning of *tremor*, the root word in the phrase *mysterium tremendum* and deployed by Otto to draw attention to the authentic *res* signalled by the holy. The first stirrings of awe, he maintained, are experienced in the feeling of 'something uncanny' which is *the* feeling which forms the starting-point for the entire religious development in history. For Heidegger it is *in der Grundstimmung der Angst* (in the fundamental mood of dread) that being in the nothingness of its authenticity first comes to life. In the moment of dread all that can be said is it feels so *unheimlich* (strange).[55] Both authors use the same German word *unheimlich* to enunciate the feeling that opens up access to the nothing and the numinous, the essence of metaphysics and the holy respectively.

Another area where there appear to be echoes of Otto in Heidegger's thought is in their common use of the term 'uncanny'. Otto tells us that *ungeheuer* (used interchangeably with *unheimlich*)[56] is the closest German rendering of the Greek word *deimos*. *Deimos*, we may likewise recall, is the word invoked by the Greeks to stir the feeling of numinous awe (insofar as such things can be conjured by human linguistic ingenuity). For instance in the choral ode of Sophocles' *Antigone*, Otto demonstrates how *deimos* is used to speak of the uniqueness of human nature: there is much in the world that is uncanny, but nothing is more uncanny than the being of man.

For our purposes it is of deep significance that in section 13 of *Hölderlin's Hymn The Ister* Heidegger offers an almost identical hermeneutic of the exact-same verse from Sophocles' choral ode. When in 1917 Otto writes 'the German *ungeheuer* is not by derivation simply "huge," in quantity or quality . . . it is that which is not *geheuer*, i.e. approximately, the *uncanny*'[57] 25 years later, in a lecture at the University of Freiburg, Heidegger says: 'the "extraordinary" need not necessarily be thought merely in the sense of the immense . . . it is properly and at the same time that which is not ordinary (*das Nicht-Geheure*). The ordinary

---

[54] While Heidegger's indebtedness to Kierkegaard's writings in this area is acknowledged (see M. Heidegger, *Sein und Zeit*, p. 190, footnote iv) it is conceivable that Rudolph Otto likewise was familiar with Kierkegaard, although he fails to mention him directly as an influence in *Das Heilige*.

[55] Literally, '. . . it is the homeless or the unhomely'.

[56] Otto says '. . . that which is not *geheuer* is approximately the *uncanny* – in a word, the numinous' [R. Otto, *Das Heilige*, p. 54. 'Dann ist ihm das Ungeheure vielmehr das *Ungeheuerlich*-unheimlich-entsetzliche'].

[57] R. Otto, *Das Heilige*, p. 54. 'Mit "ungeheuer" meinen wir heute gewöhnlich einfach das Ausmaß oder Beschaffenheit ganz Große . . . Denn "ungeheuer" ist eigentlich und zuerst das wobei uns "nicht geheuer" ist, das *Unheimliche*.'

(*das Geheure*) is what is intimately familiar, homely. The extraordinary is the un-homely.'[58] He continues:

> we mean the uncanny in the sense of that which is not at home – not homely
> in that which is homely. It is only for this reason that the un-homely (*das
> Un-heimische*) can, as a consequence also be 'uncanny' ('*umheimlich*') in the
> sense of something that has an alienating or 'frightening' effect that gives rise
> to anxiety.[59]

If there is a sense in the English translations that Otto and Heidegger are speaking with one voice, suggesting a near-perfect symmetry, something even more surprising and decisive for our claim (that Heidegger was influenced to some degree by Otto) comes into focus when we refer to the original German words used by both authors. When Otto says:

> '*ungeheuer*' *ist eigentlich und zuerst das . . .* '*nicht geheuer*' *ist, das
> Unheimliche*
>
> (The extraordinary is actuatlly and firstly for us the not ordinary, the
> unhomely.)

Heidegger reflects:

> *Das Ungeheure ist zugleich und eigentlich das Nicht-Geheure . . . ist das Un-
> heimische.*
>
> (The extraordinary is simultaneously and actually the not ordinary . . . it is
> the unhomely).

John Macquarrie believes that 'the possibility of a connection to Otto is increased when we consider . . . Heidegger's . . . use of the word 'uncanny' (*umheimlich*) in his descriptions of the mood of anxiety'.[60] This close investigation of the text has shown that the connection between Otto and Heidegger is less a 'possibility' open to refutation but more a certainty that can be precisely demonstrated.

One final area of convergence comes to light in Otto's discussion of the *Ganz Andere* (Wholly Other). As the 'numinous object' the '*Ganz Andere*' is

---

[58] M. Heidegger, *GA53 Hölderlin's Hymn 'The Ister'*, p. 86. 'Das "Ungeheure" braucht nicht notwendig nur im Sinne des Riesenhaften gedacht zu werden. Das Ungeheure ist zugleich und eigentlich das Nicht-Geheure. Das Geheure ist das Vertraute, Heimische. Das Ungeheure ist das Un-heimische.'
[59] M. Heidegger, *GA53 Hölderlin's Hymn 'The Ister'*, p. 87. 'Das Unheimliche meinen wir im Sinne dessen, was nicht daheim – nicht im Heimischen heimisch ist. Nur deshalb kann das Un-heimische in der Folge dann auch "unheimlich" sein in der Bedeutung des befremdlich und beängstigend und "furchbar" Wirkenden.'
[60] J. Macquarrie, *Heidegger and Christianity*, p. 51.

'absolutely and intrinsically other than and opposite of everything that is and can be thought'.[61] Otto observes, we have seen, that for mystics all that can be said of the Wholly Other 'numen' is that, because it is utterly beyond being (all that 'is') it is 'that which is nothing'. The nothing of being (*Sein*) beyond beings (*Seiende*) therefore is the 'numinous object', the phenomenal content of the idea of the holy.

Although Otto does not use the expression 'ontological difference' to name the otherness of the nothing from being, this expression is however at the heart of Heidegger's thinking on metaphysics as we have just seen. Macquarrie cites from the *Postscript to 'What is Metaphysics?'* to speculate about the extent Otto's *Ganz Andere* influenced Heidegger's '*schlechthin Andere*' in the following extract from the *Postscript*:

> As that which is *schlechthin Andere* (altogether other) than all beings is that which is not. But this nothing essentially prevails as being.[62]

Given the other areas where Otto's thought has been shown to influence Heidegger's philosophy, I have demonstrated (conclusively I hope) that when Heidegger says *Das Nichts* he is speaking from out of the same domain as Otto when he utters *Das Heilige*.

3.4 Conclusion

In our reading of Heidegger in Chapter 1 we found that, in order properly to get to grips with his thinking on metaphysics, it is essential to step back into the domain out of which he speaks when he recalls *das Nichts* from the oblivion of forgetfulness where it has been consigned to in-abide. *Lethe*, we discovered, is the 'where' of *das Nichts*' in-abiding. The brash assertions of science and the noise of everyday life have exiled *das Nichts* into this lonely, remote and unreachable place. In *An Introduction to Metaphysics* Heidegger says:

> We cannot talk about *das Nichts* as though it were a thing like the rain outside or a mountain or any object whatsoever. In principle, *das Nichts* remains inaccessible to science. The man who wishes truly to speak about the must of

---

[61]   R. Otto, *Das Heilige*, pp. 34–5, 'schlechthin und wesentlich Andere und Gegensätzliche zu allem was ist und gedacht werden kann'.

[62]   M. Heidegger, *Nachwort zu: 'Was Ist Metaphysik?'* in *Wegmarken* (GA9), p. 306. '. . . Dies schlechthin Andere zu allem Seienden ist das Nicht-Seiende. Aber dieses Nichts west als das Sein.' Cited and translated by Macquarrie in his *Heidegger and Christianity*, SCM Press Ltd, 1994, p. 51.

necessity become unscientific[63] . . . To speak about the *Nichts* (nothing) will always remain a horror and an absurdity for science . . . Authentic speaking about nothing always remains unusual. It cannot be vulgarized. It dissolves if it is placed in the cheap acid of a merely logical intelligence.[64]

We embarked on this enquiry, searching for a deeper understanding of *das Nichts*, guided by the conviction that in the nothing the real content of Heidegger's inaugural lecture *Was Ist Metaphysik?* is to be found. This was considered an important task since *das Nichts* cannot be silently passed over by theologians intent on theologizing after metaphysics in the light of Heidegger's thought.

Following on from our reflections we are now in a position to conclude that the full meaning of *das Nichts* comes sharply into focus when viewed in the light cast by *das Heilige*. If *das Nichts*, announced in the mood of dread or anxiety, is the uncanny and *das Heilige* in the awe-filled moment of the *mysterium tremendum* is the uncanny, then it follows that *the nothing is the holy and vice versa*.

Indeed Heidegger tells us as much when, having established that *Sein* (being) and *das Nichts* (the nothing) are the same,[65] he says . . .

. . . The thinker says *das Sein* (being). The poet names *das Heilige* (the holy).[66]

---

[63] Herein lies the rub for Chauvet, who as we noted in Chapter 1, is methodologically committed to the positivist tendencies of theological 'science'. Having dismissed a scientific approach to philosophical enquiry that researches matters from a particular standpoint or direction, Heidegger adopts a phenomenological research methodology. This 'does not characterize the what of the objects of philosophical research as subject-matter, but rather the *how* of that research'. It endeavours to 'come to terms with the things themselves' and is 'opposed to taking over any conceptions which only seem to have been demonstrated; it is opposed to those pseudo-questions which parade themselves as "problems," often for generations at a time. This maxim ["To the things themselves!"] is abundantly self-evident' [M. Heidegger, *Sein und Zeit* (GA2), pp. 27–8. 'Er charakterisiert nicht das sachhaltige Was der Gegenstände der philosophischen Forschung, sondern das *Wie* dieser . . . mit den Sachen selbst verwurzelt . . . entgegen der Übernahme von nur scheinbar ausgewiesenen Begriffen, entgegen den Scheinfragen, die sich oft Generationen hindurch als "Probleme" breitmachen. Diese Maxime ["zu den Sachen selbst!"] ist . . . reichlich selbstverständlich'].In short phenomenology means 'to let that which shows itself be seen from itself in the very way in which it shows itself from itself' [M. Heidegger, *Sein und Zeit* (GA2), p. 34. 'Das was sich zeigt, so wie es sich von ihm selbst her zeigt, von ihm selbst her sehen lassen'].

[64] M. Heidegger, *Einführung in die Metaphysik* (GA40), pp. 28–9. '. . . Man kann . . . nicht über das Nichts reden und verhandeln, als sei dies ein Ding wie draußen der Regen oder ein Berg oder überhaupt irgendein Gegenstand. Das Nichts bleibt grundsätzlich aller Wissenschaft unzugänglich. Wer vom Nichts wahrhaft reden will, muß notwendig unwissenschaftlich werden . . . Vom Nichts zu reden, bleibt für die Wissenschaft allezeit ein Greuel und eine Sinnlosigkeit . . . Das wahre Reden vom Nichts bleibt immer ungewöhnlich. Es läßt sich nicht gemein machen. Es zerrinnt freilich, wenn man es in die billige Säure eines nur logischen Scharfsinnes bringt'.

[65] M. Heidegger, *Was Ist Metaphysik?* in *Wegmarken* (GA9), p. 120. 'Das reine Sein und das reine Nichts ist also dasselbe' (pure being and pure nothing are therefore the same).

[66] M. Heidegger, *Nachwort zu: 'Was Ist Metaphysik?'* in *Wegmarken* (GA9), p. 312. 'Der Denker sagt das Sein. Der Dichter nennt das Heilige.'

The connection between being (experienced in its truth as *das Nichts*) and the holy (*das Heilige*) is again highlighted by Heidegger in *Letter on Humanism*:

> . . . *das Heilige* (the holy), which alone is the essential sphere of divinity, which in turn alone affords a dimension for the gods and God, comes to radiate only when being itself beforehand and after extensive preparation has been illuminated and is experienced in its truth.[67]

In *Elucidations of Hölderlin's Poetry* Heidegger suggests that the nothing, which cannot be named or reduced to the form of an object because it is in a perpetual state of coming or presencing, is the holy. He says . . .

> . . . *Das Heilige* (the holy) is quietly present *als Kommendes* (as what is coming). That is why it is never *vorgestellt und erfaßt* (represented and grasped) as *ein Gegenstand* (an object).[68]

Others have arrived at this conclusion albeit via different routes and with varying degrees of emphasis. In *The Mystical Element in Heidegger's Thought* for instance, Caputo, following Meister Eckhart, finds in *das Nichts* an anonymous name for the very *is-ness* of the divine:

> . . . Eckhart's 'nothing' refers to God Himself, to 'He who *is*.' In virtue of His 'immovable detachment' God transcends every being, every this or that, every determinate being. That is why for Eckhart – as for Heidegger – one can refer to this transcendent reality either as 'pure nothing' or 'pure being.' 'Pure being and pure nothing are one and the same.' That sentence from Hegel aptly depicts the nature of God in Eckhart's metaphysics too.[69]

---

[67] M. Heidegger, *Brief über den Humanismus (1946)* in *Wegmarken* (GA9), p. 338, 'das Heilige . . ., das nur erst der Wesensraum der Gottheit ist, die selbst wiederum nur die Dimension für die Götter und den Gott gewährt, kommt dann allein ins Scheinen, wenn zuvor und in langer Vorbereitung das Sein selbst sich gelichtet hat und in seiner Wahrheit erfahren ist.'

[68] M. Heidegger, *Erläuterungen zu Hölderlins Dichtung* (GA4), p. 67. 'Das Heilige ist still gegenwärtig als Kommendes. Deshalb wird es auch nie als ein Gegenstand vorgestellt und erfaßt.' In *Dieu sans L'Être* Jean-Luc Marion, following where Nietzsche's proclamation that 'God is dead' leads and to avoid further idolatrous constructions, nevertheless and in spite of his own admonitions, depicts God's being as love. Although in so doing he ascribes being to God and therefore fails to show how God can be understood without being, nevertheless his definition of love as constant flux that never comes to alight on a final term can be seen as an appropriation of Heidegger's thoughts on the holy. For example Marion says: 'it belongs to the esence of love – *diffusivum sui* – to submerge, like a ground swell the wall of the jetty, every demarcation, representation or existential, of its flux: love excludes the idol or, better, includes it by subverting it' [J.-L. Marion, *Dieu Sans L'Être*, p. 75, 'il appartient à l'essence de l'amour – *diffusivum sui* – de submerger, comme une lame de fond le mur d'une jetée, toute délimitation, représentative ou existentielle, de son flux: l'amour exclut l'idole, ou mieux l'inclut en la subvertissant'].

[69] J. D. Caputo, *The Mystical Element in Heidegger's Thought*, pp. 21–2.

3.5 Reprise

In Chapter 2, following Chauvet in his search for an understanding of *ecclesia*, the *tension* that characterizes the relation between cult and ethics was discussed. It was shown how, after metaphysics, ethics for Chauvet is the place of veri-fication, the *veritas . . .* of the Eucharist. The effect on his sacramental theology of overlooking *das Nichts* was demonstrated: sacraments reduced to symbols instaurate otherwise dispersed and disconnected individuals within an always already world of symbolic forms; their singular virtue, for Chauvet, is that they guard against the 'danger of sinking . . . in the quicksands of the "unutterable" and "touching"'.

This chapter has demonstrated that it is precisely here, in the quicksands of the 'unutterable' and 'touching'[70] which Heidegger portays as *das Nichts* and Otto *das Heilige*, that the divine in its terrifying majesty, danger and awesomeness touches and transforms human lives. The 'unutterable' and 'touching' may indeed slip the grasp of conceptual ways of understanding, defying representation in transcendent symbolic form, but as Otto has demonstrated it [the ineffable] must be in some way or other within our grasp, else absolutely nothing could be asserted about it. Both Otto and Heidegger identify feeling (albeit in a quite particular and refined sense) as the manner in which the Holy registers in human being, Otto through the *Kreaturgefühl* (creature feeling) and Heidegger through the basic mood of dread. For Heidegger it is precisely within these quicksands of the 'unutterable', which he characterizes as *das Nichts* (the nothing) or *Das reine Sein* (pure being), that God makes his presence felt:

> the experience of God and his manifestedness, to the extent that the latter can indeed meet man, flashes [eventualizes] in the dimension of being.[71]

Chauvet's failure to recognize *das Nichts* as key to Heidegger's understanding of metaphysics has profound consequences for his sacramental theology. If sacraments as symbols block access to the *sables mouvants* (quicksands) of the 'unutterable' and if, as has been demonstrated, it is within these *sables mouvants* that God reveals himself, then *Chauvet's sacramental theology actively prevents encounter with the living God construed after metaphysics as das Heilige.* In other words, Chauvet's omission leads to the formulation of a theology that denies

---

70 L.-M. Chauvet, *Symbole et Sacrement*, p. 130.
71 M. Heidegger, *Seminare* (GA15), p. 437, 'die Erfahrung Gottes und seiner Offenbarkeit (sofern sie dem Menschen begegnet) in der Dimension des Seins sich ereignet'.

salvation is experienced now in a sudden, fleeting and unexpected *augenblicke*. In short he defers our beatification to an eschatological beyond.

In the succeeding chapters it remains to consider what ethics (Chapter 4) and cult (Chapter 5) look like when these are considered from out of *das Nichts*, taken now not in the sense of a negative purposelessness and godless nihilism but as the holy, fecund and originary matrix from which all beings emerge and within which they stand. Heidegger's words '*ex nihilo omne ens qua ens fit . . .* only in the nothing of *Dasein* do beings as a whole come to themselves'[72] instruct what follows. It remains to research in what ways ethics and sacrifice come to themselves when approached, not symbolically as Chauvet's sacramental theology attempts but, in the nothing of existence.

---

[72] M. Heidegger, *Was Ist Metaphysik?* (GA9), p. 120, 'ex nihilo omne ens fit. Im Nichts des Daseins kommt erst das Seiende im Ganzen . . . zu sich selbst.'

4
Heidegger and ethics

In Chapter 2 it was seen how, for Chauvet, God presences eucharistically in the fundamental sacramental mediation of the Church in the time between the past event of Jesus' crucifixion over 2,000 years ago and the future occurrence of his coming again in the *parousia*. Such a view of the manner of God's post-crucifixion presencing protects against, it may be recalled, the illusion of an *individualism* by which we would believe ourselves to be more Christian the more we achieve immediate contact with God in the silent conversation of meditation. Henceforth, until his second coming, Jesus is incarnate as the body, *symbolized* through the testimony the Church gives about him, through the scriptures reread as his own word, the sacraments performed as his own gestures, the ethical witness of the communion between brothers and sisters.

It is the last of these elements, the communion between brothers and sisters, constituting the tri-partite structure that forms for Chauvet the essence of a postmodern understanding of *ecclesia* and Eucharistic presence, which authenticates and brings the Church, as the real, true and substantial Body of Christ, into being. To recapitulate, it is in the return-gift of an *ethical* practice, in every kind of *action* not only, interpersonal 'moral *praxis*', but also collective 'social *praxis*' that the subject 'verifies' what it has received in the sacrament. For Chauvet ethics, as a categorical *imperative* of life and action as well as being the principle which brings the *ecclesia* into being as such, is likewise the fundamental location of the Christian liturgy. It is Heidegger's philosophy, encouraging the overcoming of metaphysics, that gives Chauvet's fundamental theology of sacramentality its philosophical credentials: his meditation on Heidegger's being enables Chauvet to rediscover the importance and essence of *ecclesia*, that is, *ecclesia* as the unthought essence of the Eucharist.

In Chapter 3 the phenomenon of *das Nichts*, which Chauvet had neglected to consider in his reading of Heidegger, was examined with the aim of exploring the term taken less as a concept of thought acting within the human psyche and more as the referent indicated by the formal concept occurring within a transcendental horizon.[1] By showing the influence of Rudolph Otto on Heidegger, it was possible to demonstrate that the term *das Nichts*, although frequently misunderstood and misconstrued by those who engage with Heidegger's thought, was nevertheless evidence that for Heidegger being has something of a holy, divine character. The nothing turns out to be the non-entity which nevertheless has more being than any entity, for it is the being that comes before every entity and in virtue of which every entity *is*. Being is 'Wholly Other' to beings, it is the *transcendens* that cannot fall under the categories applicable to beings. Yet it is 'so far from being nugatory that it is the most beingful of all.[2]

It was shown that in the domain of *das Heilige*, formally indicated by *das Nichts*, God in the awe-filled moment of his overpowering fleetingly presences, never settling long enough though to be grasped conceptually.[3] In the intensified moment of his presencing, as the individual asserts itself against the subject it has become, an impenetrable mood of anxious dread overwhelms,[4] dispersing only when *das Heilige* has passed-by. This experience, flashing in the far and hidden reaches of the being of man, independently of the interventions of human subjectivity, diminishes self-esteem and reduces the self to ashes, to less than nothing. It prefigures and prompts, in the emptiness that now prevails, a creaturely feeling of intense and dreadful anxiety, in the face of the transient character of our existence, which is through and through finite and threatened with annulment. As a space devoid of meaning opens up in the encounter with God unmediated by anything transcendental (in particular symbols), the

---

[1] This is not transcendence understood as a supersensible symbolic world transcending the individual and in so doing protecting them from themselves. Rather it is a transcendence that can not stand in a positive relation with the familiar intelligible world. Hans Jonas says: 'it [transcendence] is not the essence of that world, but its negation and cancellation' [H. Jonas, *The Gnostic Religion* (2001), p. 271].

[2] John Macquarrie, *Martin Heidegger* (1968), p. 45.

[3] Kierkegaard says when the one striving for God comes to a standstill 'he sees the illusive track of an enormous being that exists when it is gone, that is and is not' [S. Kierkegaard, *Three Discourses on Imagined Occasions*, p. 20].

[4] Kierkegaard likewise speaks of 'the dangerous moment' when the subject collects himself withdrawing from his surroundings to be alone before God in 'a stillness that changes the ordinary just as the storm does'. He continues: 'he did not know the anxiety that grips him when he feels himself abandoned by the multiplicity in which he has his soul; he did not know how the heart pounds when the help of others and the guidance of others and the standards of others and the diversions of others vanish in the stillness; he did not know the shuddering when it is too late to call for human help, when no one can hear him' [S. Kierkegaard, *Three Discourses on Imagined Occasions*, pp. 36–7].

individual, instead of succumbing to desperation, is enraptured or overwhelmed by a sense of wonder.[5] Wonder recedes only as the impulsion to a more radical and fruitful engagement with others and the world increases.

It is the aim of this chapter to consider how ethics, given its significance for Chauvet, might look when viewed in the light of *das Nichts* or *das Heilige*. It has been established that when Heidegger is read in the way Chauvet reads him, so that Heidegger ends up endorsing a symbolic understanding of existence, ethics becomes an interpersonal 'moral praxis' of the communion between brothers and sisters. This chapter asks the question: if God presences after the crucifixion, not symbolically as a three-part structure of word-sacrament-ethics, but instead as the holy that eventualizes in the dimension of being, what are the implications of this postmodern understanding of divine presence for ethics? If a reading of Heidegger, which takes seriously *das Nichts* and the region of being thereby formally indicated, consequently ends up refusing Chauvet's claim, that the recognition of Jesus as Christ and Lord cannot take place through a personal contact with him but on the contrary requires acquiescence in the mediation of his symbolic body, what characteristics do the ensuing ethics acquire?[6] Put differently, if (against Chauvet and predicated on a less incomplete reading of Heidegger) the recognition of Jesus as Christ and Lord *can* take place through a personal contact with him so that there *is* a *direct line* to Jesus Christ,[7] that is, one that does not require acquiescence in the mediation of his symbolic body, then

---

5 Kierkegaard says 'where the unknown seems to manifest itself, there is wonder, and wonder is immediacy's sense of God . . . Wonder is an ambivalent state of mind containing both fear and blessedness . . . Worship is the expression of wonder' [S. Kierkegaard, *Three Discourses on Imagined Occasions*, pp. 18–19].

6 In Chapter 5 the same question will be asked in connection with cult of the liturgy of the mass.

7 Chauvet interprets resentment of the Church and resistance to its claim to be the fundamental sacrament of Christ's presence in the time in-between Jesus' First and Second Coming as a 'symptom of this "gnostic" desire for the immediate contact with Jesus Christ' [L.-M. Chauvet, *Symbole et Sacrement*, p. 192, 'symptôme de ce désir, "gnostique", de branchement direct sur Jésus-Christ']. We may recall that for Chauvet it is one of the singular virtues of his method which construes sacraments symbolically that they serve as 'an unavoidable stumbling block which forms a barrier to every imaginary claim to a direct connection, individual and interior, with Christ or a gnostic-like, illuminist contact with him' [L.-M. Chauvet, *Symbole et Sacrement*, p. 160, 'une *butée incontournable* qui fait barrage à toute revendication imaginaire de branchement direct, individuel et intérieur, sur le Christ ou de contact illuministe de type gnostique avec lui'].
    Certain Heidegger scholars, for example Crowe and Macquarrie, have speculated about the possible gnostic content of Heidegger's philosophy. Such speculation is fuelled primarily by the research interests of Hans Jonas, one of Heidegger's main students. Macquarrie, speaking of 'Hans Jonas' brilliant work in the field of Gnosticism', speculates 'whether Jonas' use of . . . Heideggerian concepts was not made possible by the even closer affinity between existentialism [i.e. Heidegger's philosophy] and Gnosticism' [John Macquarrie, *Martin Heidegger* (1968), p. 55]. Given our claim in Chapter 3, that for Heidegger God addresses man in the immediacy of pure being (i.e. *das Nichts*), this emphasizing of the gnostic content of Heidegger's thought renders his philosophy properly understood incompatible with Chauvet's sacramental theology.

what happens following this shift in understanding of divine presence, to an understanding of Christian ethics?[8] In considering this question it is hoped that at the same time a contribution is made towards answering the broader question giving direction to this research, namely: does Heidegger's philosophy conflict with orthodox Catholic doctrines (such as transubstantiation) as Chauvet claims, or does it rather resonate with them?

4.1 Methodology

To establish what ethics might look like after a reading of Heidegger that does not shy away from but seriously engages with *das Nichts*, the features of a contemporary representation of Catholic ethics will be extracted from Pope Benedict XVI's first encyclical *Deus Caritas Est*. Heidegger's thought will next be considered to see whether symmetries with these features can be identified. Heidegger's fundamental ontology will be examined, principally through a reading of *Identity and Difference*, to establish whether it offers insights into an originary ethics, that is, an ethics that moves beyond universal principles governing human behaviour and moral reflection.

This chapter takes seriously Heidegger's own question: in what relation does the thinking of being stand to theoretical and practical behaviour? It asks: what happens to ethical theory when man, dropping out or stepping back from the violent order of *techne* (whose ethic determines the being of modern man and regulates his behaviour)[9] comes into his ownmost, opening up to the infinite possibilities of his being displaying in the moment of *das Nichts* in the overpowering order of what the Greeks speak of as *dike*?[10] When man identifies himself as the *deinon*, namely, the one within whom the overpowering power compels panic fear, true fear and the collected silent awe that vibrates with its own rhythm, how does this all-consuming mood influence his relations with others? If man takes up his abode in the truth of his being, an action or an accomplishment more essential than instituting rules, and therein encounters God flashing and passing-by in the realm of being, what is the relationship between those directives that must become law and rule for man (assigned

---

[8]   This question has ramifications for ecclesiology and liturgical studies if, as Chauvet claims, ethics brings the Church into being and is 'the fundamental location of the Christian liturgy' [L.-M. Chauvet, *Symbole et Sacrement*, p. 285, 'le lieu fondamental de la liturgie chrétienne'].

[9]   Hodge, following Heidegger, says: 'in the transformation of metaphysics into technical relations there is a diminution of the ethical . . .' [J. Hodge, *Heidegger and Ethics*, p. 3].

[10] Hodge says: 'for Heidegger, a question of ethics can be posed only in relation to a new principle of order, a new *dike*' [J. Hodge, *Heidegger and Ethics*, p. 28].

during his encounter with divinity) and ethics? Put simply, this chapter explores the effect an immediate encounter with God in the abysmal depths of being has on man's behaviour. When man comes to know himself as no thing, an awareness that comes about (as we saw in the previous chapter) when he is overpowered by the *mysterium tremendum* of *das Heilige*,[11] how is this 'self' knowledge played out in his relations with others? This chapter hopes to show that for both Benedict and Heidegger to embrace a 'thing' or a 'person' in its essence means to love it. This, it will be shown, is the meaning of originary ethics or essential action as accomplishment where something or someone is unfolded into the fullness of its essence.

4.2 Pope Benedict XVIth and ethics as *Caritas*

Pope Benedict XVI sets out the aim of his first encyclical *Deus Caritas Est* in the opening paragraph: 'to call forth in the world renewed energy and commitment in the human response to God's love'.[12] To achieve this he proposes to clarify with characteristic exactitude the love which God mysteriously and gratuitously offers man in order to show the intrinsic link between God's love and the reality of human love. This intrinsic link, we will come to see, is to be found in *eros* which although an essential characteristic of love is habitually excluded from consideration in many Christian reflections on love. However, for Benedict, since it is in *eros* itself that God's creative word discourses with man, such that man's finite existence is overwhelmed by divine power, it cannot be ignored without serious implications for our relationship both to God and man. Given its avowed aim, *Deus Caritas Est* contains the potential to awaken in human hearts a joy that is otherwise turned to bitterness[13] by the Church's commandments and

---

[11] Hans Jonas says that 'when God has more of the *nihil* than of the *ens* in his concept, so also his inner-human counterpart, the acosmic self or pneuma, otherwise hidden, reveals itself in the negative experience of otherness, of non-identification and of protested identifiable reason. For all purposes of man's relation to existing reality, both the hidden God and the hidden pneuma are nihilistic conceptions' [H. Jonas, *The Gnostic Religion* (2001), p. 271].

[12] Pope Benedict XVI, *Deus Caritas Est*, [25 December 2005. Translated as *God Is Love*, (2006)], §1, 'in mundo renovata quaedam operositatis vis excitetur uti amori Dei humanum responsum'.

[13] There are echoes here of Nietzsche to whom Benedict (as we will see later) explicitly refers. For instance, Nietzsche abhors 'every morality that says: "Do not do this! Renounce! Overcome yourself!"' [F. Nietzsche, *Die Fröhliche Wissenschaft* (1986), p. 203, 'alle jene Moralen . . . welche sagen: "Tue dies nicht! Entsage! – Überwinde dich!"'] on the grounds that such morality devalues otherwise quite healthy 'natural stirrings and inclinations' [Nietzsche, *Die Fröhliche Wissenschaft* (1986), p. 203, 'natürlichen Regungen und Neigungen']. These stirrings, when foregone in obedience to commands and prohibitons, change from being potential occasions of joy and virtue into being occasions of bitterness, irritability and vice.

prohibitions grounded on an incomplete understanding of God.[14] It promises the release into the world not only of an energy to which the Church previously blocked access but also of an understanding of God as a lover with all the passion of a true love to challenge and contest a strictly metaphysical image of God.

In her review of Pope Benedict's first encyclical, Janet Martin Soskice summarizes how, through participation in the sacraments we, whose love on its own is too weak, are fed by the divine Love, and 'enter into the very dynamic of self-giving'.[15] This self-giving is heralded by Jesus' sacrifice on the Cross which, Benedict says, is love in its most radical form. By contemplating the pierced side of Christ (cf. Jn 19.37), we can understand the starting-point of the Encyclical Letter: 'God is love' (1 Jn 4.8). It is there, Benedict reminds us, that this truth can be contemplated. It is from there that our definition of love must begin.[16]

4.2.1 The closed inward-looking self and the overpowering

From this starting point, the encyclical goes on to show that 'God's love for us and ours for God must inevitably and with no exceptions *spill out in love for one another*'.[17] God is present to us face to face in the intimate encounter of an event (*Ereignis*) which, in disrupting ordinary life, opens up a new horizon. It

---

In proclaiming *Deus caritas est*, and *caritas* as disciplined *eros*, Benedict is revalidating such stirrings and inclinations as occasions of divine encounter. In so doing his encyclical, as we have just seen, hopes, by returning bitterness and vice to an originary joy and virtue, 'to excite in the world renewed energy' [Pope Benedict XVI, *Deus Caritas Est*, §1, 'in mundo renovata quaedam operositatis vis excitetur']. If God is to be found in love, in particular in *eros*, then commands that rule out natural stirrings and inclinations at the same time rule out a living experience of God or a proper understanding of God's nature. In rehabilitating *eros* (revalidating joy) Benedict is simultaneously re-divinizing human life for, in Nietzsche's terms, to reject passions is to refuse the virtuous life in the frustration of 'thy highest aim' [F. Nietzsche, *Also sprach Zarathustra* (1999), p. 35, 'dein höchstes Ziel'].

In *Also sprach Zarathustra* Nietzsche anticipates Benedict when he says: 'Once hadst thou passions and calledst them evil. But now hast thou only virtues; they grew out of thy passions. Thou implantedst thy highest aim into the heart of those passions; then became they thy virtues and joys . . . all thy passions in the end became virtues, and all thy devils angels. Once hadst thou wild dogs in thy cellar; but they changed at last into birds and charming songstresses. Out of the poisons brewedst thou balsam for thyself; thy cow, affliction, milkedst thou – now drinketh the sweet milk of her udder' [F. Nietzsche, *Also sprach Zarathustra* (1999), p. 35. 'Einst hattest du Leidenschaften und nanntest sie böse. Aber jetzt hast du nur noch deine Tugenden: die wuchsen aus deinen Leidenschaften. Du legtest dein höchstes Ziel diesen Leidenschaften an's Herz: da wurden sie deine Tugenden und Freudenschaften . . . Am Ende wurden alle deine Leidenschaften zu Tugenden und alle deine Teufel zu Engeln. Einst hattest du wilde Hunde in deinem Keller: aber am Ende verwandelten sie sich zu Vögeln und lieblichen Sängerinnen. Aus deinen Giften brautest du dir deinen Balsam; deine Kuh Trübsal melktest du, – nun trinkst du die süsse Milch ihres Euters'].

[14] That is, an understanding of God that fails to conceive his being as love and love's being as eros (albeit disciplined and purified).

[15] Janet Martin Soskice, *Heart of the Matter*, The Tablet, 4 February 2006, p. 4.

[16] Benedict XVI, *Deus Caritas Est*, §12.

[17] Janet Martin Soskice, *Heart of the Matter*, The Tablet, 4 February 2006, p. 4 (my emphasis).

is within this horizon, in a moment of decision, that I come to be as *christianus* (one who is Christian) so that thereafter my life acquires a new orientation and a decisive direction. It is this overflow *from-out-of* us, of God's love *for-and-within* us that overpowers the closed inward-looking self, that is the defining character of ethics as *caritas*. This is because in the moment of overpoweringness in which I come face to face with God I am assigned 'directives' to instruct my relations with others.

Benedict shows in the 'Christological architectonic' of the first, speculative, part of the encyclical that love-within finds its source in the unintended and gratuitous gift of *eros*,[18] which, contrary to Nietzsche's contention that Christianity has poisoned *eros*[19] is an essential feature of Christian love. Indeed were *eros* to be presented as the antithesis of love, the essence of Christianity would be detached from the vital relations fundamental to human existence, and would become a world apart, admirable perhaps, but decisively cut off from the complex fabric of human life. Faith does not set up a parallel universe that runs along side the world and which is opposed to that primordial human phenomenon which is love. Rather *eros*, disciplined and purified through its association with *agape*,[20] is foundational to Christianity's engagement with the world.

---

[18]   In 'the pre-Christian world' Benedict says that 'the Greeks – not unlike other cultures – considered *eros* principally as a kind of intoxication, the overpowering of reason by a "divine madness" which tears man away from his finite existence and enables him, in the very process of being overwhelmed by divine power, to experience supreme happiness ... *Eros* was thus celebrated as a divine power, as fellowship with the Divine' [Benedict XVI, *Deus Caritas Est*, §4. '. . . mundum ante aetatem christianam. Certissime congruentes cum aliis culturis, viderunt Graeci in illo *eros* ante omnia aliquam ebrietatem, nempe rationis ipsius oppressionem per "divinum furorem" qui hominem ad ipsius vitae limitem abripit et, quod sic potestate quadam divina percutitur, quam maximam beatitudinem facit ut ipse experiatur ... Sic celebrabatur *eros* veluti divina quaedam vis, tamquam communio cum divina natura'].

[19]   Benedict XVI, *Deus Caritas Est*, §3. '. . . christiana religio dicitur venenum bibendum dedisse ipsi *eros*.'
       Benedict directs his reader to the original aphorism (168) in Nietzsche's *Jenseits von Gut und Böse* which states: 'Christianity gave Eros poison to drink – he did not die of it, it's true, but he deteriorated, into vice' [F. Nietzsche, *Jenseits von Gut und Böse* (1999), p. 102. 'Das Christenthum gab dem Eros Gift zu trinken: – er starb zwar nicht daran, aber entartete, zum Laster']. Benedict, in his rehabilitation of *eros*, simultaneously attributes a positive value to the associated but oftentimes discredited joy 'which is itself a certain foretaste of the Divine' [Benedict XVI, *Deus Caritas Est*, §3, 'quae praegustare ... de Divina natura'] or a coming into 'fellowship with the Divine' [Benedict XVI, *Deus Caritas Est*, §4, 'communio cum divina natura'].
       This is of particular importance in the light of Chauvet's claim, examined in Chapter 2, that the sacraments protect against the illusion of an 'original beatitude' [L.-M. Chauvet, *Symbole et Sacrement*, p. 103, 'beatitude originelle'] or an '*individualism* by which we would believe ourselves to be more Christian the more we achieve immediate contact with God in the silent conversation of meditation' [L.-M. Chauvet, *Symbole et Sacrement*, p. 193, '*individualisme* par lequel on croit être d'autant plus chrétien qu'on serait davantage branché directement sur Dieu dans le silencieux tête-à-tête de la méditation'].

[20]   *Agape* is love grounded in and shaped by faith, a descending and oblative love, *amor benevolentiae* and is contrasted with *eros* as a worldly, ascending and covetous love, *amor concupiscentiae* [Benedict XVI, *Deus Caritas Est*, §7].

Christianity accepts the whole man embracing, rather than turning away from, *eros* at the heart of his being. The more *eros* and *agape* in their different aspects find a proper unity in one reality of love, the more the true nature of love in general is realized. If *eros* were to be ruled out of a Christian understanding of love or to be given poison to drink by Christianity, a caricature or at least a impoverished form of love would result.[21] Love embraces the whole of existence in each of its dimensions, including the dimension of time. Love is indeed 'ecstasy', not in the sense of a moment of intoxification, but rather as a journey, an ongoing exodus out of the closed inward-looking self towards its liberation through self-giving, and thus towards authentic self-discovery and indeed the discovery of God.[22] In other words it is in the moment of overpoweringness that God, not as a metaphysical being, is physically encountered.

Benedict points out the Old Testament Prophets used boldly erotic images to speak of God's passion for his people and make extensive use of the metaphors of betrothal and marriage. Infidelity to God, in an extension of

[21]   Benedict points out that although, in the pre-Christian world, the religion of the Old Testament opposed the Greek view that, in the overpowering of reason effected by *eros*, fellowship with the divine is granted, he nevertheless points out in addition that 'it [Old Testament monotheism] in no way rejected *eros* as such; rather it declared war on a warped and destructive form of it' [Benedict XVI, *Deus Caritas Est*, §4, 'hinc vero minime *eros* repudiavit in se, sed quasi bellum indixit eius eversioni deletoriae'].
        In one sense Benedict's encyclical can be read as an attempt to rehabilitate *eros* on the grounds that, as the site where God encounters man, it cannot be overlooked without profound ontological and theological consequences. The Greek's celebration of *eros* as divine power turns out not to be a 'counterfeit divinisation of *eros*' [Benedict XVI, *Deus Caritas Est*, §4, 'falsa divinizatio *eros*'] but holds the key to a true understanding of the being of man and God's nature.
[22]   Benedict XVI, *Deus Caritas Est*, §6.
        Soskice says: 'it is wonderful to see it [*eros*] firmly restated here, especially since a number of modern theorists of Christian love (usually not Catholic) have taken it so far in an *agape*ist direction that any whiff of human desire is immediately ruled out as "self-interest" and thus bad.' For her, Benedict's encyclical represents a 'welcome restatement of the unity of the loves' [Janet Martin Soskice, *Heart of the Matter*, The Tablet, 4 February 2006, p. 4].
        Presumably Benedict's account of the importance of *eros* in any Christian understanding of love is in response to a contemporary misconception that it has no place. Perhaps the rehabilitation of *eros* is a reaction to the vices, defined by Nietzsche as deteriorations of *eros*, that flourish when *eros*, portrayed as a thing to be protected against, is thereby poisoned. Benedict's argument seems to follow closely a path trodden by Nietzsche who showed that when *eros* is allowed to be the motive impelling human action (i.e. when it is not poisoned but positively embraced) earthly joy and an original beatitude are its fruits. This is because in *eros* God speaks his living word so that what man wills and what God wills are indistinguishable.
        For instance, Benedict says that when '*eros* comes fully into its own' [*Deus Caritas Est*, §17] it 'can awaken within us a feeling of joy' [*Deus Caritas Est*, §17] and provide 'a certain foretaste . . . of that beatitude for which our whole being yearns' [*Deus Caritas Est*, §4] (Chauvet, it may be recalled, believes sacraments as symbols block access to an original beatitude). *Eros*, because (like God) it 'is in fact more deeply present to me than I am to myself' [*Deus Caritas Est*, §17] 'calls into play all man's potentialities' [*Deus Caritas Est*, §17].
        Since it is here, in *eros*, that God's will and mine coincide in a communion of will, so that God's will is no longer for me an alien will, something imposed on me from without by the commandments, but it is now my own will. This communion of will engages the whole man.

this metaphor, becomes thus adultery and prostitution. But how does this understanding of the truth of love and the nature of God inform the essential theme of ethics?

4.2.2 From *Mandato* to *Intrinsecus Data*

If ascending *eros* best describes God's relationship with man then ethics, as man's non-violent and affirming comportment to man (or the human comportment to others), has something of this gratuitous and mysterious character. We relate to one another, not because of an imperious command to do so or out of a desire to be devout and to perform religious duties, but on the basis of an intimate coming together with God, an encounter which has become a communion of will, even affecting my feelings. It is a stirring of 'divine madness' whose intoxication overpowers reason but which is, by pushing us out into relationship with others, nevertheless, leavened by descending *agape*. No longer is it a question, Benedict says, of a 'commandment' imposed from without[23] and calling for the impossible, but rather a freely bestowed experience of love *from within*, a love which by its very nature must then be shared with others. Love is 'divine' because it comes from God and unites us to God; through this unifying process it makes us a 'we' which transcends our divisions and makes us one.

Ethics has moved on from being simply a matter of morality. It is no longer etiquette or a 'lofty idea' that regulates and governs human relations but, in the event in being unsusceptible to the manipulations and intentions of reason, directives are assigned birthing the *Christsein* and giving life a new orientation.[24] We could say that ethics, now as a fundamental ontology, is no longer attributable to the categorical imperative for beyond the categories of everyday thought,

---

[23] Nietzsche parodies ideational strictures (i.e. commands as rational imperatives) equating them with whips (because of the violence that accompanies their administration) used to steer, direct and ultimately destroy human nature (depicted as a mule). He speaks of 'those everyday souls ... like tired mules who have been whipped somewhat too often by the "whip-lashes" of ideals!' [F. Nietzsche, *Die Fröhliche Wissenschaft* (1986), p. 103. 'des Alltags der Seele ... müden Maultieren, an denen das Leben die Peitsche etwas zu oft geübt hat ... idealische Peitschenschläge gäbe!'] 'What would those people know,' he asks 'of "higher moods"' [F. Nietzsche, *Die Fröhliche Wissenschaft* (1986), p. 103. 'Was würden jene Menschen überhaupt von "höheren Stimmungen" wissen'].

[24] There are echoes of Nietzsche here. For instance, Zarathustra says '"Thou shalt not rob! Thou shalt not slay!" – such precepts were once called holy; before them did one bow the knee and the head, and took off one's shoes ... was it a sermon of death that called holy what contradicted and dissuaded from life? O my brethren, break up, break up for me the old tables!' [F. Nietzsche, *Also sprach Zarathustra* (1999), p. 210. '"Du sollst nicht rauben! Du sollst nicht todtschlagen!" – solche Worte hiess man einst heilig; vor ihnen beugte man Knie und Köpfe und zog die Schuhe aus ... war es eine Predigt des Todes, dass heilig hiess, was allem Leben widersprach und widerrieth? Oh meine Brüder, zerbrecht, zerbrecht mir die alten Tafeln!'].

in the deeper regions of being where God draws near to us or eventualizes, 'something'[25] hidden nudges and prompts us to action or relation with others. If *eros* (purified and disciplined) names the occurring within or drawing near to us of God in the overpowering of my closed inward-looking self in the ecstatic moment, then I become more and more open and concerned with the happiness of the other the more I am reduced to nothing in the encounter that overwhelms. To refuse the encounter of love as *eros* in vain attempts to preserve non-Christian being (i.e. to remain enclosed within the self) is to refuse the supreme happiness of divine life, to forego a certain foretaste of that beatitude for which our whole being hungers, to refuse a fulfilled and authentic existence that calls into play all man's potentialities. In *eros* subjectivity is no longer exhaustively determined as the Cartesian *cogito*[26] but rather the *Christsein* or being Christian emerges from the encounter with an event which gives a new horizon to life and a decisive direction. As Soskice puts it:

> In the question of love, the novelty of Christian teaching on love is not in 'what Jesus taught' but 'who Jesus was'.[27]

Ethics therefore, emerging from God's love for us, raises important questions about who God is and who we are. In other words, for Benedict without a radical understanding of being, that is, a fundamental ontology encompassing man in the full range of his possibilities, there can be no understanding of an originary ethics beyond the everyday view of ethics as dominical command.

4.2.3 Summary

The object of identifying the main features of Pope Benedict's first encyclical was twofold: first, to search for a phenomenological definition of the term 'ethics', that is, a definition that penetrates beneath a superficial view of ethics as dominical command (universal principles or moral reflection) through to the matter of ethics itself, to direct us in our determination of whether Heidegger's

---

[25] Something is placed here in parenthesis to signal that it is not a thing but rather *das Nichts* or . . .

[26] In a joking aside, Benedict dismisses Descartes' ontology based as it is on the *extensio* abstracted from the corporeal substance of matter. He recounts 'the epicure Gassendi used to offer Descartes the humorous greeting; "O Soul!". And Descartes would reply: "O Flesh!"' and concludes 'it is neither the spirit alone or the body alone that loves. Only when both dimensions are truly united, does man attain his full nature' [Benedict XVI, *Deus Caritas Est*, §5. 'Per iocum Epicureus Gassendi salutatione illa Cartesium appellavit: "O Anima!". Cui Cartesius respondit: "O Caro!" Verumtamen neque solus spiritus neque corpus solum amat. Tunc tantum, cum in unum quiddam ambo revera coalescent, plene sui ipsius fit homo'].

[27] Janet Martin Soskice, *Heart of the Matter*, The Tablet, 4 February 2006, p. 4.

philosophy has ethical consequences. Secondly, to work out a contemporary Catholic understanding of ethics, that is one that is consistent with scripture and tradition, as this has evolved over the ages, to enable us to answer the main research question, whether Heidegger's philosophy supports or subverts Catholic orthodoxy. The following essential points can be distilled from this discussion of ethics as *caritas*:

1. Love is an *ecstasis* or exodus out of a self, closed and inward-looking, which brings humankind's full potentialities into being as the *Christsein*.
2. Love cannot be mandated and therefore consciously intended, that is, it is not a 'commandment' in the sense of an imperious act subject to human intentionality. Rather, it is a freely bestowed experience of love *from within*.
3. Love is a 'unifying process' that makes us a 'we' which transcends our divisions and makes us one.
4. Being comes fully to be in the encounter with an event (*Ereignis*) at the juncture where the ascending of covetous *eros* meets the descending of oblative *agape*. Belief that God is Love is not an assent within the human intellect but is a fundamental event occurring in the profound depths of human being. True belief effects or determines the who that I am and is therefore ontologically decisive.

Having distilled these essential 'principles' from Benedict XVI's encyclical to arrive at a contemporary and originary view of ethics, it is possible now to attempt an assessment of Heidegger's philosophy to determine whether any of the motifs identified in Benedict's thought appear in Heidegger's. If this can be demonstrated our claim that Heidegger's philosophy has ethical consequences consistent with Catholic orthodoxy will be substantiated.

4.3 Heidegger and ethics as love

In *Identity and Difference* the first lecture, *The Principle of Identity*, offers a window into Heidegger's thinking. Translated into English by Joan Stambaugh, as *Identity and Difference* Heidegger considered this text to be the most important thing he had published since *Being and Time*. We shall therefore examine this text in some detail, referring to other writings where these help to unfold the sense and meaning of its main themes, before returning to the question directing our enquiry whether or not Heidegger's philosophy has ethical consequences.

It is important from the outset for us to allow for the possibility of being seized or claimed by that which is contained within the visible word-forms that make up the content of the text.[28] The authentic interpretation, Heidegger says, must show what does not stand in the words but which is nevertheless said. Not to allow the texts to address the being (and thinking) of the reader in his uninhibited openness, neutralizes their transformative potential and results in an inauthentic reading. Indeed, when thinking, Heidegger says at the start of *The Principle of Identity*, attempts to pursue something that has claimed its attention, it may happen that on the way it undergoes a change. Heidegger advises his reader therefore in what follows to pay attention to the path of thought rather than its content. To dwell properly upon the content would simply block the progress of this lecture.

4.3.1 Identity and the highest principle of thought

The essential concern of this lecture[29] is to deconstruct the principle of identity A = A which is considered the highest principle of thought. Heidegger maintains that by doing this it will be possible to ascertain identity in its essence. The formula A = A asserts that there is an equivalence or equation or 'saming' (already an action) between one thing and another. In ordinary circumstances the establishment of equivalence confers identity so that, through the referencing or identification of one with the other, the two become the same. For something to be the same, Heidegger says, one is always enough. Sameness implies the relation of '*mit*' ('with'), that is, a mediation, a connection, a synthesis: the unification into a unity.

The structure of difference once violated now collapses in the construction of identity. Although Heidegger does not explicitly say so in *The Principle of Identity*, there is a fundamental connection here between the rendering of identity as A = A and the formulation of truth as *adæquatio*. This connection is brought out into the open when attention is diverted to the German word used to translate the Latin term *adæquatio*: in *Being and Time* Heidegger uses

---

[28] Hemming points out in *Heidegger's Atheism* that certain modern Catholic theologians, although they allow Heidegger to instruct their theologies to some degree, nevertheless disallow him to challenge their fore-conceptions. This cautious approach to Heidegger's thought impinges on their theological conclusions and prevents their thinking from undergoing a change. Hemming speaks of 'a form of distinction between the provinces of theology and philosophy that result in theology only ever being informed by Heidegger's thought and never self-tested against what that thought concludes' [(2002), p. 29].

[29] *Der Satz Der Identität* was a lecture given on the occasion of the 500th anniversary of the University of Freiburg im Breisgau, for the faculty day on 27 June 1957. Heidegger was 68 years old.

'*Angleichung*' which has the same root as '*Gleichung*' translated by Stambaugh as 'equation'. What Heidegger has to say about truth as *adæquatio* therefore is inextricably bound up with his thinking on identity as equation, that is, as the highest principle of thought.

In section 44 '*Dasein, Disclosedness and Truth*' of *Being and Time* Heidegger points out that Thomas Aquinas 'also uses for "*adæquatio*" ("likening") the terms "*correspondentia*" ("correspondence") and "*convenientia*" ("coming together")'.[30] Following this observation, it could be said that there is an equivalence between the correspondence theory of truth, where 'truth consists in the agreement of knowledge with its object'[31] (*adaequatio intellectus et rei*) and the highest principle of thought, where A equates or agrees with A. In other words the truth of identity is as much uncovered in research into identity and difference as it is in an exploration into the meaning of truth. *The Principe of Identity* raises the question whether the principle of thought, represented in the equation A = A, is indeed the highest principle of thought. The mere act of questioning however implies the possibility of an alternative (perhaps higher) principle for in the driving onset of questioning, Heidegger says, there is affirmation of what is not yet accomplished, and there is the widening of questioning into what is still not weighed out and needs to be considered. What reigns here is going beyond ourselves into what raises us above ourselves. Questioning is becoming free for what is compelling, though sheltered.[32] Insofar as questioning is the allowing of what is compelling to break through everyday inertia, it signals a disruption. In other words, when the sheltered irrupts (or the undisclosed discloses or the hidden emerges from its hiding), disturbing the ordinary and the familiar, questioning begins.

4.3.2 Difference

Having proposed the highest principle of thought in the form of an equation, Heidegger then proceeds to call into question its ability to reveal the very thing it claims to reveal. The being or essential identity of A does not reside in, nor is it equivalent to 'A', for the latter is not up to the task assigned to it. In fact the tendency, that is, the care about certainty and the grasping of the world indicated

---

[30] M. Heidegger, *Sein und Zeit* (GA2), p. 214. '. . . gebraucht für adaequatio (Angleichung) auch die Termini correspondentia (Entsprechung) und convenientia (Übereinkunft).'

[31] M. Heidegger, *Sein und Zeit* (GA2), p. 215. '. . . die Wahrheit in der Übereinstimmung einer Erkenntnis mit ihrem Gegenstand besteht . . .' (This is a citation from Kant's *Critique of Pure Reason*).

[32] M. Heidegger, *Beitrage zur Philosophie (Vom Ereignis)*, (GA65), p. 10.

in the formula, leads towards the burying of existence itself. When the being or essential identity of A is disinterred, it is discovered to reside in that which *connects* A with A. The quiddity, or 'A-ness', of A, is located in the 'is-ness' of the 'is' in the improved formula A is A. Otherwise put, the essence or real identity of A shows itself, not in the phenomena of the subject and objectival characters in the statement A is A, but instead in the 'is' as the phenomenal content[33] joining the two into one-and-the-same.

Speculative idealism, epitomized in Leibniz and Kant, reads identity off from the same characters and in the process of abstracting identity there-from completely overlooks and by-passes the mediating is-ness, the cleavage, the midpoint, wherein real identity or the truth of being is to be found. In positing the being of identity at this level every entity is seen in terms of one uniform, basic level of being that is amenable to interrogation by science. But by this levelling of being, Heidegger warns, every determination of being and, in particular, that of existence already moves on a level that is no longer suitable for a genuine inquiry into being, but instead is bent solely on conceptualities and propositions about them.[34]

When the being of identity is represented in conceptualities and propositions, that is, as A is A, so that being is understood at this level, the ensuing identity is a distortion of the real identity of being. The formula purports to capture that for which it cares, in the bold proclamation that A, as subject, is owned-by or in the possession-of A, as object. However, what obtains in this process is not the phenomenal content of the phenomenon A for, as already noted, something essential remains sheltered being hidden because forgotten. Each being qua grasping, each knowing, Heidegger says, is an interpretation of existence itself, when seen in terms of the basic distorting phenomenon.[35]

This structure of distorting in the levelling of being, jumps over or flees in the face of A's real existence. In spite of the fact that A goes out in concern towards A, the is-ness of A is lost in the careful intentional act. Heidegger points out that in *care* as a basic manner of being in the world existence leapfrogs itself such that it keeps in view and keeps in its care something *that is not yet here*. In the formula A is A then the primordial and fundamental quiddity of A is surpassed;

[33] In *Sein und Zeit* Heidegger speaks of *der eigentliche phänomenale Gehalt* (the real phenomenal content), resisting *jeder mathematischen Funktionalisierung* (any sort of mathematical functionalization) that gets *nivellieren* (levelled off) when the system of relations in the context of assignments and references (as significance) are taken formally [M. Heidegger, *Sein und Zeit* (GA2), p. 88].
[34] M. Heidegger, *Einführung in die Phänomenologische Forschung* (GA17), p. 286.
[35] M. Heidegger, *Einführung in die Phänomenologische Forschung* (GA17), p. 285.

although A asserts an equality with A, through care for it, it nevertheless remains peculiarly remote from the real reality of A, the truth of its being. In the pounding down of every being to one and the same level something critical and essential gets left behind and neglected. In his discussion of Husserl's critique of naturalism Heidegger observes that each care qua care neglects something. What is neglected is precisely what the care itself claims to take care of for it disregards *what* is supposed to be normatively determined. This neglect is not simply an oversight, a failure to pay attention to something that could subsequently be done, but instead that what is here neglected is neglected in the manner of a concern for it.[36]

In *Der Satz Der Identität* Heidegger makes a similar point: in the interpretation of sameness as a belonging together the belonging *together* is 'stubbornly' misunderstood or neglected so long as everything is represented only in categories and mediations whether this representation be with or without dialectic.

4.3.3 Belonging *together*

'Belonging together', an essential theme of the lecture, is ordinarily understood with particular and implicit emphasis placed on the operative word 'together'. To belong is determined by the together, that is, to be assigned and placed into the order of a 'together', established in the unity of a manifold, combined into the unity of a system, mediated by the unifying centre of an authoritative synthesis.

The kind of unity signalled in this belonging *together* is one Heidegger treated at length in section 18 *Involvement and significance: the worldhood of the world* in *Being and Time*. When an entity can be referred or assigned back to something pre-existing in the totality of equipment making up the world, it discovers itself. Heidegger establishes that the state of reference or assignment to a larger and encompassing totality, that is, to a higher synthesis, constructs identity or is constitutive for the ready-to-hand as equipment. That which presents itself comes into existence insofar as it is read or interpreted in terms of other beings. However, the system of relations assigning being to a place within a pre-posited unity, world or togetherness, so that being shows itself, not as it is in itself, but rather in a founded-mode as being, overlooks or neglects a more originary unity, worldhood of world or *belonging* together, that is, the

---

[36] M. Heidegger, *Einführung in die Phänomenologische Forschung* (GA17), pp. 85–7.

unity wherein being, understood phenomenologically and not merely through the *noein*, in-abides.[37]

As Heidegger says, these systems of relations taken formally, result in the leveling off of phenomena such that their real phenomenal content may be lost. It is this real phenomenal content, resisting any sort of instrumentalization, that offers a clue to the existence of a deeper world (the worldhood of world) or a *belonging* together that is not contingent on the pre-established systems that transcend the individual, but rather emerges, without founding references or assignments, from out of itself. When the accent is changed in the 'belonging together', to the *belonging*, the possibility emerges of no longer representing belonging in terms of the unity of the together, but rather of experiencing this together in terms of the belonging.

4.3.4 *Das Ge-Stell*

But before we switch our concern from *belonging* together, Heidegger introduces the notion of *das Ge-Stell*[38] (the framework) to indicate the challenge human existence faces, now playfully, now urgently, now breathlessly, now ponderously to devote itself to the planning and calculating of everything. The technological world and the mode of concern that characterizes it, is determined by the *Ge-Stell* within which a strange ownership and a strange appropriation of being by man prevails. It is strange because, as that which lets us think the being of beings as presence, it exists beyond the purview of representation. As the thing that enables entities to come to be, its presence is one step removed from ordinary existence.[39] The extra-ordinary, as that which remains veiled, presents itself as the strange to those who unquestioningly acquiesce in nature as determined and

---

[37] In *Sein und Zeit* Heidegger says of Descartes' ontology that '... the foundations on which it is based have led him to *pass over* both the phenomena of the world and the Being of those entities within-the-world which are proximally ready-to-hand' [M. Heidegger, *Sein und Zeit* (GA2), p. 95. '... deren Fundamente dazu führten, das Phänomen der Welt sowohl wie das Sein des zunächst zuhandenen innerweltlichen Seienden zu *überspringen*'].

[38] M. Heidegger, *Identität und Differenz* (GA11), p. 44. The '*Ge-*' of '*Ge-Stell*' suggests the past tense that is the framework is the consequence of a event that has already happened so that man's comportment to Being in this mode is determined by the past and not as it is occurring in itself in the here and now.

[39] Heidegger makes a similar point in *Sein und Zeit*. Discussing Cartesian ontology he says 'Descartes ... prescribes for the world its "real" Being, as it were, on the basis of an idea of Being whose source has not been unveiled and which has not been demonstrated in its own right – an idea in which Being is equated with constant presence-at-hand' [M. Heidegger, *Sein und Zeit* (GA2), p. 96. 'Descartes ... auf dem Grunde einer in ihrem Ursprung unenthüllten, in ihrem Recht unausgewiesenen Seinsidee (Sein-ständige Vorhandenheit) schreibt er der Welt gleichsam ihr "eigentliches" Sein vor']. This idea of Being, like the framework, lies beyond circumspection.

defined by modern physics. Technology is not just something man has acquired as an accessory. Right now it is, says Stambaugh, what he *is*. The manner in which man and being concern each other in the world of technology Heidegger calls the framework.[40]

The reference or assignment of being to the totality of the technological world reduces everything down to man and creates the need for an ethics of the technological world. It highlights the fact that technology is the product of man's finite and delimited preoccupations and in so doing simultaneously draws attention to the fact that we fail to hear the claim of being which speaks in the essence of technology. The 'ownership' typified by the *Ge-Stell* and the relations that are regulated by it in the construction of modern being, result in the neglect of something essential/foundational in being's primordiality. And this is because, as we have seen, the overlooked real phenomenal content of being is resilient and resistant to the mathematical functionalization which characterizes the ontology of modern physics and technology. From the perspective of temporality, we could say that to view phenomena through the *Ge-Stell*, itself the outcome of an event occurring in the past, is to miss something of the urgency and futurity of that which is intensely present. The technological leads to a dislocation for the assault of *techne* against *dike* is the happening whereby man becomes homeless or ceases to be at home.

4.3.5 *Belonging* together

If the framework belying the technological world connects man and being into a belonging *together*, necessitating an ethic of the technological world, what then is the 'principle' that betroths man and being in a *belonging* together implying an alternative ethic? The key to an answer is suggested in the etymology of the German word *ge-hören*. Derived from *hören*, meaning to hear or listen, *belonging* together obtains when man is attentive to the claim being makes upon him. Instead of failing to hear its sound, being deaf to the address of being, as in the ontology characteristic of the modern world of technology, when man sensitizes to being's call allowing its sway to determine his life he enters a deeper unity which uncovers the *belonging* together of man and being. This unity or the constellation of being and man is not achieved through reference and assignment to the totality of the *Zusammen*, nor the *Ge-Stell*, but rather through immediate and direct reference of man to being. Man *is*, Heidegger says, essentially this

---

[40] Heidegger, *Identity and Difference*, pp. 13–14.

relationship of responding to being, and he is only this. A belonging to being prevails within man, a belonging which listens to being because it is appropriated to being. Being is present and abides only as it concerns man through the claim it makes on him.[41]

So if thinking, as a listening to the claim of being,[42] leads to the *belonging* together determinative of the is-ness connecting A to A in the truth of identity, and not to the belonging *together* brought about by a cogitating that evacuates the essential phenomenal content of identity in the reductive levelling off of being, then what is it that initiates this new way of beholding or thinking?

Or put differently, how does that which has been neglected, missed or leapfrogged over in the highest principle of thought (A is A), announce its presence? How can we think the neglected, that is, what still must be thought, if there is no thought beyond the principle? Surely if something cannot be thought it has no being and therefore existence that we can know about. This much is true if thinking is conceived in the narrow Cartesian sense of the *cogito*. However, when conceived phenomenologically thinking enlarges to encompass non-rational modes of awareness. Although existence is bent on blocking this possibility, because such modes of awareness do not lie explicitly in existence, it nevertheless emerges when phenomena are viewed judiciously or phenomenologically. For example, the phenomenon of anxiety as a manner of being-related-to-something is a phenomenon of existence itself that is overlooked when being is determined as intentionality. Similarly, in an extended discussion of the Greek understanding of truth in the *Parmenides* lecture series, Heidegger speaks of the sudden irruption of the 'it is' of beings, into appearance from non-appearance, addressing us from outside of the pretensions of arcane erudition. To think being in this way does not require mystical raptures, reveries and swooning for it is not a display of rare and exceptional states. Rather, all that is needed is simple wakefulness in the proximity of any random unobtrusive being, an awakening that all of a sudden sees that the being 'is'.[43]

From the level of the highest principle of thought, A is A, such modes are considered a threat. The threat against which existence defends itself, Heidegger says, lies in the fact that it *is*. *That it is* is the threat of existence itself.[44]

[41] M. Heidegger, *Identität und Differenz* (GA11), p. 39.
[42] 'Let us think of being' Heidegger exhorts 'according to its original meaning, as presence' [M. Heidegger, *Identität und Differenz* (GA11), p. 39 'Denken wir das Sein nach seinem anfänglichen Sinne als Anwesen'].
[43] M. Heidegger, *Parmenides* (GA54), p. 222.
[44] M. Heidegger, *Einführung in die Phänomenologische Forschung* (GA17), p. 289.

4.3.6 Uncanniness

The comforting reassurance, familiarity or homeliness that comes to characterize the levelling of difference into the same,[45] achieved through tranquillizing the being of knowing itself, comes under threat when the un-thought being of A, from which A took flight in the formula A is A, is thought phenomenologically for the first time. Such thinking is characterized by Heidegger as the uncanny or the eerie. That *in the face of which* existence *flees* by way of the *care about certainty*, he says, is the uncanny. Uncanniness is the genuine threat that existence is subject to. Uncanniness is the threat that is in existence of itself. Uncanniness displays itself in the *everydayness* of existence. Uncanniness is, if one asks what it is, *nichts*; if one asks where it is, *nowhere*. It expresses itself in existence's flight in the face of itself as the flight into familiarity and tranquillization.[46]

In the context of our discussion of identity and difference, it may be said that the site-less site of the no-where and thing-less thingliness of the no-thing of identity is not uncovered at the level of, nor is it at home within, the highest principle of thought as 'A is A.' Rather its truth is disclosed in the the eerie or the uncanny and is as such a homeless in-abiding. What Heidegger is attempting here is a recovery of being, though not as an 'A' or a thing as such. Being as no thing is not nothing but is rather being in its wholeness.

If being is not fully disclosed in the top down or transcendent highest principle of thought then it must be experienced anew from the bottom up. It is from here, the realm of the uncanny into which being returns in the overpowering, being dislodged from out of the homely, the customary, the familiar and the secure, in the suspension of *techne*, that the unbound powers of being come forth. The irruption that overpowers disrupts as it breaks-in. It is here in the overpowering that breaks-in upon the A = A, when identity comes into the truth of being, that those directives that must become rule and law for man are assigned. If it is these directives that constitute an originary ethics, giving life

---

[45] 'The beginning', Heidegger says 'is the strangest and mightiest. What comes afterward is not development but the flattening that results from mere spreading out; it is inability to retain the beginning; the beginning is emasculated and exaggerated into a caricature of greatness taken as purely numerical and quantitative size and extension' [M. Heidegger, *Einführung in die Metaphysik* (GA40), p. 164. 'Der Anfang ist das Unheimlichste und Gewaltigste. Was nachkommt, ist nicht Entwicklung, sondern Verflachung als bloße Verbreiterung, ist Nichtinnehaltenkönnen des Anfangs, ist Verharmlosung und Übertreibung des Anfangs zur Mißgestalt des Großen im Sinne der rein zahlen- und mengenhaften Größe und Ausdehnung'].

[46] M. Heidegger, *Einführung in die Phänomenologische Forschung* (GA17), pp. 289–90.

authentic orientation, then it follows that to resist the unbound powers coming forth in the overpowering that breaks-in upon my identity (taken as A = A), that is, to existing into the truth of being, is to be fundamentally disorientated, to be inauthentically,[47] to be imprisoned within the mundane, to be entangled in the eternal recurrence of the same.

Heidegger says it has taken Western thought over 2,000 years to realize that it is no longer possible for thinking to represent the unity of identity as mere (sameness) and to disregard the mediation[48] that prevails in unity. This is because it is into the breach between A and A (the midpoint or cleavage) that the preponderant power of being explodes in its appearing. It is this radiant emergence, in all of its uncomfortable and threatening eeriness, bursting the breach, destructuring and disrupting, that is the concern of the rest of the lecture.

---

[47] If allowing one's life to be directed by the overpowering that breaks-in is, in Nietzsche's terms, entrusting oneself to the 'free wing beat' [F. Nietzsche, *Die Fröhliche Wissenschaft* (1986), p. 204. 'freien Flügelschlage'] then if man is not orientated by the overpowering or not directed by 'whatever may henceforth push, pull, beckon, impel him from within or without' [F. Nietzsche, *Die Fröhliche Wissenschaft* (1986), p. 203, 'stoßen, ziehen, anlocken, antreiben mag, von Innen oder von Außen her'] he is afflicted by 'a peculiar disease, namely, a constant irritability at all natural stirrings and inclinations and as it were a kind of itch' [F. Nietzsche, *Die Fröhliche Wissenschaft* (1986), p. 203, 'eine eigentümlich Krankheit . . . nämlich eine beständige Reizbarkeit bei allen natürlichen Regungen und Neigungen, und gleichsam eine Art Juckens'].
Conversely, to be determined by the overpowering, that is, not to block 'whatever may henceforth push, pull, beckon, impel . . . from within or without' [F. Nietzsche, *Die Fröhliche Wissenschaft* (1986), p. 203, 'stoßen, ziehen, anlocken, antreiben mag, von Innen oder von Außen'] is to taste a joy or 'happiness unknown to humanity so far: a divine happiness full of power and love, full of tears and laughter, a happiness which, like the sun in the evening, continually draws on its inexhaustible riches, giving them away and pouring them into the sea, a happiness which, like the evening sun, feels richest when even the poorest fisherman is rowing with golden oar! This divine feeling would then be called humanity!' [F. Nietzsche, *Die Fröhliche Wissenschaft* (1986), p. 226, 'ein Glück . . . das bisher der Mensch noch nicht kannte, – eines Gottes Glück voller Macht und Liebe, voller Tränen und voll Lachens, ein Glück, welches, wie die Sonne am Abend, fortwährend aus seinem unerschöpflichen Reichtume wegschenkt und ins Meer schüttet und, wie sie, sich erst dann am reichsten fühlt, wenn auch der ärmste Fischer noch mit goldenem Ruder rudert! Dieses göttliche Gefühl hieße dann – Menschlichkeit!'].

[48] In *Sein und Zeit*, in his discussion of truth, Heidegger names this mediation 'the relation between an ideal entity and something that is Real and present-at-hand'. He continues: '. . . the relation is to be one that *subsists*. What does such "subsisting" mean ontologically? . . . Is it accidental that no headway has been made with this problem in over two thousand years?' He concludes, having pointed out 'the indispensability of clarifying the kind of Being which belongs to knowledge itself', that 'we must . . . try to bring into view a phenomenon which is characteristic of knowledge – the phenomenon of truth'. When we speak of mediation therefore we are in fact speaking of truth, the essential nature of which has remained obscured for over 2,000 years [M. Heidegger, *Sein und Zeit* (GA2), pp. 216–17. '. . . *die Beziehung zwischen ideal Seiendem und real Vorhandenem* . . . Die Beziehung soll doch *bestehen*. Was besagt ontologisch Bestand? . . . Ist es Zufall, daß dieses Problem seit mehr denn zwei Jahrtausenden nicht von der Stelle kommt? . . . die Aufklärung der Seinsart des Erkennens selbst unumgänglich wird . . . muß versuchen, zugleich das Phänomen der Wahrheit, das die Erkenntnis charakterisiert, in den Blick zu bringen'].

4.3.7 Phenomenology

How to get access to the elusive[49] phenomenal content of the highest principle of thought, that has evaded the grasp of thinkers for over two millennia, requires an approach (as suggested earlier) that is more attentive to the richer fluctuating possibilities of existence than scientific and calculative thinking has hitherto-for been. If a listening disposition is adopted, instead of just thoughtlessly mouthing the formula 'A is A', such that the principle of identity is heard in its fundamental key, then the listener finds that existence, in its uncanniness, makes a claim on him. Deafness or non-attunement to the sound of being rustling in the undergrowth of being reduces everything, in a degeneration, to a forced rattling of concepts. Everywhere, wherever and however we are related to beings of every kind, Heidegger says, we find identity making its claim on us. If this claim were not spoken, beings could never appear in their being. The claim of the identity of the object *speaks*, whether the sciences hear this claim or not, whether they throw to the winds what they have heard or let themselves be strongly affected by it.[50]

The phenomenological method of investigation, because one does not have to measure up to the requirements of an already-given discipline, allows one to become attuned to the eerie voice of the claim which ordinarily is silenced in a scientific method of investigation. Phenomenology brings into view that which is overlooked in habitual modes of consciousness allowing for a grounding attunement to the key note sounding out in the phenomenal content of phenomena. It is incumbent upon the researcher that he seek the essential where nothing more is to be found by the scientific interpretation that brands as unscientific everything that transcends its limits. In answer to the question: What is it that phenomenology lets us see? in *Being and Time* Heidegger replies:

Manifestly, it is something that proximally and for the most part does *not* show itself at all: it is something that lies *hidden*, in contrast to that which

---

[49] Heidegger says that 'elusiveness is a feature proper to the existing world as existing. Things can elude us and that is not to say they disappear. The elusiveness of things comes to life by virtue of the fact that we encounter them circumstantially. We do not see the things as subject matters in the sense that they are an object of a scientific investigation. This existence of things is much richer and affords much more fluctuating possibilities than have been thematically prepared' [M. Heidegger, *Einführung in die Phänomenologische Forschung* (GA17), p. 37. 'Die Entgänglichkeit der Dinge wird dadurch lebendig, daß sie uns in der Umständigkeit begegnen. Wir sehen die Dinge nicht als Sachen, wie sie Gegenstand einer wissenschaftlichen Untersuchung sind. Dieses Dasein der Dinge ist viel reicher und bietet viel wechselndere Möglichkeiten als das thematisch präparierte'].

[50] M. Heidegger, *Identität und Differenz* (GA11), pp. 35–6.

proximally and for the most part does show itself; but at the same time it is something that belongs to what thus shows itself, and it belongs to it so essentially as to constitute its meaning and its ground . . . That which remains *hidden* is the *being* of entities. In the phenomenological conception of 'phenomenon' what one has in mind as that which shows itself is the being of beings, its meaning, its modifications and derivatives.[51]

In the context of our investigation into identity and difference the discipline of phenomenology allows the mediation connecting A with A, that is, the is-ness in the formula A is A, to come out from the obscurity of hiddeness into the shining brightness of un-concealment. Phenomenology brings to light the truth of identity and difference which, when approached carefully and scientifically, through the discipline of mathematical geometry, is by-passed. This is because for phenomenology what matters is to bring existence into focus in a positive sense in its averageness, something rendered impossible from the outset by the interpretation of intentionality as the basic structure of consciousness. Phenomenology's concern is 'to let that which shows itself be seen from itself in the very way in which it shows itself from itself',[52] that is, to reveal the ownmost content of phenomena. The one who thinks phenomenologically, namely the creative man, is one who sets forth into the unsaid, breaks-in into the unthought,[53] compels the unhappened to happen and makes the unseen appear.

4.3.8 The leap

But if the method of phenomenology allows us to think from out of the domain of the uncanny or *belonging* together, wherein is to be found the principle of mediation connecting A to A in such manner that difference is preserved, then how is the move from the level of the highest principle of thought, the habitual and familiar site of being, to come about? If such a move cannot be carefully intended in the concern for certainty, what then instigates the return to that from which existence has fled? What realizes the possibility of downfall into

---

[51] M. Heidegger, *Sein und Zeit* (GA2), p. 35. 'Offenbar solches, was sich zunächst und zumeist gerade *nicht* zeigt, was gegenüber dem, was sich zunächst und zumeist zeigt, *verborgen* ist, aber zugleich etwas ist, was wesenhaft zu dem, was sich zunächst und zumeist zeigt, gehort, so zwar, daß es seinen Sinn und Grund ausmacht . . . Was . . . *verborgen* bleibt . . . ist . . . *das Sein des Seienden* . . . Der phanomenologische Begriff von Phänomen meint als das Sichzeigende das Sein des Seienden, seinen Sinn, seine Modifikationen und Derivate.'

[52] M. Heidegger, *Sein und Zeit* (GA2), p. 34. '. . . Das was sich zeigt, so wie es sich von ihm selbst her zeigt, von ihm selbst her sehen lassen.'

[53] It may be recalled from Chapter 2 that Chauvet calls *das Un-gedachte* the *essence impensée.*

the issueless and placeless? Heidegger devotes the remainder of his lecture to answering the question, how to enter into the domain of the *belonging* together[54] and to move beyond a thinking that never lets us glimpse the constellation of being and man and always falls short of the mark. But how can such an entry[55] come about? By our moving away, Heidegger answers, from the attitude of representational thinking. This move is a leap in the sense of a spring. The spring leaps away, away from the habitual idea of man as the rational animal who in modern times had become a subject for his objects.[56]

The German *springen* is used by Heidegger in various ways to draw attention to the primordial origins of ontology, whether constructed on rational foundations or otherwise. For instance, in *Being and Time*, in a discussion of Descartes' understanding of being, Heidegger refers to the *Ursprung*, the spring at the source of the Cartesian idea of being. The *Ursprung* is habitually *übersprungen* (passed or leapt over) when entities are accessed through a knowing that is mathematical. As we have already seen in the discussion of 'the framework', to view phenomena in this way, that is, mathematically, leads to the obstruction of the real phenomenal content of phenomena which defiantly eludes the vain graspings of rational calculation. By taking his basic ontological orientation from traditional sources and not subjecting it to positive criticism, Heidegger believes Descartes has made it impossible to lay bare any *ursprunglichen* (primordial) ontological problematic of *Dasein*; this has inevitably *obstructed his view* of the phenomenon of the world.[57]

Heidegger points out that traditional ontology operates in a blind alley when it *überspringt* (passes over) the phenomenon of worldhood, that is, the phenomenal content of world. The very fact of this *Überspringens* (passing-over) suggests that we must take special precautions to get the right phenomenal point of departure for access to the phenomenon of worldhood so that it will not get *Überspringen* (passed over).[58]

As we have already discussed above *das Ge-Stell* is not the point of departure as thinking no longer enjoys the favour of the system nor does mathematical knowledge give access to that which is passed over. Rather the *springt* is the

---

[54] The rendering of this as 'enter the domain of the *belonging* together' is one translation for *kehren* can also mean 'to turn'. Another translation might be 'turn . . . into the unity of the belonging together' although this sounds more clumsy in English.

[55] The translation of *einkehr* as 'entry' is consistent with the translation of *kehren* as 'to enter' but, as noted above, conceals an association with the important notion of *Die Kehre*.

[56] M. Heidegger, *Identität und Differenz* (GA11), pp. 40–1.

[57] M. Heidegger, *Sein und Zeit* (GA2), p. 98.

[58] M. Heidegger, *Sein und Zeit*,(GA2), p. 66.

starting point and phenomenology opens access onto the ownmost content of phenomena that has defied the grasp of Western thinking for over 2,000 years. Thinking has needed more than 2,000 years, Heidegger says, really to understand such a simple relation as that of the mediation within identity.[59]

But having determined that a spring is needed in order to experience authentically the *belonging* together of man and being it is important at this juncture to attempt to say something about what the *Sprung* is in itself. We have already seen that it brings about an entry, or more accurately, a re-turn to, that domain of being neglected in ordinary thinking. In the English translation of *Contributions to Philosophy (From Enowning)* the translators have rendered *Der Sprung*, one of six key themes of the text,[60] as the leap. It is referred to as a *going under*, that is, man's leaping-into *Dasein* in which the one leaping is consumed by the fire of what is deeply sheltered[61] and is en-owned/appropriated by be-ing. In other words, those who are *going under* sacrifice themselves. In becoming questionable to themselves they abandon (sacrifice) familiar being and become free for what is fascinating though hidden, for what is compelling, though sheltered. Those who go-under, Heidegger says, are the ones who constantly question. Disquiet of questioning is not empty insecurity, but the enopening and fostering of that stillness which, as gathering unto the most question-worthy (enowning), awaits the simple intimacy of the call and withstands the utmost fury of the *Seinsverlassenheit* (abandonment of being).[62]

The worth of the turning relation and the riches it yields are immeasurable and incalculable because of their resistance to mathematical reckoning. In opening himself out towards being present in the openness of the clearing, man is appropriated or enowned in a belonging that occurs beyond the *ratio*. This *Spring*, Heidegger says, is the abruptness of the unbridged entry into that belonging which alone can grant a toward-each-other of man and being, and thus the constellation of the two.[63]

The 'toward-each-other' of the *belonging* together, announced by the leap, is unmediated by the *Ge-Stell* and as such is indicative of a temporality that presses

---

[59] M. Heidegger, *Identität und Differenz* (GA11), pp. 49–50.
[60] The others are *Der Anklang*, the Echo, *Das Zuspiel*, the Playing-Forth, *Grundung*, Grounding, *Die Zukünftigen*, the Ones to Come and *Der Letzte Gott*, the Last God [M. Heidegger, *Beiträge zur Philosophie (Vom Ereignis)* (GA65), p. 9].
[61] There are detectable echoes of Nietzsche here. For instance in *Vom Wege des Schaffenden* (The Way of the Creating One) Nietzsche says: 'Ready must thou be to burn thyself in thine own flame; how couldst though become new if thou have not first become ashes?' [F. Nietzsche, *Also sprach Zarathustra* (1999), p. 65. 'Verbrennen musst du dich wollen in deiner eignen Flamme: wie wolltest du neu werden, wenn du nicht erst Asche geworden bist!'].
[62] M. Heidegger, *Beitrage zur Philosophie (Vom Ereignis,* (GA65), p. 397.
[63] M. Heidegger, *Identität und Differenz* (GA11), p. 41.

forwards away from the traditions of the past and into the future. Tradition prevails, Heidegger says, when it frees us from *Nachdenken* (thinking back) to a *Vordenken* (thinking forward), which is no longer a planning. The constellation of the two emerging from the leaps speaks of an encounter within which 'man and being have already reached each other in their active nature, since both are mutually, extended as gift, one to the other'.[64]

There is no loss of self in the belonging *together* of the constellation but rather a mutual appropriation that confirms man and being as each really are in themselves. The nature of both man and being mutually claim one another, for outside of a thinking that measures, each hears the song of the other sounding in 'the playing forth'. There is no flight-from nor abandonment-of being in the betrothal that takes place in the leap. The leap, and the *belonging* together that comes out of it, lead to the mutual authentication in the embrace of man and being. Nothing is passed over, left behind or neglected except that disposition which resulted in the *Überspringen* of the phenomenal content of man and being in the first place. As Heidegger reaffirms:

> ... man and being reach each other in their nature, achieve their active nature by losing those qualities with which metaphysics has endowed them.[65]

4.3.9 The event

The spring away from the ground of habitual identity, in being consumed in the fire of what is deeply sheltered, removes man from the familiar place of de-limited being or displaces him from out of where he runs aground. The encounter of man and being in this appropriation, within the open of the clearing and beyond the grasp of calculating thinking, is the new kind of thinking, a knowing awareness or *actual historical* knowledge which Western culture has anticipated for over 2,000 years. As a kind of thinking that does not rely on the framework it neither offers a doctrine nor brings about a moral action. Rather, *this thinking-saying is a* directive. *It indicates the free sheltering of the truth of be-ing in beings as a necessity, without being a command.* Such thinking never lets itself become

---

[64] M. Heidegger, *Identität und Differenz* (GA11), pp. 41–2. '... Mensch und Sein einander je schon in ihrem Wesen erreicht haben, weil beide aus einer Zureichung einander übereignet sind.'

[65] M. Heidegger, *Identität und Differenz* (GA11), p. 46. '... Mensch und Sein einander in ihrem Wesen erreichen, ihr Wesendes gewinnen, indem sie jene Bestimmungen verlieren, die ihnen die Metaphysik geliehen hat.'
   The losing of those qualities with which metaphysics has endowed man, so that man and Being reach each other, recalls Benedict's 'ongoing exodus out of the closed inward-looking self towards its liberation through self-giving' [Benedict XVI, *Deus Caritas Est*, §6, 'stabilis exodus de persona in se ipsa clausa adversus propriam liberationem in dono sui ipsius'].

a doctrine and withdraws totally from the fortuitousness of common opinion. But such thinking-saying directs the few and their knowing awareness retrieving them from the chaos of not-beings (metaphysical entities) and plunging them into the swirl of the deep for the passing of the last god. The *Ereignis* (event of appropriation), bringing man and being together in the leap, is therefore a key term in the service of thinking. As such a key term, Heidegger continues, it can no more be translated than the Greek *logos* or the Chinese Tao. The term *Ereignis* (event of appropriation) here no longer means what we would otherwise call a happening, an occurrence. It now is used as a *singulare tantum*. What it indicates happens only in the singular. Actually, not in any number at all, but uniquely.[66]

It is as though the whole of the lecture *The Principle of Identity* has been pressing towards the transformation of the frame into the event of appropriation representing, as it does, a possible resolution to the problematic of technology and Cartesian ontology. Within the *Ereignis* thinking has undergone a transformation: from a thinking that calculates and reckons to an inceptual thinking that brings the intimacy of the *Kehre* (turning) into the sheltering that lights up. Identity finds itself phenomenologically and the world of technology falls from the throne it has usurped, from its dominance back to its servitude. Even though Heidegger cautions against attempting a translation of the word form, since it can no more be translated than the Greek *logos* or the Chinese Tao,[67] he breaks his own rule when he says:

> Das Ereignis is that realm, vibrating within itself, through which man and being reach each other in their nature, achieve their active nature.[68]

Man comes into his truth or achieves the greatness of be-ing in the moment of decision,[69] in the opening up of that which before was closed off. The event of appropriation or enowning is, otherwise put, the enopening of a completely other time-space or the grand stillness of the most sheltered and concealed self-knowing. When I come to know my self for the first time as enownment I no

---

[66] M. Heidegger, *Identität und Differenz* (GA11), p. 45.
[67] M. Heidegger, *Identität und Differenz* (GA11), p. 45.
[68] M. Heidegger, *Identität und Differenz* (GA11), p. 46. 'Das Er-eignis ist der in sich schwingende Bereich, durch den Mensch und Sein einander in ihrem Wesen erreichen, ihr Wesendes gewinnen.'
[69] Benedict likewise speaks of the decisiveness of 'the encounter with an event [*Ereignis*] which gives life a new horizon and decisive direction' [Benedict XVI, *Deus Caritas Est*, §1, 'congressio datur cum eventu quodam . . . quae novum vitae finem imponit eodemque tempore certam progressionem' ('*die Begegnung mit einem Ereignis . . . die unserem Leben einen neuen Horizont und damit seine entscheidende Richtung gibt*')].
    The fundamental decision, with decisive ontological consequences, is when '*we come to believe in God's love*' [Benedict XVI, *Deus Caritas Est*, §1, '*nos Dei caritati credidimus*'].

longer go out of myself in pursuit of external goals but rather come under the originary essential sway of the truth of being.

It is here in the abandonment of being, in my estrangement from myself, in the eerie silence that befalls, that I come face to face with God in truth as the one who resonates unto and in-itself. When I come into my truth I am overwhelmed by *die Stille* (the stillness) of the passing of the *letzten Gottes* (last god). This is because the *letzte Gott* is sheltered within the essential swaying of the truth of be-ing, in *Ereignis* and as *Ereignis*.[70] In other words the *ereignis* is the site for the passing of the last god, the place where God, having been dislodged from the metaphysical realm where before, as the unchanging and Supreme Being, he was eternally present, now occurs in an enlivening presencing. It is here, *in der Mitte des Seyns* (in the midpoint of be-ing), and not in mediating symbols, that God and man collide. God overpowers man, Heidegger says, and man surpasses God – in *unmittelbar* (immediacy), as it were, and yet both only in *Ereignis* (enowning), which is what the truth of be-ing itself is.[71]

In the immediacy of the colliding of God and man that occurs in the *ereignis* God assigns his directives, hinting his purpose for man. Here, beyond sameness, the command of the difference gently impels and resounds in the peal of stillness.[72] Enowning places me into the call as I am brought before the passing of the last god. In the aloneness of the sacrifice as I depart from the regular familiar world of clamourous everyday being in my going under the law of the last god winks at me. The great individuation in Da-sein comes to pass in my listening to *this call* of the utmost hinting. The *essential swaying* within the hint is the how of God's manifestation to man once the intellectual presuppositions and calculating determinations that construe God metaphysically and give him a lion's voice for all commanding, have been surpassed. Although with the death of this God, all theisms collapse, man is not abandoned to godlessness for the holy now speaks its call in the moment of the shining and sheltering-concealing of the hint of the last god. Within the passing of God, Heidegger says, the empowering of man to God's necessity becomes manifest.[73]

---

[70] Heidegger's observation here is diametrically opposed to Chauvet's claim that God cannot be encountered in the immediacy of direct contact but must be experienced symbolically.

[71] M. Heidegger, *Beiträge zur Philosophie (Vom Ereignis)* (GA65), p. 415.

[72] In *Die stillste Stunde* Nietzsche articultes something similar when he says: 'Then was there again spoken unto me without voice: ". . . The dew falleth on the grass when the night is most silent". . . Then was there again spoken unto me as a whispering: "It is the stillest words which bring the storm. Thoughts that come with doves' footsteps guide the world"' [F. Nietzsche, *Also sprach Zarathustra* (1999), p. 153. 'Da sprach es wieder ohne Stimme zu mir: ". . . Der Thau fällt auf das Gras, wenn die Nacht am verschwiegensten ist." . . . Da sprach es wieder wie ein Flüstern zu mir: "Die stillsten Worte sind es, welche den Sturm bringen. Gedanken, die mit Taubenfüssen kommen, lenken die Welt"'].

[73] M. Heidegger, *Beiträge zur Philosophie (Vom Ereignis)* (GA65), p. 414.

What is said by God in the call that sways the being of man cannot be a 'doctrine' and 'system' but is rather what obliges. Heidegger refreshes the Gospel beatitudes to say: 'Blessed is the one who dares to belong to the unblessedness of be-ings cleavage in order to be the one who hears the always inceptual dialogue of the solitary ones, to whom the last god beckons because in its passing it is embeckoned by them.'[74]

To refuse the call, to resist be-ing's essential sway, to turn a blind eye to the hints of the last god, where, in the mystery of enownment the law of the last god is to be found, is to be condemned to the endless etcetera of what is most desolately transitory. To deny every question-worthiness is to reduce God and man, to hold them fast, as an end. Once a posture towards beings that is determined by 'metaphysics' is overcome, God is made present no longer in cults and churches but he appears solely in the abysmal 'space' of be-ing itself.[75]

For the hinting of the last god to wink, a new understanding of sacrifice is needed, namely, the sacrifice of those who are on the way back. This resists the most insidious form of the most acute godlessness that upholds that man has to wait for the *parousia* until he can meet God face to face. Heidegger is adamant that God is waiting to be encountered here and now in the midpoint of being. God awaits the grounding of the truth of be-ing and thus man's leaping into *Dasein*. Attentiveness and response to this self-vibrating realm engenders a *belonging* together where we must experience simply this owning in which man and being are delivered over to each other. Where, before the leap identity was conceived at the propositional level of A is A, with the neglect and passing over characteristic of this realm, after the *Ereignis,* inviting the jump away from the ground into the ab-ground or abyss of non-delimited being, identity comes into its own. But this displacement from the familiar home of being, in the uncanny moment of self-vibration, puts an end to isolation and opens up instead a primordial and timeless togetherness where man and being reach each other in their essentiality. Not only does this new thinking have a *rigour* of another kind: 'the freedom of joining its jointure' but it offers man a view of his real identity, as he is in his unmediated and uncompromised ownmost. 'Principle of identity' means now, Heidegger says, a spring demanded by the essence of identity because it needs that spring if the *belonging* together of man and being is to attain the essential

---

[74] M. Heidegger, *Beiträge zur Philosophie (Vom Ereignis)* (GA65), p. 409. 'Selig, wer der Unseligkeit seiner Zerklüftung zugehören darf, um ein Höriger zu sein in der immer anfänglichen Zwiesprache der Einsamen, in die der letzte Gott hereinwinkt, weil er durch sie in seinem Vorbeigang erwunken wird.'

[75] This is of critical importance for my argument for Heidegger shows here that his fundamental ontology has implications for liturgy (examined more closely in Chapter 5) and ecclesiology.

light of the appropriation. On its way from the principle as a statement about identity to the principle as a spring into the essential origin of identity, thinking has undergone a transformation.[76]

4.3.10 Recapitulation

Heidegger begins *The Principle of Identity* with the observation that, when the highest principle of thought is conceived as A = A, the ontological difference at the root of identity is effaced such that all difference is reduced to sameness. It was noted that identity according to this equation bears a profound resemblance to the presentation of truth as veritas. 'Truth' as it is ordinarily expressed in banal titles like '*veritas*' does not give us anything to think and still less anything to represent 'intuitively'. No amount of ordinary reflection on the term, as it is normally presented, is going to lead us into an experiential domain that ontologically engages and essentially grips us. The same can be said for identity as A = A. The truth of identity rather lies somewhere else than in the *adæquatio* or *correspondentia* characteristic of the highest principle of thought.

A = A is not the principle of identity but a structure of distorting that, through conceptualities and propositions, levels off being into manageable and familiar being. In asserting an equivalence between A, the real being of A is leap-frogged and in the final analysis neglected. Heidegger concludes therefore that the formula behind the principle of identity that has prevailed for over two millennia is no longer suitable for a genuine inquiry into being.

Sameness is deconstructed though when being is no longer belittled by a reduction to propositions but instead is viewed as the 'is' in the reworked formula A is A. Difference is to be recovered in the mediation, that is, the 'is'. It is into and through this breach that the preponderant power of being bursts in its appearing and that the unbound powers of being come forth and are accomplished in history. The wherein of the mediating 'is' is the belonging together. When the together is emphasized being is referred or assigned back to the unity of the manifold. Being is mastered by the *Ge-Stell* and cannot conceive itself independently from this pre-ordained unifying and authoritative synthesis that is constantly and ever present. The togetherness induced by the *Ge-Stell*, that grounds an ethics of the technological world, intentionally though discreetly enforces a strange ownership and a strange appropriation of being by man. The framework comes to define, if not constitute, being in the age of technology. Man is reduced to

---

[76] M. Heidegger, *Identität und Differenz* (GA11), p. 48.

a measurable phenomenon while the real phenomenal content of his being,[77] though sonorous, resounds and plays forth undetected by the instruments of modern physics evading the co-ordinates of modern geometry. And this because real being is no longer existence (A = A) but rather ek-sistence which, located in the breach, between the two 'A's', answers the claim of the nihilation illumined.

When the emphasis is switched from the *Zusammen* to the *Gehören*, in mediation's '*belonging* together', a different kind of unity comes into view that is not grounded in the framework. As the root *hören* in *Gehören* indicates, a listening and attentive disposition is required to 'think' outside the parameters of everyday rationality. Instead of referring and assigning being back to a pre-existing/pre-conceived totality of propositions to confer significance, that is, being, upon being, unfounded being is discovered to have a 'significance' and ex-istence *in itself* that exerts a claim and solicits man *in himself*. Be-ing's shimmering does not need the *stasis* of being in order to shine.

The discipline of phenomenology gives access to existence enquivering beyond the standards of everyday thinking. Because being has been severed from the familiar propositions and conceptualities that levelled it down to being and within which it was at home, the is-ness of A in the reworked formula 'A is A' and from which A has taken flight, is experienced as the uncanny. Nevertheless, phenomenology's resoluteness attunes the inner ear to the 'key note' resounding in phenomena which is ignored in the thinking that typifies traditional ontology. When man goes under, departing the customary and familiar ground of his identity as A = A, he becomes, in the acquisition of a new identity, the strangest of all.

The re-positioning of identity from the propositional level, where A is simultaneously subject and object in similitude, to the ab-ground or abyss of the in-between *belonging* together, wherein the truth of A is disclosed as difference, is enacted in *der Sprung* (the spring or leap). This opens up access to the *belonging* together that up until now has remained elusive. Here, in the there, a toward-each-other of man and being plays forth that enables the constellation of the two in an immediate embracement and authenticating betrothal. The reaching of man and being, extended as gift, one to the other, is a mutual appropriation where each reaches the other in their active nature. We might say that in the *belonging* together, inhering in the mediation between A as proposition, man and

---

[77] Heidegger names the *sum*, overlooked in the ontologically determinative Cartesian principle 'cogito ergo sum', 'the phenomenal content of Dasein' [M. Heidegger, *Sein und Zeit* (GA2), p. 46. '. . . den phänomenalen Bestand des Daseins'].

being activate each other in mutual engendering that overwhelms degenerate forms of being. In Zusammen*gehören*, the active nature of the modern world is disabled as a result of the intensity of the togetherness effected by *das Ereignis*, less an appropriation of man by being, in the sense of a subject taking possession of an object, and more an emergence from the intimate within of man and being of what is deeply sheltered. There is no loss of self or identity in the Zusammen*gehören* but rather a radical and intensified recovery of the truth of self or identity as man and being authenticate each other. In other words, when *dike* overpowers *techne* I cease being available to others as a subject that can be manipulated and put to use but instead enter into engagement with them in the uncanniness of radical encounter.

Das Ereignis effects the Zusammen*gehören* signalled by the 'is' in the formula A is A. It, and not the *Ge-Stell* (which has been transformed in *das Ereignis*), is the living foundation of being and belonging together and as such is the ab-ground of identity. *Das Ereignis* is the call of the active nature of identity between man and being which, if responded to and not *überspringt*, opens up the definitive and final Zusammen*gehören* of man and being.

4.4 Conclusion

This discussion of ethics was undertaken because in Chauvet's model of *ecclesia* (word – sacrament – ethics) it is ethics, as man's conduct towards himself and others, that verifies what he has received in both word and sacrament. Put differently, if that which is received in word and sacrament does not influence man's comportment towards himself and others, God is not made present in the world in the form of the fundamental sacrament that is the Church, in this time in between Jesus' crucifixion and his second coming. In other words, the *ecclesia*, which following the Berengarian controversy was no longer acknowledged as being the site of God's Eucharistic presence, comes into its truth through ethical practice. God, when metaphysics is overcome, is no longer to be consigned solely and exclusively to the consecrated Eucharistic species but is to be found now, after metaphysics, within the living stones that variously go to make up the fabric of the Church.

For Chauvet, we saw, ethics is the categorical *imperative* of life and action, that is every kind of *action* not only interpersonal 'moral *praxis*' but also the collective 'social praxis'. Given the priority Chauvet assigns to language, that universe always-already spoken into a 'world' before each subject comes to be, ethics is for him the present enactment of a narrative or script drawn up in advance of man's coming into being. Ethics, as that which transcends the individual, rescues man from an *individualism* by which we would believe ourselves to be more Christian the more we achieve immediate contact with God in the silent conversation of meditation. Chapter 2 demonstrated how Chauvet's theological conclusions are informed by an idiosyncratic and incomplete reading of Heidegger's philosophy.

This chapter set itself the task of examining the character ethics might have acquired had Chauvet read Heidegger in a more complete way without the omissions identified in Chapter 1. More precisely, it set out to explore the possibility of a relationship between fundamental ontology (that sees the being of man coming to fruition in *das Heilige* or *das Nichts*) and human conduct. Given Chauvet's claim (which is not contested) that ethics verifies the Church, in the sense that it is the truth of the *ecclesia*, the view of ethics developed in this chapter will have repercussions for ecclesiology and for a post-metaphysical understanding of how God presences after Nietzsche's announcement that 'God is dead'.

Benedict's encyclical *Deus Caritas Est* offered a contemporary representation of Catholic ethics. It was hoped that, if Heidegger's thought could be shown to be congruous with this, Chauvet's thesis, that Heidegger's philosophy supports the subversion (in the sense of a radical reinterpretation) of Catholic doctrine, could be challenged. In the review of *Deus Caritas Est* it was seen that the consequence of man's face-to-face encounter with God in *eros*, in which the closed inward-looking self is overpowered, was an openness and concern for the happiness of the other. Ethics for Benedict cannot be reduced to a series of commandments and prohibitions for these prevent a certain foretaste of that beatitude for which our whole being yearns and turns to bitterness the feeling of joy excited by encounter with God as *eros*. It is during the event of this encounter in drawing near to the other that life acquires a new horizon and a decisive direction. The ground of ethics is not, for Benedict, to be found in something, a dominical command or a pre-determined mandate, but rather in the no-thing of a encounter with an event. Man is impelled to authentic action in the moment of his overpowering;[78] it is when he is reduced to nothing in the moment of *eros* that he can draw close to and engage authentically with his neighbour.

---

[78] We may recall from Chapter 3 that 'the moment of overpoweringness' [R. Otto, *Das Heilige*, p. 22. 'das moment des Übermächtigen'] is one of the essential characteristics of the Holy for Otto. We have shown in this chapter that it is a defining characteristic of *eros* and as such is the key to a contemporary understanding of God and an originary ethics.

In a discussion of Heidegger's thought, centred around his lecture *Der Satz Der Identität*, we saw that for man to acquire an authentic identity his understanding of himself in terms of the highest principle of thought must be disrupted. In other words, for man to come into the truth of his being he must break out of that strange ownership and appropriation of his being by the *Ge-Stell*, the pre-existing framework that orders the technological world. It is from *das Unheimlichen* into which I am cast by the overpowering, that the unbound powers of being come forth so that what overpowers now breaks-in. The assault of *techne* against *dike* is reversed when the new ordering principle (*dike*) overwhelms being. The ethics of the technological world is replaced in the *ereignis*, that event in being whereby man and being reach each other in their nature activating one another. Instead of being brought together or combined into the unity of a system by the unifying centre of an authoritative synthesis (the *Ge-Stell*) that orders the technological world, once being's preponderant power erupts in its appearing through the breach in the principle 'A is A' of everyday identity, there is an authentic belonging together. It is the Zusammen *gehören* which alone grants a toward-each-other of man and being in the constellation of the two. When those qualities with which metaphysics has endowed man are lost, man and being reach each other in their nature.

It seems clear now there are definite symmetries between Benedict and Heidegger's thought. The motif of a moment of overpowering-ness or *das Unheimlichen* into which I am cast by the overpowering, that opens up a new horizon onto an unfamiliar world, distinct from the technological, appears in both authors. For Benedict 'the closed inward-looking self' of my being is overpowered or disrupted in the event of *eros* wherein I encounter not 'a strictly metaphysical image of God' but God as a living intoxicating presence; for Heidegger my understanding of my identity in terms of correspondence (i.e. as A = A) is overpowered, disrupted or sacrificed in the *Ereignis* when the unbound powers of being come forth offering a glimpse of the order of the gods, *dike*. It is in this decisive moment, 'the colliding of God and man' in 'the midpoint of be-ing', that God's will and mine coincide in a communion of will so that God's will is no longer for me an alien will, something imposed on me from without by the commandments, but it is now my own will. It is here beyond sameness at 'the midpoint of be-ing', in 'the stillness of the passing of the last god', that 'the command of the difference' gently impels, resounding in 'the peal of stillness'.

When I am relocated to 'the strange and uncanny' realm into which I am cast by 'the overpowering', for Benedict, I become more and more open and concerned with the 'happiness of the other' and for Heidegger 'a toward-each-other of man and being' and 'thus the constellation of the two' is granted. For both, the overpowering of our everyday and habitual identities has profound ethical consequences.

To conclude, an originary ethics is not performance of a word or narrative always-already spoken, but the bringing into fruition or fullness the being of man. It is not conduct we instigate, human behaviour driven by goals, but rather the consequence of what befalls us, a freely bestowed gift of heavenly provenance. We can heed the peal of the stillness to renew the face of a desecrated earth or we can refuse its holy appeal to further planetary desolation in an eternal recurrence. Ethics is not primarily concerned with moral praxis or universal principles that go before the individual. It is rather accomplishment, a bringing of being into the fullness of its essence. For Benedict, as for Heidegger, it is *caritas* for 'to embrace a "thing" or a "person" in its essence means to love it'.[79] To break with the norms that guide the everyday and the familiar, to burst through the mediation of habitual identity as A is A, to disrupt the order of *techne* with that of *dike* is the commission of those ones on the way back. It is, in a word, sacrifice, the central theme of the final chapter.

[79] M. Heidegger, *Brief über den Humanismus (1946)* in *Wegmarken* (GA9), p. 316. 'Sich einer "Sache" oder einer "Person" in ihrem Wesen annehmen, das heißt: sie lieben.'

Heidegger and sacrifice

5.1 Recapitulation

In the first chapter, following an evaluation of Chauvet's reading of the writings of Martin Heidegger it was discovered that Chauvet had omitted any serious consideration of the nothing. Chauvet's attempt to come to terms with Heidegger's thinking on metaphysics was compromised as a consequence of this oversight. In Chapter 2 the genealogy of Chauvet's sacramental theology was traced with the aim of demonstrating how his incomplete reading of Heidegger informed his theological conclusions. Chapter 3 considered the nothing in some detail with a view to recalling it from the oblivion to where it had been consigned by Chauvet. The possibility that the nothing and *das Heilige* speak from the same region of being was explored. Chapter 4 attempted an interpretation of ethics, as the 'for whom' or *ad-esse* of Eucharistic presence, in the light of a reading of Heidegger that does not ignore the uncanny domain formally indicated by the nothing. In thinking ethics after metaphysics from out of this district, symmetries between Heidegger's philosophy and Catholic teaching began to emerge.

The final chapter revisits the question of Eucharistic presence, as the *esse*, this time bringing a more inclusive reading of Heidegger's philosophy into conversation with this perplexing and often-times disquieting phenomenon. It asks the general question: what is the phenomenal content of 'eucharistic presence'? And more particularly: what is the manner and 'how' of Jesus' presencing after the crucifixion and before his Second Coming?

5.2 Methodology

The chapter begins with a consideration of John Macquarrie's lecture, *Thinghood and Scaramentality*, which was delivered in 1994 as the second Derek Allen Lecture on Sacramental Theology.[1] Allen's concern in establishing the Lecture was to promote a deeper understanding of sacramental theology in order to draw out the social implications of the Eucharist for, he believed, without 'a sound theology there is unlikely to be a true prayer'. In his lecture Macquarrie set out to consider sacraments in the light of Heidegger's writings on the fourfold with a view to demonstrating how this may contribute to a contemporary understanding of substance or thinghood in the context of the Eucharist. Having presented the main lines of Macquarrie's argument, supplementing these with direct citations from Heidegger's lecture *The Thing*, and having identified areas of further research following a critique of this argument, the chapter considers Heidegger's thoughts on being-towards-death with a view to understanding Eucharistic presence after metaphysics. The words of the institution, spoken by the priest over the Eucharistic species during the consecration of the Catholic Mass, are then examined to demonstrate how Heidegger's philosophy, without the omissions identified in Chauvet's reading, can inform a postmodern understanding of Eucharistic presence offering a fundamental reflection on this phenomenon central to Christian worship.

5.3 A new way for theology

Eucharistic presence is viewed against the background of Heidegger's phenomenology since, in his lectures on Paul's epistles to the Galatians and the Thessalonians, Heidegger demonstrates that phenomenology can make a valuable contribution to the explication of themes traditionally viewed from within a theological frame of reference. A new way for theology is opened up, he says, only with phenomenological understanding.[2]

In spite of appearances to the contrary, this endeavour is not theological (in the ordinary sense of the word) because it approaches Eucharistic presence

---

[1] John Macquarrie, *Thinghood and Sacramentality*, The Centre for the Study of Theology in the University of Essex, 1995, p. 4. These citations are taken from the foreword written by Barry Thompson, Canon Theologian of Chelmsford Cathedral.

[2] M. Heidegger, *Phänomenologie des religiösen Lebens* (GA60), p. 67. 'Ein neuer Weg für die Theologie.'

without the support of metaphysical preconceptions and propositions offered by tradition. As a consequence it has the potential to call into question, if not to undo altogether, prevailing theological explications that dictate the way we presently view the event happening in the epiclesis of the Eucharist.

In recalling from forgetfulness the phenomenal content of Eucharistic presence, exiled into oblivion as a result of the delimiting and fracturing nature of the conceptualities and propositions deployed to speak about it, what follows has the prospect of yielding surprising, if not dangerous, results. Historical life as such,[3] Heidegger writes, does not let itself be shattered into 'a non-authentic thingly manifold' which one now exhaustively studies. Historical life protests against this.[4] Phenomenology provides access to the life which lies concealed and obscured beneath the veil of the non-authentic thingly manifold. It heeds the protestations of its 'object' otherwise pounded down to one and the same level[5] in the desertification and levelling off that characterizes a metaphysical and theological approach to Eucharistic presence. Heidegger does not shy away from the radical potential latent in the application of phenomenology to theological concerns. The concept of theology, he says, remains entirely suspended for it cannot be avoided that the discovery of phenomenal complexes changes from the ground up the problematic and the formation of concepts. The discovery offers authentic measures for the *destruction* of Christian theology and Western philosophy.[6]

The destruction of Christian theology is a provocation which Heidegger nevertheless issues precisely to highlight phenomenology's promise. In *Being and Time* he insists that hardened tradition must be loosened up, and the concealments it has brought about must be dissolved. This process of destruction

---

[3] Which encompasses Eucharistic presence, since as Heidegger later shows, the word 'presence' implies a show or epiphany of being here and now in the present moment. For Heidegger, presence is, in other words, being viewed within a horizon of temporality. He says: '. . . the meaning of Being as *parousia* or *ousia* . . . signifies, in ontologico-temporal terms, "presence". Entities are grasped in their Being as "presence"; this means that they are understood with regard to a definite mode of time – the *"Present"'* [M. Heidegger, *Sein und Zeit* (GA2), p. 25.'. . . des Sinnes von Sein als *parousia* bzw. *ousia* war ontologisch-temporal "Anwesenheit" bedeutet. Seiendes ist in seinem Sein als "Anwesenheit" gefaßt, d.h. es ist mit Rücksicht auf einen bestimmten Zeitmodus, die *"Gegenwart"*, verstanden.'

[4] M. Heidegger, *Phänomenologie des religiösen Lebens* (GA60), p. 130.

[5] M. Heidegger, *Einführung in die Phänomenologische Forschung* (GA17), p. 283.

[6] M. Heidegger, *Phänomenologie des religiösen Lebens* (GA60), p. 135.
   In *Heidegger's Religious Origins* (2006), Crowe traces the influence of Luther on Heidegger especially in the latter's deployment of the term *Destruktion*. The 'ultimate aim' of Crowes study is 'to grasp Heidegger's understanding of philosophy as *Destruktion*' [B. Crowe, *Heidegger's Religious Origins*, p. 163]. Such a philosophy is not 'merely . . . a handmaiden to the sciences (positivism), a construction of a priori values (neo-Kantian) but . . . a comrade in the struggle aganst inauthenticity. Learning from Luther', Crowe claims, 'Heidegger called his philosophy *"Destruktion"*' [B. Crowe, *Heidegger's Religious Origins*, p. 66].

requires an enquiry into being or substance as presence since we are confronted with the task of interpreting the basis of ancient ontology in the light of the problematic of temporality. When being is surveyed in its historicality as the event of occurring, time as an eternal stretch of endless duration, thought as a string of connected 'nows', becomes the urgency of unsettled presencing, a sudden flash that lightens and plunges into darkness even before the present moment can be conceived (as such) as a 'now'. The whole experience of being 'authentically historical' is summed up for Heidegger by the term 'conscience'. There is a vital connection between the sense of historical experience and the sense of the phenomenon of conscience for, as Heidegger observes, conscience is a 'historically defined "how" of experiencing the self'.[7]

The no-longer and the not-yet of time authentically construed, unsettles and destabilizes the foundation of ordinary existence which must remain oblivious to the occurring of historical life (as conscience) if it is to secure its world into the future and protect the environs of the familiar and homely. Under pressure, though, from an event that makes history, 'the ontotheological temple of metaphysics', the sacred space in which the disciplines of theology and philosophy are enacted, starts 'crumbling'.[8] But it is a disintegration and demolition that has to happen before being can emerge in the holy of its wholeness. The 'spiritual "house" of the "new man" is only constructed', says Crowe in a discussion of Luther's comments on St Paul's letters to the Romans and Hebrews, 'by means of the destruction inflicted upon the "old man" by God'.[9]

In the context of our present discussion we might paraphrase Heidegger to say that until we arrive at those primordial experiences in which we achieved our first ways of determining Eucharistic presence, we are to carry out the *destruction* of the traditional content of sacramental theology. This destruction then is far from having the *negative* sense of shaking off sacramental theology altogether, burying the past in nullity. Rather, it is a destruction of conventional and traditional formulations that proudly and confidently claim to say more than they possibly ever can, so that those originary experiences, held in check if not obliviated by tradition, are excavated into unconcealment. At this point, that which has been destroyed will return to fulsome fascinating life, though perhaps not in a form that is instantly recognizable. In this sense, destruction signifies

[7] M. Heidegger, *Ammerkungen zu Karl Jaspers* in *Wegmarken* (GA9), p. 33, 'historisch charakterisiertes Wie des Selbsterfahrens'.
[8] Ben Vedder, *Heidegger's Philosophy of Religion . . . From God to the Gods*, Duquesne University Press, 2007, p. 274.
[9] B. Crowe, *Heidegger's Religious Origins*, p. 62.

less an arbitrary purposeless obliteration and more a suspension or holding at bay, so that the holy as the truth of being may come to a presencing.

In his *Phenomenological Explication of Concrete Religious Phenomena in Connection with the Letters of Paul* Heidegger believes that 'what is crucial is not to have our understanding led away from the object – that is to say, interpreting the object on the basis of a ready-made framework and inserting it therein'.[10] If for any reason we allow ourselves to be seduced by prior structures of meaning, arriving at our object with already-formulated preconceptions, so that we fail to allow what lies before us to address us, as it is in and from itself, we will have failed to approach Eucharistic presence in an authentically Heideggerian way. Heidegger is emphatic on this point: *it is crucial to make an effort to show the object in itself in a particular way and to lift it into an explicitly phenomenological understanding.* This understanding remains outside of the differentiation of rational-conceptual grasp. It is peculiar to phenomenological understanding that it can understand the *incomprehensible*, precisely in that it radically *lets* the latter *be* in its incomprehensibility.[11]

Let us approach Eucharistic presence then as Heidegger would want us to do setting aside any psychological schema so that the phenomenon can present itself in all its originality. The truth of Eucharistic presence will never come to disclose itself or be attained by way of a deduction. Throughout our enquiry presence must, if it is to remain true to Heidegger's thought, be examined within the horizon of time, the central theme of his major text *Being and Time*. This is not time calculated and measured mathematically. Rather it is time taken as the sudden irrupting of historical life in the surprising and startling event of occurring itself.

5.4 Thinghood and sacramentality – Macquarrie's argument

It is propitious for our purposes that John Macquarrie, who had devoted a good deal of his life's work to translating and commenting upon the writings of Martin Heidegger, should have considered Heidegger's thoughts on thinghood in the context of sacramentality generally and the Eucharist in particular. It provides

---

[10]   M. Heidegger, *Phänomenologie des religiösen Lebens* (GA60), p. 130. 'Es gilt: nicht vom Gegenstand wegverstehen, d.h. ihn zu deuten aufgrund eines fertigen Rahmens und in diesen hinein.'

[11]   For Heidegger hermeneutics 'is itself not philosophy. It wishes only to place an object which has hitherto fallen into forgetfulness before todays's philosophers for their "well-disposed consideration"' [M. Heidegger, *Ontologie* (*Hermeneutik der Faktizität*) (GA63), p. 20].

a helpful starting point to consider the contribution Heidegger's thought can make to a postmodern understanding of Eucharistic presence. Macquarrie's lecture will serve as a point of departure in our reflections on the Eucharist after metaphysics and following a reading of Heidegger that avoids the omissions identified in Chauvet's own reading.[12]

Macquarrie begins his lecture with what he confesses many may think merely a silly question . . . 'What is a thing?'[13] Most typically, he says, we answer that a thing refers to a real, solid, material object located in the physical world and thinghood to the state of existing that is typified by 'the solid enduring physical object'. On this view, solid objects are held out to be the obverse of the spiritual so that matter is kept at a distance by 'those who pursue spiritual ends'. This position however, Macquarrie believes, is subverted by the great religions wherein 'an affirmative attitude toward matter and material things' is nourished by the doctrine of creation as found in the Hebrew scriptures.

Here things and their thinghood are regarded as the creation of God and so are seen, not as isolated and disconnected objects, but infused with a common and shared divine light.[14] This attitude is further reinforced in Christianity by the doctrine of incarnation, which claims 'the Word became flesh', and in addition by sacramental worship, most especially the Eucharist. The doctrine of creation, refined in the doctrine of the incarnation and sacramental worship, thus opens up the possibility of a relation between God and the solid matter of objects.[15]

Macquarrie turns to discuss the nature of this relation, contrasting schools of thought where God's transcendence is emphasized, for example Protestant theologians from Calvin to Barth, with writers where God's immanence is highlighted. Principal among the latter are St Thomas Aquinas, who claims 'God

[12]   Chauvet's major work *Symbol et Sacrement* was first published in 1987 seven years before Macquarrie delivered his lecture, sponsored by the Confraternity of the Blessed Sacrament, in 1994.
In Chapter 2 we saw how Chauvet relied heavily on Heidegger's notion of the appropriating fourfold in his attempt to say something about substance, after metaphysics. Macquarrie likewise invokes the fourfold, in a way that resembles Chauvet, to support his contention that transignification speaks more eloquently than the traditional doctrine of transubstantiation about the *res* of Eucharistic presence. Macquarrie says: 'one form of the doctrine of transignification, a change in the meaning of things', is to be found 'within the rich understanding of a thing in threefold or fourfold relations . . .' (p. 23). No attempt is made though to demonstrate how this view provides a satisfactory exegesis of Jesus' claim in Jn 6. 51 ('*panis quem ego dabo caro mea est*' ['The bread which I give is my flesh']), offensive to the Jews and the reason many disciples deserted Jesus.
[13]   In this section all quotations in parenthesis and without an associated footnote reference are taken from John Macquarrie's *Thinghood and Sacramentality*, The Centre for the Study of Theology in the University of Essex, 1995.
[14]   Teilhard De Chardin names this '*le milieu Divin*'.
[15]   In the previous chapter we saw how, in human beings, the *intrinseco vinculo* (intrinsic link) between the physical and the spiritual realms is found in *eros disciplina et purificatione* (disciplined and purified). In *eros* God's *creandi Verbi* (creative word) stirs within human hearts determining the course of historic events.

is everywhere, in substance, power and presence,' and Teilhard de Chardin, the theologian who went furthest in this direction. De Chardin believes that, by virtue of the creation and still more of the incarnation, nothing here below is profane for those who have eyes to see. 'In the life that wells up in me and in the matter that sustains me', he says, 'I find much more than your gifts. It is you yourself whom I find, you who make me participate in your being, you who mould me.'[16]

Macquarrie finds in Teilhard de Chardin a reworking of Aristotle's principle that asserts the possibility of there being something more to the thinghood of a thing than at first meets the eye: 'one does not simply ask what something is, but what it has in it to become.' Even the discipline of physics, with its tendency to atomize the created order, is coming to acknowledge the potentialities inhering in the physical and to recognize that matter, even in its humblest form, is highly organized and highly active and capable of 'many transformations and transmutations'. In setting a *rationale* for incarnation, that is to say, for the idea of incarnation, Macquarrie asserts a connection between the Word who became flesh and the sacramental.

His argument can be seen to unfold in a methodical sequence, each step forward representing the next 'link in the chain': (i) a real, solid, material object located in the physical world points to (ii) creation which in turn speaks of (iii) the immanence of divine presence which suggests (iv) the incarnation (the Word becoming flesh) which finally can be identified with (v) the sacramental.[17] The sacraments constitute, he says, a new stage in that 'hierarchy of presencing', which he traces through the steps of creation, immanence, the gift of the divine image to the human family, the realization of this gift in Jesus Christ.

The purpose of structuring his argument in this way is to highlight the link between thingliness and sacramentality so that what can be said of a thing can likewise be said of a sacrament, for example, if a thing by virtue of participation in creation contains immanent divinity so too, by extension, do sacraments as things. Having identified the links of the chain, Macquarrie then turns to the philosophers to see whether any of them can throw light on 'the nature of thinghood'. It is no small surprise that he alights on Martin Heidegger as one

---

[16] J. Macquarrie, *Thinghood and Sacramentality*, 1995, p. 12.
[17] Macquarrie cites Edward Schillebeeckx's *Christ the Sacrament* (1963) to justify his identification of Jesus with the sacramental order. Schillebeeckx establishes this link because without it the sacraments are in danger of being confused with and belittled as 'mere objective "being there," which is proper to the things of nature' (p. 17). Schillebeeckx's introduction of a difference between mere objects and sacraments enables the latter to be taken 'in such a way as to become vehicles for a personal encounter' with God (p. 17).

who spent considerable effort in exploring what we mean when 'we talk of things and thinghood'.

Heidegger continually took issue with the contemporary tendency to think of a thing primarily as an object standing over against us for such thinking dangerously overlooks the concreteness of things. No representation of what is present, in the sense of what stands forth and of what stands over against as an object, he says in *The Thing*, ever reaches the thing *qua* thing. Science always encounters only what *its* kind of representation has admitted beforehand as an object possible for science. The thingness of the thing therefore remains concealed, forgotten. The nature of the thing never comes to light, that is, never gets a hearing.[18]

To think of a thing in this kind of way is to succumb to nihilism for the thing as thing remains proscribed, *nichtig* (nil), and in this sense is annihilated.[19] A thing rather should be thought in the way of the Greeks whose word for thing, *pragma*, signifies 'something with which we have to do, not so much something that we observe as something we encounter in our concernful dealings (*praxeis*)'.[20] For Heidegger there is therefore an originally more active and pragmatic way into the thinghood of a thing than the simple reduction of that which is present into an object standing over there wholly distinct from and unconnected with me here as a subject. This pragmatic way, we might say, allows the thing's thingness, otherwise concealed and forgotten, to come to light or to be recollected.

Objects solicit a response from me as a self and in so doing lose their disconnectedness, the characteristic that allowed them to be named objects in the first place. For the thing's thingness to show it must first have laid claim to thought. This relational aspect of presence presupposes a totality within which each thing has a position. The world, as human beings see and understand it, is a unity in which every item is related to every other item and each has a place in the practical concerns of human beings.

Macquarrie cites the example used by Heidegger in *Being and Time* of a hammer: considered outside the totalizing unity of world a hammer is just a physical object whose characteristics can be analysed, for example, the nature

---

[18] M. Heidegger, *Das Ding* in *Vorträge und Aufsätze* (GA7), pp. 170–2.In other words, a thing is not 'what something is, but what it has in it to become' [J. Macquarrie, *Thinghood and Sacramentality*, 1995, p. 13].

[19] M. Heidegger, *Das Ding* in *Vorträge und Aufsätze* (GA7), p. 172.

[20] L. Hemming, in *Transubstantiating Ourselves . . . A Phenomenological Basis for the Theology of Transubstantiation*, elaborates the Greek understanding of the being of matter when he says 'substance, strictly speaking, is intended here not as stuff, nor even as *ousia*, but as our own co-presence to the knowability of what is known, what the Greeks named *noein*, intellection, or *noeim*, intellecting' [*Heythrop Journal*, Vol. 44 (October 2003), p. 432].

of the metal and the wood of which the object is made. But in this manner of knowing a thing we would entirely miss the being of the hammer, so to speak, what makes it a hammer rather than, say, a musical instrument. Rather, when we locate the thing within a totalizing unity, so that the bare object, viewed from a transcendental perspective, is referred to a wider universe of entities, it becomes something more than mere metal and wood: we perceive the hammer *as* a tool that is used in the act of hammering. This is the fundamental everyday human way of viewing the world which is different from the scientific view that abstracts from all human interests and tries to show us isolated things, disconnected from our concerns.

Heidegger's illustration is particularly relevant to the sacramental question because when we perceive anything (including the Eucharistic species) it already bears a meaning. We do not first have a bare sensation and then attach a meaning to it. We do not see just a patch of colour – we see a field; we do not hear just a noise, we hear an automobile. Meaning is not something like a label that we stick on to 'some bare objective datums'. Meaning has already been conferred within the context of relations, the 'world', in which we encounter 'the datums'.[21]

But, Macquarrie cautions, there is a problem with this construal since it is too closely tied to the everyday routines of life – like hammering – to have any obvious significance for the problem of sacramental meaning. Heidegger recognized that this rendering of how structures of significance give meaning and being to the present-at-hand needed further refinement since it was too utilitarian and needed broadening to take in other dimensions of human experience. To counter an exploitative functional view of nature as existing solely or chiefly for human use, a view which allows no room for the dignity and beauty of things in themselves, Heidegger therefore set out his 'mature view of thinghood', Macquarrie believes, in *The Thing*.

Heidegger chose the term the fourfold, the fourfold, to develop and explicate, Macquarrie says, his 'new theory of the thing'. Instead of ascribing meaning to the 'bare object' through referential structures constituting 'world' by positioning the particular within a wider universe of things, each thing has 'four dimensions all of which give it meaning . . . earth and sky, mortals and gods'. We saw earlier in Chapter 2 how Heidegger uses the example of a pitcher to demonstrate what he intends in the substitution of the fourfold, as the progenitor of being and significance, for referential structures of meaning. Thinghood does not come from and is not conferred or caused by a pre-existing totalizing structure

[21] J. Macquarrie, *Thinghood and Sacramentality*, 1995, p. 20.

transcending the thing in itself but is instead found imminently within the interplay of the four dimensions. The inexplicable and unfathomable character of the world's worlding lies in this, Heidegger says, that causes and grounds remain unsuitable for the worlding of world. As soon as human cognition calls for an explanation it falls short of world. The human will to explain just does not reach to the 'simple-ness of the simple onefold of worlding'.[22]

Although Macquarrie does not say anything further about the fourfold it is possible to say a little more about this 'new theory'. In answer to his own question 'what then is the thing as thing that its essential nature has never yet been able to appear?' Heidegger responds that it is the pure, giving gathering of the *einfältigen Gevierts* (onefold fourfold) into *eine Weile* (a single time-space, a single stay).[23]

Even though, as Macquarrie observes, some may feel that with such a designation of thinghood Heidegger has moved over from philosophy into the realm of myth or poetry this would not worry Heidegger very much, because for him poetry is by no means merely emotional or non-cognitive: the poet too sets forth truth, and truth at its deepest level. In the *Translator's Introduction* to *Elucidations of Hölderlin's Poetry* Keith Hoeller reaffirms this point in his observation that 'what Heidegger discovered in the year's following the publication of *Being and Time* in 1927 was that, if he is to retrieve the forgottenness of being, he will also have to retrieve the language that will enable him to say the truth of being, and that this language is a fundamentally poetic one'.[24] Heidegger himself points out that it is in *poesis* first of all that the homecoming takes place. *Poesis* means to be in the joy which preserves in words the mystery of nearness to the most joyful. To name poetically means to let the high one himself appear in words.[25]

Heidegger's new theory takes its direction from the etymology of the Old High German word *thing* which means a gathering. This is not mere word-play based on the accidents of an etymological game. Rather 'etymology', Heidegger says, 'has the standing mandate first to give thought to the essential content involved in what dictionary words, as words, denote by implication'.[26] There is nothing arbitrary therefore about the sense of gathering[27] that the word *thing* calls to

---

[22] M. Heidegger, *Das Ding* in *Vorträge und Aufsätze* (GA7), p. 181. 'Einfache der Einfalt des Weltens.'

[23] M. Heidegger, *Das Ding* in *Vorträge und Aufsätze* (GA7), p. 175.

[24] M. Heidegger, *Elucidations of Hölderlin's Poetry*, 2000, p. 11.

[25] M. Heidegger, *Erläuterungen zu Hölderlins Dichtung* (GA4), pp. 25–7.

[26] M. Heidegger, *Das Ding* in *Vorträge und Aufsätze* GA7), pp. 176–7. 'Etymologie darauf verwiesen bleibt, zuvor die Wesensverhalte dessen zu bedenken, was die Wörter als Worte unentfaltet nennen.'

[27] As distinct from referring or assigning.

mind. A thing is the four dimensions, given in an outpouring, each one of which appropriates the other, gathering or ringing into a single onefold that lingers for a while. This lingering of the poured out and then gathered fourfold is the presencing of the thing. Otherwise put, it is in the gathering that the *verborgen* (hidden) and *vergessen* (forgotten) thinghood of a thing is remembered so that the thingness of the thing comes to light and gets a hearing. But, Heidegger says, how does the thing presence? The thing things. Thinging gathers. Appropriating the fourfold, it gathers the fourfold's stay, its while, into something that stays for a while: into this thing, that thing.[28]

The four must not be taken in isolation, for thinghood lies in *das Spiel* (the play) that betroths each of the four to each through the enfolding clasp of their mutual appropriation. None of the four insists on its own particularity. Rather, each is expropriated, within their mutual appropriation, into its own being. This expropriative appropriating, Heidegger says, is the mirror-play of the fourfold. Out of the fourfold, the simple onefold of the four is ventured. The united four are already strangled in their essential nature when we think of them only as separate realities, which are to be grounded in and explained by one another.[29]

Having asserted that Heidegger's contribution to Eucharistic theology is to be found in 'the quadrate', given the link between thinghood and sacramentality, Macquarrie completes the chain that has led from incarnation to the sacraments with a disingenuous move: he contends that the fourfold is in fact a threefold. We can do away with the heavens or the sky on the grounds that 'most of the elements in the earth's crust were formed originally in the stars'. The fourfold is now reduced to the three – 'earth, the human race, the gods'.

It is vital for Macquarrie to make this move, for his argument concludes with a consideration of the offertory prayers recited in various Christian churches. These begin with a benediction of God – 'blessed are you, Lord God of all creation' – and a prayer of thanksgiving for the thing present-at-hand – 'through your goodness we have this bread to offer' – and then a recollection of the two remaining of the three – '. . . which earth has given and human hands have made'. Having invoked the threefold constituting the thinghood of the thing (i.e. the bread being offered) the prayer concludes with a statement affirming its changed nature – 'it will become for us the bread of life'.[30] All this, Macquarrie concludes,

---

[28] M. Heidegger, *Das Ding* in *Vorträge und Aufsätze* (GA7), p. 175.
[29] M. Heidegger, *Das Ding* in *Vorträge und Aufsätze* (GA7), p. 181.
[30] A similar prayer is offered over the chalice and the wine, 'fruit of the vine and work of human hands'. If there is no heaven, though, where is this becoming to take place? What, in other words, is the *topos* of the species' thinghood no longer forgotten but recollected in a thinking that recalls?

may be considered one form of 'the doctrine of transignification, *a change in the meaning of things*, within the rich understanding of a thing in threefold or fourfold relations, and in continuity with and ultimately derived from the doctrine of incarnation'.[31]

In arriving at the end of his argument Macquarrie believes that Heidegger's philosophy of thinghood therefore supports contemporary endeavours to interpret the doctrine of transubstantiation, which he accepts was 'a very good attempt to elucidate the Eucharistic mystery', as the change in *meaning* and not the substantiality of the substance. In other words, and in similar vein to Chauvet, Macquarrie claims that Heidegger's thought gives philosophical credence to the doctrine of transignification. We must now critically evaluate Macquarrie's lecture.

5.4.1 An evaluation – Macquarrie's achievement

By moving beyond prevailing definitions of thinghood, as atomized earthly objects standing over and against me as a subject, to a view in which I am personally involved in the bringing into being of the thing (so that without me no thing can be) Macquarrie succeeds in offering an answer to the question he set himself at the start of the lecture 'What is a thing?' Through an invocation of Heidegger's the fourfold Macquarrie is able to show the meaning or being of the thing need not rely to any extent on structures of significance that ordinarily construct our familiar world instrumentalizing it for utilitarian purposes. Rather, when we take a step back from the thinking that merely represents – that is, explains – to *das andenkende Denken* (the thinking that responds and recalls), the glory and mystery of the thing's thinghood, as the *Spiegel-Spiel* (mirror-play) between heaven and earth, gods and mortals, comes strangely into view. Macquarrie successfully depicts this refinement of the quiddity of thinghood so that it is no longer something standing over and against the human self but something instead by which mortals are appropriated or into which they are gathered.

5.4.2 An evaluation – Macquarrie's omissions

5.4.2a *Human self*

In spite of his achievements however, Macquarrie fails (perhaps due to the constraints of a formal public lecture) to consider how this change in the thinking

---

[31] J. Macquarrie, *Thinghood and Sacramentality*, 1995, p. 23.

of thingliness effects and modifies the being of the one whose thinking no longer represents but now responds and recalls. In other words, if the world where habitually I reside and which makes me the what that I am[32] is by-passed in this new way of thinking a thing, who do I become and what is the character and the where-in of the me that appropriates the truth of the thing as the ringing of the world's *Spiegel-Spiels*? In the by-passing of utilitarian structures of significance I too, as a publicly constructed and useful being, am passed by and left behind.

Heidegger offers an answer to the ontological implications of the fourfold for the one open to its claim: man as mortal being dies (though he does not perish as an animal in the biological sense). In a passage from *The Thing*, filled with significance for our investigation into a postmodern understanding of Eucharistic presence, Heidegger says that death is the shrine of the nothing. In other words, it is through death that I am opened up to something more than what merely exists, namely, that which nevertheless presences as the mystery of being itself or as the nothing. As the shrine of the nothing, death is the shelter of being. This observation allows Heidegger to call mortals, mortals – not because their earthly life comes to an end, but because they are capable of death as death. 'Mortals are who they are, as mortals, present in the shelter of being. They are the presencing relation to being as being.'[33]

Man is involved in the coming to be of a thing not simply, as Macquarrie concludes, by his industry, the work of his hands, but by his non-activism, his *death*. Real thinghood is more than mere human artistry and craftsmanship; it implies and requires the unreserved life of man himself. The true being of the thing in the plenitude of its wholeness (or the mystery of being), never merely exists, but rather shows as the nothing, whose enclosure is broken into when I cease to be as a useful and publicly interpreted being. The *Dingheit* (thingness) of the thing, concealed and forgotten when I stand as subject in relation to world as object, for the first time gets a hearing (or comes to be spoken) when I die to myself as subject. It is my becoming mortal in my dying that allows me to reach the thing *qua* thing.

In other words, it is only in my death (befalling me rather than instigated by me) that the beingfulness of beings (which from the vantage point of beings is no longer merely a thing, that is, the nothing) is released from *verborgenheit* (entombment/concealment) in a thinking that remembers what (before my

---

[32]   World as a totality of equipment that instrumentalizes me as subject and the thing as object.
[33]   M. Heidegger, *Das Ding* in *Vorträge und Aufsätze* (GA7), p. 180. 'Die Sterblichen sind, die sie sind, als die Sterblichen, wesend im Gebirg des Seins. Sie sind das wesende Verhältnis zum Sein als Sein.'

death) was *verborgen* (forgotten). In short, without sacrifice, as my dying to myself or (as we saw in the last chapter) my going under, there can be no fullness of life, as *Seinsfülle* (beingfulness) or the nothing.[34] Unless I become questionable to myself I cannot become free for what is compelling, though sheltered. It is, we may recall, in the aloneness of the sacrifice that the law of the last god is hinted at. It is when I am emplaced in the district of the forgotten and sheltered that, in addition to coming into the fullness of my being, I am at the same time open to the possibility of an actual encounter with divinity. It is only when I know myself to be no thing (i.e. when I know myself to be more than merely an existing thing in the recollection of the once forgotten phenomenal content of who I am) that the law of the last god (not revealed in ordinances and statutes) hints and, in my response to the hint, orients my being. If sacrifice brings things to the fullness of their being and if ethics is accomplishment we may get an early glimpse that when sacrifice and ethics are viewed from the vantage point of the nothing they can be seen to be inextricably bound together: just as through sacrifice I am filled with the fullness of my being in the recollection of what before the moment of sacrifice was forgotten so too in ethics, rightly construed as accomplishment, the other is brought to the fullness of their being.[35]

5.4.2b Macquarrie's method

Macquarrie develops his argument, as we have seen, in a linear sequence beginning with the thing standing over against me as an object (the first link in the chain) and ending with the thing infused by the divine as a sacramental incarnation of Christ's presence. His invocation of Heidegger's fourfold introduces a new set of relationships which, supplanting the structures of significance reducing it along the way to an item of equipment to be used and exploited

---

[34] Although Macquarrie does not deal explicitly with the theme of sacrifice in *Thinghood and Sacramentality*, elsewhere he supports this view when he says: 'the fundamental purpose of sacrifice is the bestowal of life. This statement puts life rather than death at the centre of sacrifice . . . In any discussion of Eucharistic sacrifice, we must put away any ideas which think of atonement as a negative transaction designed to save us *from* some unhappy fate, and see it in affirmative terms as making human beings "at one" with God, bringing them new life from God' [J. Macquarrie, *A Guide to the Sacraments*, p. 136].

   Our present experience of death, in the shadow of Christ's own, in which (as we have shown) the beingfulness of beings comes into view, offers, Macquarrie says, 'a foretaste of the kingdom which Christ inaugurated' [J. Macquarrie, *A Guide to the Sacraments* (1997), p. 139]. In other words, it is not necessary for man to wait for the *parousia* until he can meet god face to face. Macquarrie seems to be concurring here with Heidegger who warns that to believe otherwise is to succumb to *die verfänglichste Form der tiefsten Gottlosigkeit* (the most insidious form of the most acute godlessness).

[35] If being brought into the fullness of being is being made whole or holy then sacrifice means being made holy.

at will by the human subject, confer thinghood on the thing. The new set of relationships between God, man and the earth/heavens is where the thing now finds its thinghood, coming into the truth of its being. The prayer of consecration over the bread and wine bring the Eucharistic species, for Macquarrie, into being in a new way as the outcome of an interaction between God, earth and man: 'Lord of all creation' through whose goodness the bread, '. . . which earth has given and human hands have made', is offered.

At no point does Macquarrie allow the phenomenal content of the Eucharistic species to address and claim him phenomenologically. Rather, in a mechanical and systematic way, he strips away one referential structure (the totality of equipment) promising a disclosure that uncovers, only to relocate the Eucharistic phenomenon within an enclosing new structure of significance, the quadrate. The fourfold may well function as a counter-paradigm to onto-theological thinking but it is a paradigm nevertheless that conceals and covers-up in its own way.

Macquarrie, in other words, approaches the Eucharist with an already-worked-out schema which determines how he views things and disallows thereby the Eucharist to speak from out of itself as it is in its self as such without reference to any preconceptions whatsoever. The latter, being loaded with their own meanings, import a significance to the phenomenon at hand so that the thinghood of the bread and wine gets overlaid.[36] It is a betrayal of Heidegger's *wege*, which does not permit anything to be reached by way of deduction.[37] The incomprehensible can only be brought to an understanding when it is allowed to be in its incomprehensibility. By deserting its phenomenal content in favour of the familiar, recognizable and comprehensible, the *Seinsfülle* of the phenomenon at hand (Eucharistic presence), is forgotten and concealed, albeit in new ways that are seemingly more acceptable to the modern imagination.

This begs the question though that if Heidegger's contribution to a postmodern understanding of Eucharistic presence is not to be found where both Macquarrie and Chauvet say that it is, namely in the fourfold, then where are we to turn?

The Thing may well represent Heidegger's 'mature' view about the being of a thing but its reference to the nothing and its suggestion that mortals have the capacity to undergo death as death without this earthly life coming to an

---

[36] In *Platon: Sophistes* Heidegger lectures that, for Plato, taking orientation from an idea is to put a certain face on phenomena. Whereas this disposition, through hiding the actual *what* of the thing, leads to deception, being oriented by the phenomena and seeing the whole (i.e. the actual *what*) conversely, allows phenomena to be disclosed and encountered in their truth.

[37] That is, arriving at the phenomenon to be interpreted with pre-formulated ideas which are then corroborated.

end, points the attentive reader back to Heidegger's more comprehensive and earlier text *Being and Time*. Indeed, it is surprising that Macquarrie makes use of Heidegger's illustration of the hammer and how this is endowed with meaning and significance by its participation within an encompassing totality, in reference to which it becomes 'environmentally ready-to-hand' as an item of useful equipment, without acknowledging that this description of being occurs in the early stages of *Being and Time*. It therefore does not represent Heidegger's early view of thinghood as Macquarrie implies when he says *The Thing* represents his 'mature view of thinghood'.[38] We are about to see now that, in the later stages of *Being and Time*, Heidegger works out a view of being or thinghood which discredits the view that the 'environmentally ready-to-hand' represents his developed thoughts on the subject in 1927. Section 40,[39] for instance, points out that what is environmentally ready-to-hand sinks away in anxiety, and so, in general, do entities within-the-world. Anxiety thus takes away from *Dasein* the possibility of understanding itself, as it falls, in terms of structures of significance and the way things have been publicly interpreted.[40]

We shall examine now Heidegger's writings on being-towards-death to see how thinghood is to be understood after the destruction of structures of significance, whether as a totality of equipment or as the fourfold, in the moment when being comes to a disclosing, before drawing final conclusions about possible implications of his philosophy for Eucharistic theology.

5.5 Being-towards-death (*Sein zum Tode*)[41]

Having evaluated Macquarrie's attempt to bring Heidegger's philosophy into conversation with sacramental theology, which culminated with his view that things are constituted ontologically in their thinghood not by substance but by having a place in a world or totality of meanings, the remainder of this chapter offers an alternative phenomenological interpretation of the Eucharistic rite. With the aid of Heidegger's thoughts on being-towards-death a different understanding is offered of what Jesus meant when he said:

---

[38] J. Macquarrie, *Thinghood and Sacramentality*, 1995, p. 12.
[39] M. Heidegger, *Sein und Zeit* (GA2), pp. 184–91. *Die Grundbefindlichkeit der Angst als eine ausgezeichnete Erschlossenheit des Daseins* (The Basic State-of-mind of Anxiety as a Distinctive Way in which *Dasein* is Disclosed).
[40] M. Heidegger, *Sein und Zeit* (GA2), p. 187.
[41] M. Heidegger, *Sein und Zeit* (GA2), p. 235.

Take this, all of you, and eat of it: for this is my Body which will be given
up for you. Take this, all of you, and drink from it: for this is the chalice of
my Blood, the blood of the new and eternal covenant which will be poured
out for you and for many for the forgiveness of sins. Do this in memory
of me.[42]

5.5.1 Preliminary clarifications

*If we have grown up in the pattern of his death we shall share also in his
resurrection.*[43]

Before Heidegger sets out his existential interpretation and analysis of death he
clarifies certain matters which threaten to confuse the issue being investigated.
First, it is important to recognize what he is not talking about when he asserts
that *Dasein* has the possibility of finding its wholeness and completion in
being-toward-death. He is not intending the termination of the physical being
when he claims that *Dasein* reaches its ownmost in dying. To highlight this
distinction he reserves the terms perishing or demise for the phenomenon of
physical death. *Dasein*'s going-out-of-the-world[44] in the sense of *Sterben* (dying)
must be distinguished from the *Aus-der-Welt-gehen* of that which merely has
life. In Heidegger's terminology the ending of anything that is alive is denoted
as perishing. When *Dasein* dies – when it dies authentically – this is not a
biological or factical demising. Precision is to be gained, Heidegger insists, in
the distinction between the existential conception of dying and mere perishing
and the 'experience' of a demise.[45]

[42] From the present English translation of the Roman Missal.
    The words of consecration are based on Jesus' words at the Last Supper recorded in Mt. 26. 26–8
and Mk 14.22–4. Jesus ensures the words of consecration have a literal meaning when he says in Jn
6.51 'αρτος δε ον εγω δωσω η σαρξ μου εστιν' ('This bread is my flesh' or 'the bread that I shall give
is my flesh').
    Mt. 26:26–8 says: Ἐσθιόντων δὲ αὐτῶν λαβὼν ὁ Ἰησοῦς τὸν ἄρτον καὶ εὐλογήσας ἔκλασεν καὶ
ἐδίδου τοῖς μαθηταῖς καὶ (while they were eating, Jesus took bread, and when he had given thanks,
he broke it and gave it to his disciples) saying Λάβετε φάγετε τοῦτό ἐστιν τὸ σῶμά μου (Take and
eat; this is my body). καὶ λαβὼν τὸ ποτήριον καὶ εὐχαριστήσας ἔδωκεν αὐτοῖς (then he took a cup,
and when he had given thanks, he gave it to them) saying Πίετε ἐξ αὐτοῦ πάντες (drink from it, all
of you) this γὰρ ἐστιν τὸ αἷμα μου τῆς διαθήκης τὸ περὶ πολλῶν ἐκχυννόμενον εἰς ἄφεσιν ἁμαρτιῶν
(is my blood of the covenant, which is poured out for many for the forgiveness of sins).
[43] Rom. 6.5, εἰ γὰρ σύμφυτοι γεγόναμεν τῷ ὁμοιώματι τοῦ θανάτου αὐτοῦ ἀλλὰ καὶ τῆς ἀναστάσεως
ἐσόμεθα.
[44] Going *Aus-der-Welt* (out-of-the world) is going *Unter* (under). In the previous chapter – *die unter-
gehenden* in the Leap from the metaphysical realm of being was shown to have sacrificial overtones:
die unter-gehenden sich opfern (those who are going under sacrifice themselves).
[45] M. Heidegger, *Sein und Zeit* (GA2), pp. 240, 247 and 251.

Death, as the dying of Dasein, is rather a way to be, which *Dasein* takes over as soon as it is. 'As soon as man comes to life, he is at once old enough *zu sterben* (to die).'[46]

Secondly, death for Heidegger is not something that stands outside of *Dasein* simply because it eludes in principle any possibility of getting experienced at all. Even though the physical demise of *Dasein* is not yet a factical occurrence death as the 'not- yet' is nevertheless constitutive of *Dasein's* being. The problem is not getting into our grasp the *Noch-nicht* (not-yet) which is of the character of *Dasein* but rather pertains to the possible *Sein* (being) or *Nichtsein* (not-being) of this 'not-yet'.[47] If *Dasein* is really to come into its own it must, as itself, *werden* (become) – that is to say, *sein* (be) – what it is not yet.

Not being the evasive, because ungraspable, 'not-yet' is my coming-to-be or my be-coming. For *Dasein* to comport itself towards something whose 'isness' is not-yet, (i.e. towards no-thing or being's possibilities that as yet are unrealized) *Dasein*, because it can be no longer as something actual, is undone as something now here. Heidegger uses the analogy of unripeness in the being of a fruit, an entity to whose kind of being becoming belongs, to illustrate his point: the ripening fruit is not only not indifferent to its unripeness as something other than itself, but it *is* that unripeness as it ripens. The *Noch-nicht* has already been included in the very being of the fruit, not as some random characteristic, but as something constitutive of it.[48]

Corresponding to this, as long as existence *is*, it too *is already* its not-yet. To be its 'not-yet' is to forego its being here and now for when existence reaches its wholeness in death, it simultaneously loses the being of its 'there'. In other words, ordinary everyday existence 'there' cannot embrace the wholeness of life, allowing it to presence in the un-refracted beam of fulsome human possibility. When the brightness of the fullness of being shines on ordinary being, the customary, habitual and familiar withers, consumed by the fire of what is deeply sheltered.[49] Since dying is constitutive of who, what and how I am, death does not stand outside me but is quintessential to my being. Just as with ripeness the fruit fulfils itself so too, in one sense, I come into my own, achieving the fullness of my

---

46   M. Heidegger, *Sein und Zeit* (GA2), p. 245. 'Sobald ein Mensch zum Leben kommt, sogleich ist er alt genug zu sterben.'
47   The *Noch-nicht* (not-yet) represents *Dasein's* possibilities which because they have 'not yet' been realized are the *Noch-nicht*.
48   M. Heidegger, *Sein und Zeit* (GA2), pp. 243–4.
49   It may be recalled from the previous chapter that in *Vom Wege des Schaffenden* (The Way of the Creating One) Nietzsche says: 'Ready must thou be to burn thyself *in deiner eignen Flamme* (in thine own flame); how couldst though *neu werden* (become new) if thou have not first *Asche geworden bist* (become ashes)?' [F. Nietzsche, *Also sprach Zarathustra* (1999), p. 65].

being, with my dying. But the moment I come to my end in my comportment to the 'not-yet', unlike the being of the fruit that completes itself, I come to nothing, albeit a no-thing-ness that is the where-in of *Dasein*'s wholeness. Unlike the fruit which comes to its end in the ripening, *Dasein* discovers a new beginning in its dying; where a road that is under construction breaks off, Heidegger figuratively illustrates, a pathway may nevertheless continue.

No one can take my dying away from me given that it is specific and determinative of my being mortal. Dying is essentially mine in such a way that no one can be my representative: no one can take the Other's dying away from him.[50] Heidegger's reflection on being-towards-the-end offers an ontological characterization of the kind of being in which the end enters into the average everydayness of *Dasein*. But it is an end, as we have seen, that offers the promise of a new beginning or a becoming new and which invites speculation as to what *may be after death*.

Having considered these preliminary clarifications, namely that death is not a biological perishing or demise but an ontological dying, and that death is constitutive of the being belonging to *Dasein* to the extent that someone other than me cannot take my dying away from me if I am to be authentically, it is necessary now to direct our attention to the existential-ontological structure of death.

5.5.2 The existential-ontological structure of death

If, then we die with Christ, we believe that we shall share his life.[51]

In a preliminary sketch of the phenomenon, Heidegger outlines the main features of existence's ownmost potentiality-for-being which, when I stand before it, I dissolve in death. The possibility that opens and to which I have access, has to do with my being-in-the-world: in dying the possibility no-longer being-able-to-be-there presents itself so that all relations to any existence dissolves.[52] This uttermost possibility that presents itself in my 'being-towards-death' is my

---

[50] M. Heidegger, *Sein und Zeit* (GA2), p. 240.
[51] Rom. 6.8. εἰ δὲ ἀπεθάνομεν σὺν Χριστῷ πιστεύομεν ὅτι καὶ συζήσομεν αὐτῷ.
[52] Kierkegaard highlights that when God is loved absolutely, such that the individual emerges, disentangled from the delimitations of the universal, all other relationships dissolve. He points out that this is the difficult teaching of Jesus found in, for example, Lk. 14.26 but one which few can bear to hear and which 'people very seldom talk about' [*Fear and Trembling . . . A Dialectical Lyric*, p. 103]. This is because 'men are afraid to give others their freedom; they fear the worst from the moment the Individual is pleased to behave as the Individual' [*Fear and Trembling . . . A Dialectical Lyric*, p. 108]. They prefer the shrewdness of finitude than the adventurous Individual educated in accordance with the dread-filled prospects of his infinity.

ownmost non-relational possibility-of-being. It is not something I procure for myself but is, as we have seen, a fundamental character of my existence into which I have been thrown. When it solicits I am overwhelmed by the mood of dread[53] if for no other reason than my regular and habitual relations with others are threatened with dissolution in my potential recollection of what is *verborgen* (forgotten). Thrownness into death reveals itself to existence, Heidegger says, in a more primordial and impressive state-of-mind of 'anxiety'. Anxiety in the face of death is anxiety 'in the face of' that potentiality-for-being which is one's ownmost, non-relational and not to be outstripped.[54]

This anxiety is not fear of biological perishing or physical demise but amounts to the disclosedness of the fact that *Dasein* exists as 'thrown being towards its end' inviting a departure from beings, a *going under*. My death, made factical in the dread of anxiety,[55] reveals me to be a kind of being that is 'still more' than just an item of equipment, environmentally ready-to-hand about which one can be concerned. Instead, I show to be something other than and different from a merely relative being characterized in terms of some involvements.

After these preliminary remarks, Heidegger proceeds next to fill in some of the detail. Given death's corrosive effect on my relations to other beings (to the extent that these are undone) and as, in my departure from the world, I cease to be involved in the world as totality of equipment, the they constructs its defence:[56] death gets interpreted as a public phenomenon which, although afflicting individuals, belongs to nobody in particular. By levelling off and depersonalizing death in this way, the everyday world of the they succeeds in keeping its phenomenal content, my individual possibilities, completely veiled.[57] For the they, the forgotten is better left unsaid, for the nature of the thing in its

---

[53] Kierkegaard asserts something similar when he says the one 'educated by possibility' (Heidegger's *eigenste, unbezügliche Seinsmöglichkeit*) is 'educated by dread' into 'his infinitude' [*The Concept of Dread*, p. 139]. This education, discovering the deceptions of those imprisoned in the Universal, consumes 'all finite aims' [*The Concept of Dread*, p. 139] constraining out the petty and trivial. In short to open up to my *eigenste, unbezügliche Seinsmöglichkeit* or to be educated by possibility, is to be in dread, even unto death. In Heidegger's terms, this is the essence of *sein zum tode*; for Kierkegaard, it is the true meaning of faith for one must 'have faith' to 'be educated' by possibility [*The Concept of Dread*, p. 140]. Dread, though trivialized and devalorized by shrewd and calculating finitude, never lets one escape 'neither by diversion nor by noise, neither at work nor at play, neither by day nor by night' [*The Concept of Dread*, p. 139].

[54] M. Heidegger, *Sein und Zei*, (GA2), p. 251.

[55] We will see later how my ownmost potentiality for being or fulsome existence is attested (reveals itself) ontically to the me that participates in the they.

[56] Reminding us why the phenomenal content of things lies forgotten (in the oblivion of being) in the first place.

[57] Kierkegaard observes something similar when he remarks 'in "the public" . . . the individual is nothing, there is no individual . . . *Apart* from the "the public" the individual is nothing and neither is he anything, more deeply understood, *in* "the public"' [*Attack Upon 'Christendom'*, pp. xxx–xxxi].

thingness disturbs and disrupts (when it comes to light) what is familiar and ordinarily upheld to be holy.

The distinctive potentiality-for-being which belongs to my ownmost self gets lost through such devices, to the extent that *Dasein*, as factical, is in the 'untruth'. Inauthenticity or our everyday falling evasion *in the face of* death, comes to typify that kind of being into which *Dasein* can divert itself and has for the most part always diverted itself. This *constant tranquillization about death* takes away from me *the courage for anxiety in the face of death*;[58] anxiety comes to be portrayed as a weakness with which no self-assured *Dasein* may have any acquaintance. Dying, instead of being seen as an occurrence that makes possible being-a-whole in the fullness of my individuality is instead represented as a social inconvenience, if not a downright tactlessness, against which the public is to be guarded. This evasive concealment in the face of death, Heidegger says, dominates everydayness so stubbornly that, in *Miteinandersein* (being with one another), the 'neighbours' often still keep talking the 'dying person' into the belief that he will escape death and soon return to the tranquillized everydayness of the world of his concern.[59]

But I do not necessarily and constantly have to divert myself into this kind of being. Heidegger is enabled by his phenomenological approach to unearth that potentiality for being which the intrigues of the they otherwise cover-up by assigning it to the oblivion of forgetfulness. These same intrigues offer us a clue that points in the direction of the phenomenon they serve, in a calculated way, to conceal. In the light of what it evades this very evasion attests phenomenally that death must be conceived as one's ownmost possibility which, when it breaks in, breaks up all relations in an absolute and unsurpassable way. The possibility of being, after extraction from involvement with the environmentally ready-to-hand, can happen at any moment. Not only is my ownmost possibility certain therefore; it is likewise indefinite. But, asks Heidegger, given the they's tendency to publicly interpret my death as a weakness to be avoided and thereby to render

---

[58] To be immunized to anxiety or the question-worthiness of being is to be anaesthetized to my infinitude, to be closed off from the holy wherein the divine moves and enters into congress with being. While coming face to face with what is forgotten is terrifying, because my individuality or ownmost potentiality for being has not been habilitated in the they's familiar and homely world, to cheat on or to defraud the possibility which ought to educate me is never to arrive at faith. Rather, it is to be schooled in 'the sagacity of finitude' [*The Concept of Dread*, p. 157] and equates to the positioning of being.

[59] M. Heidegger, *Sein und Zeit* (GA2), p. 253. 'Das verdeckende Ausweichen vor dem Tode beherrscht die Alltäglichkeit so hartnäckig, daß im Miteinandersein die "Nächsten" gerade dem "Sterbenden" oft noch einreden, er werde dem Tod entgehen und demnächst wieder in die beruhigte Alltäglichkeit seiner besorgten Welt zurückkehren.'

me inauthentic, is it possible for *Dasein* to maintain itself in an authentic being-towards-its-end?

Given the indefinite[60] character of my infinite possibilities, such that I never know for sure when my dying will happen, Heidegger speaks of anticipation as an important disposition of being-towards-death. To expect something as possible is always to understand it and to 'have' it with regard to whether and when and how it will be actually present-at hand. Expecting is not just an occasional looking-away from the possible to its possible actualization, but is essentially a *waiting for that actualization.*

Anticipation is a perpetual disposition of being-towards-death because, even with the arrival of a sense of what I can become, the possibility still remains something not actualized or existent. Death, as possibility, gives *Dasein* nothing to be 'actualized', nothing which *Dasein*, as actual, could itself *be*. It is the possibility of the impossibility of every way of comporting oneself towards anything, of every way of existing. In the anticipatory revealing of this potentiality-for-being, Heidegger says, *Dasein* discloses itself to itself as regards its uttermost possibility. Anticipation turns out to be the possibility of understanding one's *ownmost* and uttermost potentiality-for-being – that is to say, the possibility of *authentic existence.*[61]

I come into my ownmost when, through anticipation, I am wrenched away from the 'they'. Through disseverance from the public world of being, I am individualized down to myself. This authentication highlights that all being-with others will fail us when our ownmost potentiality of being is the issue. I come into authentic existence when my concern is not the possibility of the they-self but rather myself as I truly am. Relinquishing myself and all that I (as they-self) hold to be precious becomes the uttermost possibility of my existence. By anticipation one becomes free for one's own death, one is liberated from one's lostness in those possibilities which may accidentally thrust themselves upon one. Anticipation discloses to existence that its uttermost possibility lies in giving itself up (*Selbstaufgabe*),[62] and thus it shatters all one's tenaciousness to whatever existence one has reached.[63]

---

[60] Indefinite because it resides in a domain inaccessible to the structures of significance which ordinarily give definition to world.

[61] M. Heidegger, *Sein und Zeit* (GA2), pp. 262–3.

[62] If 'relinquishing myself and all that I (as they-self) hold to be precious' is sacrifice then sacrifice is the 'uttermost possibilty of my existence'.

The *Oxford-Duden German Dictionary* (1997) suggests, as a possible rendering of the English word 'sacrifice', the German word *Aufgabe*. The uttermost possibility of my existence lies then, in this rendering, in sacrifice.

[63] M. Heidegger, *Sein und Zeit* (GA2), p. 264.

Although in anticipating that which is 'not-yet' I am disentangled and extricated from the artifices of public interpretation, having no further utilitarian and functional relations with existence, nevertheless and for the first time, I am free to go out to Others in the truth of *their* being; having recovered now my authentic self, when I go out in concern for the Other, instead of engaging them as publicly interpreted things in the public arena, I embrace them in their authenticity which before my own recovery remained concealed to me. As the non-relational possibility death individualizes – but only in the manner that, as the possibility which is not to be outstripped, it makes existence, as being-with, have some understanding of the potentiality-for-being of others.

We saw earlier how the 'threat' of individualizing death, that reveals me in my ownmost, is disclosed: the 'not-yet' of anticipation shows as the mood of anxiety to the ordinary me publicly interpreted and configured by the they. Through *Stimmung* (mood) existence is brought face to face with the thrownness of its 'that it is there'. But the state-of-mind which can hold open the utter and constant threat to itself arising from one's ownmost individualized being, is anxiety. In this state-of-mind, being finds itself *face to face* with the 'nothing' of the possible impossibility of its existence. Anxiety is anxious *about* the potentiality-for-being of the entity so destined and in this way it discloses the uttermost possibility.[64]

However, the evidential character which belongs to the immediate givenness of experiences, of the 'I', or of consciousness in the state-of-mind of anxiety, is the echo of death's occurrence. It must necessarily lag behind the certainty which anticipation includes. Heidegger concludes therefore that *the ontological structure of death, being-towards-death, is essentially anxiety.* No other factical state-of-mind could befall me once anticipation discloses my lostness in the they-self. In my impassioned freedom towards death or my decent or down-going into the forgotten or sheltered (the expectation of which locks me in dread), I am released from the illusions of the they which do their utmost to remove all trace of the life of my ownmost individualized being. When it nevertheless asserts itself, in spite of and in the face of the manoeuvres of the they-self,[65] it is at first beheld as alien and unfamiliar inciting the dread of anxiety.

Heidegger turns his attention next to a fuller explication of how *Dasein* gives testimony, from its ownmost potentiality-for-being, as to the possible *authenticity* of existence. The mood of anxiety provides an initial clue to the

---

[64] M. Heidegger, *Sein und Zeit* (GA2), pp. 265–6.
[65] We may recall an earlier observation that dread, though trivialized and devalorized by shrewd and calculating finitude, never lets one escape 'neither by diversion nor by noise, neither at work nor at play, neither by day nor by night' [*The Concept of Dread*, p. 139].

ontical character of the ontological being-towards-death and how this registers
with the they-self. Anxiety is the bearer of nuances though, which need further
to be explored if we are to get to grips more fully with the ontological structure
of death or being-towards-death of our mortality.

5.6 Voice of conscience – how authentic Being shows itself

If I myself as they-self am not the 'who' of the being that I am, then what
'form', Heidegger asks, can authentic being-one's-self take? We have seen that
anxiety modifies the they the moment the who that I can become asserts itself
but, Heidegger asks, what does this modification imply? *Dasein* is ensnared in
inauthenticity, we saw, as long as the they succeeds in preventing it from being
claimed and gripped by that factical potentiality-for-being which is closest to it.
The moment I bring myself back from the superficies of a public life there is an
existentiell modification of the they-self so that I become *authentic* being-my-
self. But how is *Dasein* 'shown' to itself in its possible authenticity? The mood of
anxiety may overwhelm me, having been released from the illusions of the 'they'
in the epiphany of my authentic being, but how is my potentiality-for-being-
myself attested?[66] Heidegger's answer is simple:

as the 'voice of conscience'.

Since in conscience, a primordial phenomenon of *Dasein* lies before us,
Heidegger embarks on an ontological analysis which is prior to any psychological
description and classification of experiences of conscience. It has nothing to do
with a theological exegesis which relies more on revelation and tradition than the
phenomenon as it is in itself. Conscience is taken as an universally established
and ascertainable fact whose being is different from what is environmentally
present-at-hand. It reveals itself as a *call* (*Ruf*) which in itself is a mode of
discourse. The call of conscience has the character of an *appeal* (*Anrufs*) to *Dasein*
by calling it to its ownmost potentiality-for-being-its-self; and this is done by
way of *summoning* it to its ownmost being-guilty.[67]

In the appeal which summons, my authentic potentiality-for-being is attested
or given concrete and substantial form rooted in my ek-sistence. But the appeal

66 Another possible way of rendering the same in English would be 'what in substance or in concrete
terms is my potentiality-for-being myself'.
67 M. Heidegger, *Sein und Zeit* (GA2), p. 269.

of conscience, portrayed as a *Ruf*, resounding in the depths of my being, can be a misleading image in the same way as Kant's depiction of conscience as a court of justice. These figurative portrayals are familiar pictures which can be situated within routine structures of significance with which we are at home and at ease. But is that which the appeal brings to our understanding something that admits such familiarity? Do we understand what conscience has to tell in the same way that we comprehend the discourses that take place in our everyday world? Heidegger raises a doubt when he says 'in some way' conscience gives us something to understand. He attempts now to explicate the way in which the something conferred by conscience may differ from normal modes of understanding.

The discourse in which conscience engages me is not conventional inasmuch as it does not involve a vocal utterance. It 'speaks' from that part of me who wants to be brought back from exile and lostness in the publicness and the idle talk of the they. It therefore cannot resort to the categories and customary practices constitutive of and familiar to the they-self. The 'voice' is taken rather as a 'giving-to-understand'. The disclosure belonging to it cannot be represented in word forms which would define or determine, and in the process compromise the integrity of, its primordial and originary urgency. If, to communicate its call, the 'voice' merely mimicked the language of all-too-familiar they-talk, as much would be concealed as revealed. Its tendency to disclose would be frustrated. Heidegger warns that we must not expect to be told something obviously practical and currently useful concerning possibilities for action. This is because the call of conscience fails to give any such 'practical' injunctions. In other words, the call is dangerous because it summons one to an action whose outcomes cannot be known beforehand and cannot be calculated in advance. Acts impelled by conscience are unsafe because, as daring adventure, they are not predictable performance.

The mode of discourse, rather, that characterizes the appeal is the momentum of a push – of an abrupt arousal[68] that presses forward in a sure and certain

---

[68] '*Aufrüttelns*' means literally to 'shake somebody out of his/her sleep'. The discourse in which conscience engages me is less one that leads to the transmission of something readily comprehensible and interpretable within a particular structure of significance and is more an unexpected nudge or brusque wake-up call. Sheehan shows that Heidegger gives pre-eminence to this state-of-being following the latter's exegesis of chapter 5 of St Paul's first *Letter to the Thessalonians*.

Given that 'the day of the Lord will come like a thief in the night' and Paul's injunction therefore not to sleep but instead 'to stay awake and be sober', Heidegger concludes, Sheehan says, that 'to relate authentically to the Parousia [i.e. the day of the Lord] means to be "awake," not primarily to look forward to a future event. The question of the "when" of the Parousia reduces back to the question of the "how" of life – and that is "*wachsam sein*," to be awake ... The Christian's state of wakefulness in factical experience means a *constant, essential and necessary uncertainty*' [T. Sheehan, 'Heidegger's *Introduction to the Phenomenology of Religion*, 1920–21', pp. 56–7].

direction. Abrupt momentum that impels makes no sound, for conscience discourses solely and constantly in the mode of keeping silent. Silence preserves the full perceptibility of the 'voice', an aspect of which is drowned out and unheard the moment it gets drawn by the they-self into general discussions. It follows that anyone who keeps silent when he wants us to understand something must have something to say. What conscience says in the call of its silent appeal is, strictly speaking, nothing. The 'voice' nothings for it asserts nothing, gives no information about world-events, has nothing to tell. The fact that what is called in the *Ruf* has not been formulated in words, does not give the phenomenon the indefiniteness of a mysterious voice, but merely indicates that our understanding of what is called is not tied up with an expectation of anything like a communication. *Der Ruf* does not report events; it calls without announcing anything.[69]

To hear the 'voice' of conscience, given the silence that characterizes it, requires a kind of listening from existence that no longer *listens away* to the they, a listening-away during which in our existing we *fail to hear* its own self; rather an altogether different kind of hearing is prerequisite, one that interrupts the 'hubbub' and the shallow novelty of everyday idle talk. In its preoccupation with listening to what the they has to say, *Dasein* fails to hear itself. Another kind of hearing, with an altogether different character, is needed to attune to the call of conscience otherwise drowned out by the general noise of life.[70]

But what happens to *Dasein* when, attuning to the resounding silence and yielding to the pressure of the directing 'abrupt arrival', it surrenders to the momentum of the push? Something unprecedented in the history of our existing takes place in the quiet and surreptitious displacement that attends *Dasein's* attentiveness to the appeal: I die to the they of my they-self for the they is overlooked and passed by in the call of conscience, calling for my departure from beings (the they) in my going under and my going back. In a word, I am sacrificed for, as Heidegger clarifies, sacrifice is the departure from beings on the path to preserving the favour of being; those who are *going under*, we may recall, sacrifice themselves. In the previous chapter it was shown that the law of the last god is hinted at in the aloneness of the sacrifice of those who are *Rückwegigen* (on the way back).

That which remains unaddressed and unsolicited by the 'voice', that is, the they, dissolves in an implosion so that what remains after the break-down is my ownmost *potentiality*-for-being-its-self. The call, Heidegger says, calls me forth

---

[69] M. Heidegger, *Sein und Zeit* (GA2), pp. 273–7.
[70] M. Heidegger, *Sein und Zeit* (GA2), p. 271.

in my existing and 'forward' into being's ownmost possibilities. I am summoned to be the self from which the they (and me as a they-self) are in flight. The sort of *Dasein* which is understood after the manner of the world both for others and for itself, gets *passed over* in this appeal; this is something of which the call to the self takes not the slightest cognizance. And because only the *self* of the they self gets appealed to, the *they* collapses.[71]

Because my they-self is deprived of its lodgement and hiding-place in the they when it attends to the appeal, it is held (now as self) no longer to *be* from the perspective of the everyday and public self. In other words, I die to life in my attunement to the nothing that summons me, in being-towards-death. When *'nichts'* gets called to this self it shatters all one's tenaciousness to whatever existence one has reached and reduces me to nothing, where-in *Dasein* finds its ownmost *potentiality*-for-being-its-self. In my response to the appeal, which dispenses with all public announcements and altogether refuses to be voiced in words, I am called, not to what *Dasein* counts for, can do or concerns itself with in being with one another publicly, but into the reticence of my *own self*.

5.6.1 Who does the calling? – an alien power

But, Heidegger asks, can we claim to have adequately interpreted conscience without mention of *who* does the calling and how I am related and interconnected ontologically with the caller? We have seen how, in attending to the summons, I am emptied of my 'what' in a dying (sacrifice) that opens up the prospect, through being-towards-death, of authentic being-my-self. If the call is addressed to me in my nothingness, about which little can be said, what hope have we of saying much about that which issues the summons?

Heidegger concedes that if the caller is asked about its name, status, origin or repute, it not only refuses to answer, but it likewise defies all attempts to make it into something with which one can be familiar in an ordinary and everyday sense. But although getting considered and talked about goes against its kind of being so that the caller holds itself aloof from any way of becoming well-known, nevertheless Heidegger maintains these characteristics are distinctive for it in a positive way if for no other reason than it will not let itself be coaxed.[72]

---

[71] M. Heidegger, *Sein und Zeit* (GA2), p. 273.
[72] In *Beiträge zur Philosophie (Vom Ereignis)* Heidegger is less cautious about who it might be who does the calling. We may recall him saying that when I am placed *in den Zuruf* (into the call) I am brought *vor den Vorbeigang des letzten Gottes* (before the passing of the last god).

On the one hand it seems that *Dasein* calls itself, being *at the same time* both the caller and the one to whom the appeal is made. However, although the call comes *from* me, it appeals against our will in a way that is counter-intuitive. Given that the 'voice', calling out from an unfamiliar and unhomely domain, makes us anxious in its invitation, subverting our expectations, the caller must be considered an alien power by which *Dasein* is dominated. That which does the calling, though part of me, is nevertheless unfamiliar and alien to me when I take myself to be as the they prescribes.

In its 'who', the caller is definable in a 'worldy' way by nothing at all.[73] The caller is *Dasein* in its uncanniness: primordial, thrown being-in-the-world as the not-at-home – the naked and bare 'that-it-is' in the 'nothing' of the world. The caller is unfamiliar to the everyday they-self; it is something like an *alien* voice. What could be more alien to the 'they', lost in the manifold 'world' of its concern, than the self which has been individualized down to itself in uncanniness and has been thrown into the 'nothing'?[74]

The caller then is not a wholly distinct presence standing over and against me but is a part of me which, as such, I am not therefore at liberty to ignore. If the caller were construed as an alien power wholly separated and distinct from me I would have some justification to take no notice of its appeal. Since however it speaks from out of that part of me consigned to the oblivion of forgetfulness by the 'they', an obscure and remote part but a part of me nonetheless, I am not free to dismiss its call as having nothing to do with me without profound and radical ontological consequences.

We need not resort to powers with a character other than that of *Dasein*; indeed, recourse to these is so far from clarifying the uncanniness of the call that instead it annihilates it.[75] If the caller is named 'the Good' or 'God' and not

---

[73] Given that when I am placed 'into the call' [M. Heidegger, *Beiträge zur Philosophie (Vom Ereignis)* (GA65), p. 407. 'in den Zuruf'] I am brought 'before the passing of the last god' [M. Heidegger, *Beiträge zur Philosophie (Vom Ereignis)*, (GA65), p. 4, 'vor den Vorbeigang des letzten Gottes'] Heidegger here hints that after metaphysics and following Eckhart God, not as the caller but as the one who 'eventualises (flashes) in the dimension of being' [*Seminare*, (GA15), p. 437, 'in der Dimension des Seins sich ereignet'] is nothing.

We may recall the concluding citation from Chapter 3: 'Eckhart's "nothing" refers to God Himself, to "He who *is*". In virtue of His "immovable detachment" God transcends every being, every this or that, every determinate being. That is why for Eckhart – as for Heidegger – one can refer to this transcendent reality either as "pure nothing" or "pure Being." "Pure Being and pure nothing are one and the same." That sentence from Hegel aptly depicts the nature of God in Eckhart's metaphysics too.'

[74] M. Heidegger, *Sein und Zeit* (GA2), pp. 276–7.

[75] Heidegger has in mind here the common practice of attributing the call of conscience to an onto-theological God. Human beings, not seeing themselves as divine and having no aspirations to be gods, have no reason to attend to its call and can ignore its appeal without detriment, so it would seem, to their own being.

Dasein, it follows that, if I do not believe in the 'Good' or 'God', I can dismiss its call, in a dispassionate recognition without self-compromise and with impunity. This interpretation, however, is only a fleeing in the face of conscience – a way for *Dasein* to escape by slinking away from that thin wall by which the they is separated, as it were, from the uncanniness of its being. If the Good or God is the caller then I am alienated from the uncanniness of who I am and, immunized now to the threat to my lostness in the they, consigned indefinitely to the idle chatter sustaining my 'they-self' and turbulence characteristic of the they. By substituting *Dasein* for these other possible callers Heidegger makes available being-a-whole to those existentialists, atheists and nihilists, who have no time for God. In setting up the problematic in this way and expressing it in these terms to ignore the call is not to ignore God or the Good but rather to cheat on my self. The call then, discoursing in the uncanny mode of *keeping silent*, is nothing other than *Dasein* individulized down to itself in its uncanniness having been thrown into the 'nothing'. *Unheimlichkeit* is the basic kind of *In-der-Welt-seins* (being-in-the-world), even though in an everyday way it has been covered up. Out of the depths of this kind of being, existence itself, as conscience calls. The 'it calls me' is a distinctive kind of discourse for existence. The call whose mood has been attuned by anxiety is what makes it possible first and foremost for existence to emerge in its ownmost *potentiality-for-being*.[76]

But this is not to say that Heidegger is diminishing conscience so that it becomes something 'merely subjective'. Rather, the caller calls from out of my being, beyond they-subjectivity (the 'merely subjective') and, in asserting the *Unheimlichkeit* of thrown individualization, denies the they-self its dominion. Indeed were the caller to be someone other than *Dasein* individualized down to itself in uncanniness there would be no sense of guilt in the passing over of conscience's call; I can reject God or the God with impunity and without remorse if I do not accept or believe in either. As it happens, however, when I ignore the summoning call, my indifference registers ontically as being guilty for in rejecting the call I am rejecting myself, albeit my self in a transcending and uncanny register of being.

---

[76] M. Heidegger, *Sein und Zeit* (GA2), p. 277.
    We may recall from Chapter 3 Otto's demonstration, following his reflection on the choral ode of Sophocles' *Antigone*, of how *deimos* is used to speak of the uniqueness of human nature: *Viel gibt es des Ungeheuren. Doch nichts/Ist ungeheurer als der Mensch* (there is much in the world that is uncanny, but nothing is more uncanny than the being of man).

5.6.2 Being-guilty

Only those who acknowledge their guilt can go free.[77]

Being-guilty is a definite kind of being that obtains in any failure to hear the call or any incorrect hearing of oneself. Something always ensues when the call utters its appeal in the uncanny mode of keeping silent: if, in relinquishing the public interpretations of the they, the nothing directs me then I am called back into the reticence of un-refracted being. In understanding the call I have effectively chosen myself since, in positively responding to the appeal, *Dasein* is in thrall to its ownmost possibility of existence allowing its *ownmost self* take action in itself. Heidegger calls this reticent self-projection upon one's ownmost being-guilty in which one is ready for anxiety, resoluteness.[78]

If, on the other hand, in the cultivation of a '"superior" indifference' the they denies me the courage for anxiety in the face of death so that I ignore its summons, the call cries 'Guilty!' made concrete to me in my experience of myself as being guilty. In either case awareness of the call indicates the possibility of being-guilty.

Heidegger takes care to point out that conscience's call of 'Guilty!' is inaudible to the they-self because it resounds in a region to which it (the they-self) is closed off. The fact that they, he says, who hear and understand nothing but loud idle talk, cannot 'report' any call, is used to discredit conscience as *'stumm'* ('dumb') and manifestly not really there at all or present-at-hand.[79] If the they has any sense of 'guilt' at all it locates its significance at the surface level of infractions of manipulable rules and public norms. In this superficial understanding of 'guilt' as morality, distinct from the more primordial 'being-guilty', the they has slunk away from its ownmost being-guilty so as to be able to talk more loudly about making 'mistakes'.[80] This state, of being 'asleep' to primordial being-guilty, reveals what Heidegger terms nullity. If conscience is the basis for my authentic being then my decision not to respond resolutely to its appeal in my care for existentiell concerns gives rise to a nullity which becomes instead the basis of my now inauthentic being. *Dasein*, projecting itself in care as factical existence, is by default guilty. Not only can entities whose being is care load themselves

[77] S. Kierkegaard, *Attack Upon 'Christendom'*, p. xxxii.
[78] M. Heidegger, *Sein und Zeit* (GA2), pp. 296–7.
[79] M. Heidegger, *Sein und Zeit* (GA2), p. 296.
[80] M. Heidegger, *Sein und Zeit* (GA2), p. 288.

with factical guilt, but they *are* guilty in the very basis of their being. Being-guilty constitutes the being to which we give the name of care.[81]

Uncanniness, in hearing the appeal correctly, takes up the possibility of its ownmost potentiality-for-being and at the same time reveals nullity to be the evasion and flight from the world. The call comes from the soundlessness of uncanniness, and the being which it summons is called back into the stillness of itself, and called back as something that is to become still. But this calling back into the stillness of my ownmost potentiality-for-being, which because unfamiliar to me is me in my uncanniness, does not result in an isolation from others.

5.6.3 *Das Eigentliche Miteinander*

In retreating from the 'they', which the call passes over and thereby brings to collapse, it could be maintained my being-towards-death means I have no relationship with other beings. How can there be a unity or togetherness with others if, in attending to conscience's call, I die to the structures of significance that position me, as they-self, within an encompassing totality? Is the they not correct to perpetuate the subterfuge that the call of conscience is dumb and to portray the dying of Others as a social inconvenience, if not a downright tactlessness, against which the public is to be guarded? Heidegger concludes his discussion of being-towards-death with an emphatic rejection of such preposterous suggestions. Resoluteness, as *authentic being-one's-self*, does not detach *Dasein* from its world, nor does it isolate it so that it becomes a free-floating 'I'. Indeed, how could it possibly do this when resoluteness as authentic disclosedness, is *authentically* nothing else than being-in-the-world? Resoluteness brings the self into authentic engagement with the world, pushing it into solicitous *Mitsein mit den Anderen* (being-with with others).[82]

We saw at the end of the last chapter how, when I am opened up to the nothing, aroused abruptly to authentic life in the dread-filled moment when the uncanny stirs, instead of becoming submerged in an obliteration of self, the action of the nothing rather pushes me back to the world, not into distorting structures of significance that result in utilitarian human relationships, but into association with others in their authenticity, an association that allows their beingfulness to accomplish itself. The recovery of my ownmost potentiality-for-being in my dying, in my listening away from the general chit-chat of the they to the call of

---

[81]   M. Heidegger, *Sein und Zeit* (GA2), p. 286.
[82]   M. Heidegger, *Sein und Zeit* (GA2), p. 298.

conscience discoursing in the disturbing sound of silence, brings *Dasein* face to face with its world as world, and thus brings it face to face with itself as being-in-the-world. It could not be more different from the displacement and isolation of the subject into 'the innocuous emptiness of a worldless occurring'. In other words, although leaping out of the world may do away with customary and familiar forms of human association or togetherness, the one who comes into his own is not thereby condemned to isolated lonely, solitary existence. Rather, new forms of belonging together become possible in the going under, ones which allow others to be as they are in their infinite possibilities.[83]

Heidegger concludes that resolute existence frees itself for its world rather than abstracting itself from it. Being's resoluteness towards itself is what first makes it possible to let the others who are with it 'be' in their ownmost potentiality-for-being, and to co-disclose this potentiality in 'the solicitude which leaps forth and liberates'.[84] When *Dasein* is resolute, it can become the 'conscience' of others. Only by authentically being-their-selves in resoluteness can people authentically be with one another. There *is* a form of human sociality transcending the jealous stipulations and talkative fraternizing in the they and resisting what they want to undertake.[85]

5.7 A final resolution

dying can *be the highest 'act' of living.*[86]

We set out on this enquiry in search of a view of thinghood, overlooked by Macquarrie but pointed out by Heidegger in *The Thing* in the latter's enigmatic

---

[83] Kierkegaard alludes to something similar when he says 'I want to do away with the public, and yet, if possible, to have *everyone* become the "individual" – *in unity*' [*Attack Upon 'Christendom'*, p. xxxii].

[84] Heidegger is referring here to section 26 *The Dasein-with of Others and Everyday Being-with*. In this section he highlights that, in 'its positive modes, solicitude has two extreme possibilities'. In the second of these he says 'solicitude . . . does not so much leap in for the Other as *leap ahead* of him in his existentiell potentiality-for-Being, not in order to take away his "care" but rather to give it back to him authentically as such for the first time'. The 'authentic care' that characterizes this kind of solicitude goes out 'to the existence of the Other, not to a "*what*" with which he is concerned; it helps the Other to become transparent to himself *in* his care and to become *free for* it' [M. Heidegger, *Sein und Zeit* (GA2), p. 122, 'einer Fürsorge, die für den Anderen nicht so sehr einspringt, als daß sie ihm in seinem existenziellen Seinkönnen *vorausspringt*, nicht um ihm in die "Sorge" abzunehmen, sondern erst eigentlich als solche zurückzugeben . . . die eigentliche Sorge . . . die Existenz des Anderen betrifft und nicht ein *Was*, das er besorgt, verhilft dem Anderen dazu, *in* seiner Sorge sich durchsichtig und *für* sie *frei* zu werden'].

[85] M. Heidegger, *Sein und Zeit* (GA2), p. 298.

[86] M. Heidegger, *Vom Wesen und Begriff der Phusis* in *Wegmarken* (GA9), p. 254 and p. 297. 'Das Sterben *kann* der höchste "Akt" des Lebens sein.'

statement that death is the shrine of the nothing, that is, of that which in every respect is never something that merely exists, but is instead that which presences as the mystery of being itself. The mystery of being in its fullness, in other words, opens up to me when I die to life metaphysically represented. We discovered that Heidegger's fully worked-out understanding of where thinghood is to be found, once structures of significance have been undone in my sacrifice or going-under, is contained in his writings on being and death (being-towards-death) in *Being and Time*. A question that presents itself is whether the origins of the idea the fourfold are to be found in *Being and Time*.

Certainly it seems that when, in *The Thing*, Heidegger says 'mortals are human beings . . . they are called mortals because they can die . . . to die means to be capable of death as death . . . only man dies . . . the animal perishes . . . it has death neither ahead nor behind it'[87] he has in mind (and is thereby referring his reader back-to) his writings on being-towards-death in *Being and Time*. We have seen how, in the latter, when man relinquishes the illusions of the they, going out of the ordinary everyday world of familiar average existence, a new potentiality for being and relating to others emerges. After my dying I am, in terms of *The Thing*, no longer something that merely exists but am instead a coming into presence, a self unfolding emergence of the mystery of being itself.

Although Heidegger does not explicitly invoke God or the gods in *Being and Time* in the way that he does in *The Thing*, nevertheless something other than man, an alien power, which transcends his mere existence, appeals to him in the call of conscience. Whereas in *The Thing* God is counterposed to man, who in the divine appropriation dies to mere existence, in *Being and Time* Dasein (in its uncanniness) summons the self of my they-self, so that the they collapses in my listening away to its call. Similarly, as the *topos* of God's abode is Heaven and man's dwelling is Earth in *The Thing* so in *Being and Time* the they-self inhabits the totality of those entities which can be present-at-hand within the world in contrast to being-in-its-ownmost that resides in the ontological existential worldhood. This suggestion in *Being and Time* of two different worlds, with two different associated ways of being, foreshadows and

---

The preceding part of the paragraph from which this citation is taken reads as follows: *Das sich entfaltende Aufgehen* (the act of self-unfolding emergence) is inherently *ein In-Sich-zurückgehen* (a going-back-into-itself). With its very coming-to-life every living thing already begins *zu sterben* (to die) . . ., and conversely, *das Sterben* is but a kind of living, because only a living being has the ability *zu sterben.*

[87] M. Heidegger, *Das Ding* in *Vorträge und Aufsätze* (GA7), p. 180. 'Die sterblichen sind die Menschen. Sie heißen die Sterblichen, weil sie sterben können. Sterben heißt: den Tod als Tod vermögen. Nur der Mensch stirbt. Das Tier verendet. Es hat den Tod als Tod weder vor sich noch hinter sich.'

is germane to the heaven and earth, God and man, of the fourfold in the later *The Thing*.

Having demonstrated that *Being and Time* in some way adumbrates the notion of the fourfold discussed in *The Thing*, and having highlighted the significance of mortals in the fourfold, on account of the fact mortals are capable of death as death and can thereby gain entry to the shelter of being wherein the mystery of being itself abides, we can justify now turning to being towards death in *Being and Time* to examine how it might assist with our main purpose: to obtain an understanding of the thinghood of Eucharistic substance after metaphysics. Before we attempt this, a recapitulation of the essential themes from the two sections, is necessary given the complexity of the ideas.

5.7.1 The birth of a dancing star – recapitulation

The following were discussed as preliminary clarifications essential for an understanding of Heidegger's main ideas:

1. Death, understood as ontological dying, is different in kind from biological perishing and demise or going-out-of-the-world of that which merely has life.
2. Death as not-yet is constitutive of *Dasein* in the truth of its being and cannot be re-assigned to an other.

A preliminary sketch of the existential-ontological structure of death was then drawn:

3. When my ownmost potentiality-for-being asserts itself relations to other *Dasein*s (as they-selves) disintegrate. In other words, in my ownmost I am non-relational[88] in the sense of having no involvement in a transcendent unifying totality which, in dispersing my individuality into a manifold, facilitates inauthentic engagement with others.
4. The mood of anxiety reveals my throwness into inauthentic existence, showing me up to have been instrumentalized as a functional being with a particular use, that is, in Hediegger's terminology, to be an item of equipment, environmentally ready-to-hand.

---

[88] This non-relationality does not preclude relations with others in the authenticity and solicitude of their and my being. Dying, as we have shown, prefigures resoluteness and the engagement characteristic of *mitsein*. My being non-relational when I come into my ownmost means simply that I do not read off my existence from or with reference-to other beings as entities metaphysically construed.

The preliminary sketch was then filled-in with the following detail:

5. The they de-individuates dying reducing it to a public event that is beyond my concern. In so doing it introduces untruth into factical *Dasein* and alienates me from the uncanniness foundational to my being.

6. Evasive concealment in the face of death or running for cover when I hear the strange and unfamiliar voice of conscience takes away my courage for dread and closes the prospect of being-a-whole.[89]

7. Anticipation breaks the invasive hegemony of the they wrenching me away from lostness in the they and re-opening the prospect of authentic existence.

8. The uttermost possibility of *Dasein* is revealed in the they's giving up of itself or sacrifice, allowing for authentic existence.

9. *Dasein's* dying (its *selbstaufgabe*) is brought about simultaneously with the assertion of new ontological possibilities that cause the they of the they self[90] to collapse.

10. *Sein zum Tode* registers not as an actual thing that can be calculated and rationally comprehended but as the *Nichts* of the possible impossibility of our existence arousing the dread of anxiety that never reaches a tranquillizing point of settlement. Its non-teleological character means it avoids any kind of comforting hypostasis whatsoever and the familiar nullity characteristic of habitual care.[91]

---

[89] Nietzsche speaks of this closure from the higher life (signalled in Heidegger's being-a-whole) as the eternal return of 'the man of whom thou art weary, *der kleine Mensch* (the small man)' [F. Nietzsche, *Also sprach Zarathustra* (1999), p. 229, 'der Mensch, dess du müde bist, der kleine Mensch']. To be evasively concealed in the face of death means 'the plexus of causes returneth in which I am intertwined . . . I come again eternally to this identical and selfsame life' [F. Nietzsche, *Also sprach Zarathustra* (1999), pp. 231–2, 'der Knoten von Ursachen kehrt wieder, in den ich verschlungen bin . . . ich komme ewig wieder zu diesem gleichen und selbigen Leben']. To have become too weary even for dying is to 'keep awake and live on – in sepulchres' [F. Nietzsche, *Also sprach Zarathustra* (1999), pp. 231–2. 'wachen . . . und leben fort – in Grabkammern!'].

[90] In *A Transcendental Hangover*, Laurence Paul Hemming, makes the same point when he says 'to die well means to have drawn myself out of the "*Man-selbst*" as *eigentlich*' (*Studies in Christian Ethics*, 18.2 (2005), p. 62).
      Nietzsche's Zarathustra declares that 'only where there are graves are there resurrections' [F. Nietzsche, *Also sprach Zarathustra* (1999), p. 116, 'nur wo Gräber sind, giebt es Auferstehungen'].

[91] *Dasein* in this register approximates the holy being of divinity or higher life. Nietzsche for example calls Jesus a 'free spirit' for 'he cares nothing for what is fixed: the word *killeth*, everything fixed *killeth*' [F. Nietzsche, *Der Antichrist* (1990), p. 229. '"freien Geist" . . . er macht sich aus allem Festen nichts: das Wort *tötet*, alles, was fest ist, *tötet*']. Zarathustra asks ' Where is the frenzy with which you should be inoculated?' and answers 'Lo, I teach you the Superman: . . . he is that frenzy!' [F. Nietzsche, *Also sprach Zarathustra* (1999), p. 12. 'Wo ist der Wahnsinn, mit dem ihr geimpft warden müsset? Seht, ich lehre euch den Übermenschen: der ist dieser Blitz, der ist dieser Wahnsinn!']. Later on he counsels 'I tell you: one must have chaos in one, to give birth to a dancing star' [F. Nietzsche, *Also sprach Zarathustra* (1999), p. 15. 'man muss noch Chaos in sich haben, um einen tanzenden Stern gebären zu können'].

Having proposed that the mood of anxiety overwhelms me when I entertain the ownmost potentiality for being, in my going-out from the world to that which has no existence, the 'not-yet', Heidegger turned his attention next to the means by which (the 'how') the epiphany of my authentic being occurs. If suddenly I am no longer immersed in the they's world, there alongside such and such things, alongside such and such people, alongside these vanities, these tricks, this chattering but instead am taken into the nothing, Heidegger explains how this concretely comes about. The ontological-existential structure of death (outlined above) comes to reveal itself as follows:

1. Anxiety, as the show of authentic being, is attested by the voice of conscience.
2. Conscience is not merely a theological concern but, as a primordial phenomenon of *Dasein*, has a significance for fundamental ontology.
3. Conscience is not specific to particular structures of significance and the environmentally present-at-hand but, common to all, is universally established and ascertainable by all those who participate in being. This is not to say though that it may not undergo a different interpretation in each individual in accordance with its own possibilities of understanding.[92]
4. The call of conscience has the character of an appeal that summons *Dasein* to its ownmost self. It is the kind of understanding that does not rely on a deductive and metaphysical way of thinking.[93]
5. The call, to communicate its utterance, does not resort to words. It speaks to that part of me negated in conventional they-talk. Summoning from outside the world of familiar chatter, the call is uncanny. It discourses in the uncanny mode of keeping silent.[94]

---

[92] M. Heidegger, *Sein und Zeit* (GA2), p. 274.

[93] Nietzsche likewise speaks of 'a new deep murmuring, and the voice of a new fountain! . . . a ruling thought is it, and around it a subtle soul . . .' [F. Nietzsche, *Also sprach Zarathustra*, (1999), p. 78, 'ein neues tiefes Rauschen und eines neuen Quelles Stimme . . . ein herrschender Gedanke ist sie und um ihn eine kluge Seele']. He continues: 'beauty's voice speaketh gently; it appealeth only to the most awakened souls' [F. Nietzsche, *Also sprach Zarathustra* (1999), p. 95, 'der Schönheit Stimme redet leise: sie schleicht sich nur in die aufgewecktesten Seelen'].

[94] There are echoes of Nietzsche here whose Zarathustra says: 'Ah, abysmal thought, which art my thought! When shall I find strength to hear thee burrowing, and no longer tremble? To my very throat throbbeth my heart when I hear thee burrowing! Thy muteness is like to strangle me, thou abysmal mute one!' [F. Nietzsche, *Also sprach Zarathustra* (1999), p. 168. 'Ach, abgründlicher Gedanke, der du mein Gedanke bist! Wann finde ich die Stärke, dich graben zu hören und nicht mehr zu zittern? Bis zur Kehle hinauf klopft mir das Herz, wenn ich dich graben höre! Dein Schweigen noch will mich würgen, du abgründlich Schweigender!']. And earlier in 'The Stillest Hour' Zarathustra says: 'then was there again spoken unto me as a whispering: "It is the stillest words which bring the storm. Thoughts that come with doves' footsteps guide the world"' [F. Nietzsche, *Also sprach Zarathustra* (1999), p. 168. 'Die stillsten Worte sind es, welche den Sturm bringen. Gedanken, die mit Taubenfüssen kommen, lenken die Welt'].

6. Conscience, calling without announcing anything, is instead a momentum that pushes and rudely awakens tranquillized *Dasein* to its authentic possibilities in the silent discourse of its appeal. If conscience is reflected upon and reduced to a general communication, albeit to oneself, something essential gets lost.

7. Conscience is nothing since, calling without uttering anything, it is deprived of words that normally bring things to be as an enduring presence.

8. In hearing the call of conscience and listening-away from the 'they', existence hears itself as uncanniness in the murmurings of authentic being, perhaps for the first time.[95]

9. The effect of attending to the call of conscience is that the they of the inauthentic they-self, constructed from the hubbub of idle talk, collapses and dies. Whatever existence one has reached shatters in the call's silent utterance passing-over the 'they'.[96]

10. My death makes possible now entrance into the reticence of my own-self.

11. The caller is an alien power, that unfamiliar part of me nullified in the chatter of idle-talk and the reduction of existence down into a they-self.[97]

12. The caller, as nothing that can be brought into vocal utterance, is existence in its uncanniness whose epiphany as the nothing locks me in dread.[98] If I ignore its appeal I do so, not in disobedience to an external moral authority disconnected from me, but rather at the cost of myself.[99]

---

[95] Nietzsche's Zarathustra says 'Did perhaps a new knowledge come to thee, a bitter, grievous knowledge? Like leavened dough layest thou; thou soul arose and swelled beyond its bounds' [F. Nietzsche, *Also sprach Zarathustra* (1999), p. 227. 'Kam wohl eine neue Erkenntniss zu dir, eine saure, schwere? Gleich angesäuertem Teige lagst du, deine Seele gieng auf und schwoll über alle ihre Ränder'].

[96] Zarathustra speaks of 'the consummating death ... which becometh a stimulus and promise to the living' [F. Nietzsche, *Also sprach Zarathustra* (1999), p. 73. 'Den vollbringenden Tod zeige ich euch, der den Lebenden ein Stachel und ein Gelöbniss wird'] for 'freed at last is my nose from the smell of all human hubbub!' [F. Nietzsche, *Also sprach Zarathustra* (1999), p. 194. 'Erlöst ist endlich meine Nase vom Geruch alles Menschen wesens']. To be creators 'much bitter dying must there be in your life ... Thus are ye advocates and justifiers of all perishableness' [F. Nietzsche, *Also sprach Zarathustra* (1999), p. 87, 'viel bitteres Sterben muss in eurem Leben sein ... Also seid ihr Fürsprecher und Rechtfertiger aller Vergänglichkeit'].

[97] Nietzsche complains, through Zarathustra, that 'noise killeth thought – and just now there came to me such delicate thoughts' [F. Nietzsche, *Also sprach Zarathustra* (1999), p. 87. 'Lärm mordet Gedanken, und eben kommen mir so zärtliche Gedanken'].

[98] In *'Die stillste Stunde'* Zarathustra recounts the dread aroused in being spoken to 'without voice'. He says: 'never did I hear such stillness around me, so that my heart was terrified ... cried in terror at this whispering, and the blood left my face ...' [F. Nietzsche, *Also sprach Zarathustra* (1999), p. 87, 'ohne Stimme ... nie hörte ich solche Stille um mich: also dass mein Herz erschrak ... ich schrie vor Schrecken bei diesem Flüstern, und das Blut wich aus meinem Gesichte'].

[99] This kind of sacrifice is referred to by René Girard as sacred violence, being essential for the foundation of social and religious groups. That is, social groups flourish in proportion to the extent that individuals sacrifice or hold themselves in check. His theory is incomplete for it does not recognize the necessity of dying to the they-self, a sacrifice that brings me into the fullness of my being or my ownmost potentiality for being.

For Nietzsche 'all suppressed truths become poisonous' [F. Nietzsche, *Also sprach Zarathustra*, (1999), p. 87, 'alle verschwiegenen Wahrheiten werden giftig'].

13. Being guilty is not something extrinsic to my being, a mood aroused in my breach of an external ethical code designed by an alien moral authority. Rather, it is an existential state-of-mind that grips me when I ignore myself in the uncanniness of my being, fraudulently cheating on myself.[100]

14. I experience resoluteness when, in choosing myself, I allow the momentum of my *ownmost self* to determine the course of my actions.

15. Nullity, the default position of the they-self, is the condition of deafness to the call, whether it cries 'Guilty!' or confers stillness in resoluteness.

16. Being individuated down to myself in all its uncanniness is not solipsistic but allows authentic engagement with others in their uncanniness. The disenchantment of existential despair is overcome when I am pushed into solicitous being-with-others.

5.7.2 Towards a post-metaphysical theology of Eucharistic presence

So what has any of this to do with the central concern of our enquiry, namely to explore how Heidegger's philosophy can inform a contemporary understanding of Eucharistic presence after metaphysics? If we are now displaced from the terrain of classical metaphysics, from whose standpoint until now we have viewed the Real Presence, what does the Body of Christ look like, not on Chauvet's *voie du symbolique* (path of symbolism), but from the uncanny and holy being of man? How can an analysis of the fundamental structures of *Dasein*, in particular my being-towards death, throw any light upon what happens to the accidents of bread and wine during the consecration of the Mass? Should our focus not be confined exclusively to the thinghood of the Eucharistic elements, the *Esse*, in our search for a contemporary understanding of Eucharistic presence?

We have already seen how Macquarrie, borrowing both Heidegger's observation that for the Greeks a thing is that which one has to do with in one's 'concernful dealings'[101] and his paradigm of the fourfold, believes that the meaning of the thinghood of a thing cannot be uncovered by viewing it as being 'over there' wholly disconnected from me 'over here'. Rather the thing's thinghood emerges from the intercourse and interplay between earth, sky mortals and gods.[102] We

---

[100] In his *Letter to the Romans* Paul says: ἄχρι γὰρ νόμου ἁμαρτία ἦν ἐν κόσμῳ (sin existed in the world long before the law was given [Rom. 5.13]).

[101] M. Heidegger, *Sein und Zeit* (GA2), p. 68, 'besorgenden Umgang'.
    In other words, *Dasein* is implicated in the coming to be of something so that without me there are no things.

[102] J. Macquarrie, *Thinghood and Sacramentality*, 1995, p. 21.

noted how Macquarrie neglected to highlight the significance of the meaning of mortals, as they who are capable of *Tod als Tod* (death as death) although not death in which earthly life comes to an end. The foregoing discussion of *Dasein*'s ontological structure, given man's interplay in all that exists, is therefore of significant importance for any understanding of the *res* or thinghood of the Eucharist or sacramental presence. Man as mortal, expropriating from his they-self in his appropriation by the fourfold, allows for the staying a while or the presencing of all things. When, being educated in accordance with his infinity, he drops out of the finite universe of petty mortal concerns plunging into the swirling vortex of nothingness, the impossibility of the 'not-yet' now becomes possible.[103] It remains for us to show why and how this is so.

When I attend to the infinite possibilities of my being, as they assert themselves, I cease to be as a being susceptible to public interpretation. In my departure or going out from the ordinary, everyday world of programmed association, so that the familiar relations with others that previously sustained me and constructed my world disintegrate, my dying to the *man-selbst* in my becoming (or coming to be) incites holy terror and dread.[104] With this disintegration my ability to refer or assign that which is present-to-hand to an already-existing universe of transcendent ideas or symbols, involving it in a universal totality, is paralysed. That which stands before me ceases to be any longer as a thing publicly interpreted or defined ontologico-categorially. Instead, I stand face to face in an unmediated encounter with what lies nakedly present-to-hand, appropriating it and being appropriated by it, in a dynamic interplay.

The question arises: what does the thing now sunk into insignificance and having no involvement in a metaphysical universe that ordinarily ascribes meaning to things, come to be? Put differently, when *Dasein* withdraws altogether from its 'worldly' possibilities, being taken back into its naked uncanniness as the possibility of an *authentic* potentiality-for-being, what happens to the thinghood of the thing or the *res* of the sacrament? Heidegger has an answer:

---

[103] Before the fall it was in God's original plan that man, made in God's image and likeness and in continuous fellowship with Him, co-create with God. Having created the heavens and the earth from out of a formless void, in the darkness that hovered over the deep, God commissioned man and woman to be fruitful and multiply, filling the earth and subduing it and having dominion over the fish of the sea, over the birds of the air and over every living thing that moves on the earth.

[104] In the previous chapter it was noted how Kierkegaard likewise speaks of the human subject being gripped by anxiety 'when he feels himself abandoned by the multiplicity in which he has his soul . . .' [*Three Discourses on Imagined Occasions*, pp. 36–7].

. . . the present-at-hand must be encountered in just *such* a way that it has *no* involvement *whatsoever*, but can show itself in an empty mercilessness[105] . . . our concernful awaiting finds nothing in terms of which it might be able to understand itself; it clutches at the *Nichts* of the world.[106]

We might re-phrase this to ask: what do the accidents of bread and wine become when they have *no* involvement *whatsoever* in structures of significance that ordinarily bring them into existence as bread and wine? When I go out of myself (in my naked uncanniness) towards the bread and wine now severed from any involvement and showing in an empty mercilessness in the *Nichts* of the world, at what or to whom am I going out towards?

The words of institution spoken over the Eucharistic species during the consecration of the Mass are unambiguous:

Take this, all of you, and eat of it:
this is my body which will be given up for you.
Take this, all of you, and drink from it:
this is the chalice of *my blood,*
the blood of the new and eternal covenant.
which will be poured out for you and for many
for the forgiveness of sins.
Do this in memory of me.[107]

---

[105] Kierkegaard observes something similar when he says 'the person who renounces the world shudders at the emptiness that seems to manifest itself' [*Three Discourses on Imagined Occasions*, p. 14].

[106] M. Heidegger, *Sein und Zeit* (GA2), p. 343. 'Es muß gerade begegnen, damit es *so gar keine* Bewandtnis mit ihm haben und es sich in einer leeren Erbarmungslosigkeit zeigen kann . . . das besorgende Gewärtigen findet nichts, woraus es sich verstehen könnte, es greift ins Nichts der Welt.'
    We may recall from Chapter 2 that in Chauvet's approach to the sacraments and Eucharistic presence involvement in a symbolic structure of significance is critical if the Eucharistic species are to come to their truth and subjects are to be rescued from an exaggerated individualism. Without symbolization, that is involvement or instauration within a symbolic universe that transcends the self, 'one is in danger of sinking in the swamps of an exacerbated subjectivism, in the quicksands of the "unutterable" and "touching," in the vaporous mysticism of some para-psychological or para-religious esotericism' [L-M. Chauvet, *Symbole et Sacrement*, p. 130, 'on est en effet menacé de sombrer dans les marais d'une subjectivité exacerbée, dans les sables mouvants de l'"indicible" et du "touchant", dans la vaporeuse mystique d'un ésotérisme "para-psychologique" ou para-religieux']. Without symbolization, *the charge sémantique du pain et du vin* (semantic richness of bread and wine) is lost so that, for example, bread no longer designates (as it did in the universe of the Bible) the one food that none can do without. After Chauvet's reading of Heidegger however, bread is thought symbolically, not only in terms of its ability to nutrify and sustain biological organisms but also in terms of its ability to bring individuals together or to mediate fellowship. In other words, Chauvet's symbolic view locates Eucharistic presence in the very essence of bread itself which, when broken, reveals and manifests its ultimate reality and true essence to be *de pain-nourriture, de pain-repas, de pain-partage* (bread-as-food, bread-as-meal, bread-for-sharing).

[107] From the present English translation of the Roman Missal.
    Macquarrie, having cited from the Anglican-Roman Catholic Commission's report *Eucharistic Doctrine* that 'the Eucharistic memorial is no mere calling to mind of a past event or of its significance, but the effectual proclamation of God's mighty acts,' believes that if Heidegger's

The bread and wine now stripped of any involvement in the network of references that assign significance to and breathe life into the thinghood of the present-to-hand suddenly, in their release and fall into nothingness, have now no recognizable, familiar and identifiable thinghood. It is as though the substances of bread and wine are returned to the primeval void from which God created at the dawn of creation. Because the void is formless the morphologies of the bread and wine dissolve into indeterminate nothingness. As God hovers over the darkness of the deep, his spirit moving over the surface of the waters, 'they' (albeit indistinguishable from the nothingness) await God's spoken word before coming to be as any thing again. Just as God said, at the dawn of creation, 'Let there be light,' and there was light, so when Jesus said 'this is my body'[108] and 'this is indeed my blood'[109] so the 'bread' and 'wine', though now unrecognizable in the nothing, resurface at the sound of God's voice as the Body and Blood of Christ. Chauvet's claim that bread, after the consecration and understood symbolically, remains essentially still bread, albeit bread-as-food, bread-as-meal, bread-for-sharing, is inconsistent with a phenomenological understanding of Eucharistic presence in the light of Heidegger's the nothing.

It was noted earlier that the nothing does not engulf and consume to the extent that identity is wholly subsumed and submerged in a total obliteration of being. Rather, having been released from the illusions of the they and having gained phenomenological access by holding in abeyance our interpretative tendencies (which disallow entities to be encountered as they are in themselves) the bread (and the wine) are pushed back out from nothingness into 'existence', though this time not as all-too-familiar and useful *earth*ly entities (i.e. bread-as-food, bread-as-meal, bread-for-sharing) but as they are in the interplay between earth, heaven, God and man ... the Body and Blood of Jesus. Displaced from the public arena (earth), where they are defined ontologico-categorially as bread and wine, the body and blood stay their while within the uncanny realm of authentic being wherein heaven, earth, God and man interflow.

When Jesus says 'I am the Bread of Life'[110] he is deliberately moving beyond or dropping out of the biblical universe of meanings that ascribed the provenance of the 'bread from heaven'[111] to Moses. The ultimate reality and true essence of

philosophy is to have any application whatsoever to the sacrament of the Eucharist it is principally 'to explain the exegesis of the word *anamnesis* given in the ARCIC document' [*A Guide to the Sacraments* (1997), p. 140].

[108] Mt. 26.26 τοῦτό ἐστιν τὸ σῶμά μου.
[109] Mt. 26.28 τοῦτο γάρ ἐστιν τὸ αἷμά μου.
[110] Jn 6.35 Ἐγώ ἰμι ὁ ἄρτος τῆς ζωῆς.
[111] Jn 6.32 τὸν ἄρτον ἐκ τοῦ οὐρανοῦ.

bread is not found in its functional ability to physically maintain biological life or to symbolically mediate fellowship as *bread-as-food, bread-as-meal, bread-for-sharing* but in its ontological capacity to be a life-giving mortal human being, albeit one who, on earth, is in uninterrupted fellowship with God in heaven. The thingness of the bread now becomes indistinguishable from living human flesh for as Jesus says: 'This bread is my flesh'.[112] The thinghood (substance) that was there before, when the bread present-to-hand was referred to a universe of (biblical) meanings, disintegrates in its disengagement from this transcendent universe that hides and conceals more than it reveals. The bread has changed in form from Moses' manna that sustains the body, to Jesus' flesh that gives eternal life for, as Jesus says, 'whoever eats my flesh and drinks my blood has eternal life'.[113]

The only feature that remains in common after the event of consecration is that the bread-wine and the body-blood are substances that have the potential to sustain life, the one an earthly existence constructed intentionally by man from totalizing structures of significance, the other a heavenly life whose outburst requires the death of man in his coming-to-be in resoluteness. Importantly, the words of the consecration effect not only the Eucharistic species but also the worshippers who, as mortals, are co-creative of the bread and wine. The words encourage a *transitus* from a transcendent world mediated by the senses to the infinitely personal world of a formless void or the *Nichts* of the possible impossibility of existence wherein God and man, Heaven and earth coincide and wherefrom beings or things emerge.

When I know myself as limitless possibility I view the things that stand before me, the bread and wine, not in their accidental actuality but in the nothing of their possible impossibility. Bread viewed through the open eyes of the senses,[114] in its actual presencing, now in the present moment, may physically sustain biological life and symbolically mediate fellowship, but viewed more primordially through the open eyes of faith (through the optic of the nothing), whose vision does not rely upon sensual mediation,[115] it (the bread that is now flesh) nourishes the

---

[112] Jn 6.51 ο αρτος η σαρξ μου εστιν.

[113] Jn 6.54 ὁ τρώγων μου τὴν σάρκα καὶ πίνων μου τὸ αἷμα ἔχει ζωὴν αἰώνιον.

[114] This kind of seeing, in which things in their nakedness are repulsive and need to be covered up, is spoken of in *Genesis* as a consequence of the fall of man and woman: ([Gen. 3.7]. And the eyes of them both were opened and they knew that they were naked).

[115] Heb. 11.1 'Now faith is the evidence of things unseen' (Ἐστιν δὲ πίστις πραγμάτων ἔλεγχος οὐ βλεπομένων.

human soul and gives eternal life. Just as *Dasein* is overwhelmed with dread, wonder and awe when it comes face to face (in an empty mercilessness) with its authentic being, revealing itself in the voice of conscience,[116] so too when I look out at the bread taken back now into its naked uncanniness, so that it shows to me in the emptiness of my authenticity as flesh, my blood runs icy cold, my flesh creeps, I shudder with horror at what I see before me.[117]

5.7.3 *Durus est Hic Sermo* – this is a hard teaching

How can this man give us his flesh to eat?[118]
This is a hard teaching.
Who can accept it?[119]

But what does Jesus mean when he says the bread is his body and the wine is his blood? To answer this, *'this is my body'* and *'this is my blood'* need to be contextualized into the remainder of the Words of Institution. Heidegger's thoughts on being-towards-death will now be brought into conversation with these Eucharistic words. To do this the Words of Institution will be divided into seven sections before bringing them back together again in a final and decisive synthesis:

1. *Take this, all of you . . .*
2. *. . . and eat of it: . . . and drink from it*
3. *. . . this is my body . . . this is the chalice of my blood*
4. *. . . which will be given up for you . . . It will be poured out for you and many . . . .*

---

[116] When man and woman heard the sound of God walking in the garden in the cool of the day, overwhelmed with fear they attempted to hide themselves among the trees. In response to God's call 'Where are you?' man confesses: I heard thy voice in the garden and I was afraid because I was naked and I hid myself.

[117] Kierkegaard speaks of how the heart pounds and the body shudders in the stillness of the dangerous moment when the worshipper, collecting himself from manifold dispersions, withdraws from his surroundings to stand alone in emptiness before God. The stillness of worship that must not be disturbed or violated is 'a stillness that changes the ordinary just as the storm does' [*Three Discourses on Imagined Occasions*, p. 36]. Proper worship is 'to think highly of God and lowly of yourself' [*Three Discourses on Imagined Occasions*, p. 32] (this sense of one's own worthlessness, it may be recalled from Chapter 3, is referred to by Rudolph Otto as *Kreaturgefühl* – creature feeling). It is in the diminishing self-esteem, when 'a person feels himself as a nothing, as less than nothing' [*Three Discourses on Imagined Occasions*, p. 29], as awareness of God dawns, that he is gripped by 'fear and trembling' [*Three Discourses on Imagined Occasions*, p. 27]. Worship is therefore 'simultaneously a mixture of fear and blessedness' [*Three Discourses on Imagined Occasions*, p. 18]. Of the person who attempts to belittle the importance of fear in true worship Kierkegaard cautions 'let him see to it that he does not leave out the discovery' [*Three Discourses on Imagined Occasions*, p. 24].

[118] Jn 6.52 Πῶς δύναται οὗτος ἡμῖν δοῦναι τὴν σάρκα φαγεῖν.

[119] Jn 6.60 Σκληρός ἐστιν οὗτος· ὁ λόγος τίς δύναται αὐτοῦ ἀκούειν.

5. ... *the blood of the new and eternal covenant* ...
6. ... *for the forgiveness of sins* ...
7. ... *Do this in memory of me.*

1. *Take this, all of you* ...

The voice of conscience[120] must be understood as a giving-to-understand and not dismissed as an alien power of no importance and significance to my being. The 'this', that is taken, is the call of the appeal. In 'taking this' in my appropriation, I am not running for cover or taking flight-from the summons in spite of its unfamiliar, unhomely and thus terrifying demeanour. Taking, in this sense, is allowing the momentum of a push to arouse me abruptly, allowing my listening-away to the they to be interrupted by the call. Given the ontological character of the 'this', if I am desirous to be truly and authentically what I am, I am not at liberty to refuse what is given in the offer; to do so is to defraud and cheat on myself. I can take 'this' in its emptiness to become all that I am in my bare nakedness in the urgency of my uncanniness. Alternatively, I can barricade myself from life, hiding like Adam and Eve among the trees of the garden at the sound of God's voice,[121] taking flight to the tranquillization of the familiar and the homely that drowns out the sound of transcending, risen life.[122]

2. ... *and eat of it:* ... *and drink from it*

Having heard the voice of conscience and blocked my ears to the noisy doings of the crowd's confused collective scream (Heidegger's 'hubbub' of the manifold ambiguity which idle talk possesses), eating and drinking signify the

---

[120] For the sake of bringing Heidegger's thought into conversation with the Eucharistic words of the Institution, a project Heidegger might have resisted given his persistent concern to keep the disciplines of philosophy and theology distinct but a project which nevertheless contemporary theologians are inclined to undertake, I am assuming here that conscience, whose caller is 'Dasein in its Unheimlichkeit: primordial, thrown Being-in-the-world als Un-zuhause (as the "not-at-home")' [M. Heidegger, Sein und Zeit (GA2), p. 276.] calls from the same domain as the Risen Christ.
     It could be argued that the meaning of uncanny as unheimlichkeit, the un-homely, and (as we showed in Chapter 3) das Heilige, resonates with 'risen' understood in the sense of no-longer-being-at-home in the world. The experience of the disciples on the road to Emmaus, in which 'their hearts burned within them', illustrates anecdotally that the Risen Christ speaks without utterance. As with conscience what is im Ruf Gerufenen (called in the call) is un-worded, that is, not expressed in word-forms. Giving a sense of life beyond that which is merely given in general, it can not speak ordinarily because speech translates me into the universal. Emplacing me outside the universal, it is the demonic-divine life stirring within me.

[121] Gen. 3.8.

[122] Kierkegaard says; 'You have probably heard big words and loud talk and noisy doings to get rid of the stillness in order to have, instead of conscience and stillness and God's voice delivering judgement in stillness, a nature echo from the crowd, a confused collective scream, a general opinion in which one, out of cowardice, fearing for oneself, is not alone' [Three Discourses on Imagined Occasions, p. 11].

taking action within me of my *ownmost self*, an enlivening intoxication.[123] I am sustained now, not by the idle chatter of the they (by whose common consensus the Eucharistic species are taken to be bread and wine), but instead by the agitating summons of the call discoursing in the uncanny mode of keeping silent.[124] Gathering myself up from dispersion, in the reunification of my fractured being, I rise transfigured into a transcending life where the prospect of authentic engagement with others (the solicitude which leaps forth and liberates), opens out before me. Until I have eaten the Body and drunk the Blood 'given up' for me, a reconciliation with that uncanny part of me, dissevered, disfigured and mutilated by the discriminations of the they, I cannot hope to enter into mutually accomplishing relations with others so that we can authentically be with one another. Eating the Body and drinking the Blood given up in sacrifice, is *Dasein's* coming in the stillness into *die Entschlossenheit* (resoluteness). It implies a listening-away from the big words, loud talk and generalizations of the crowd, a rejection of 'ambiguous and jealous stipulations and talkative fraternising in the they'.[125]

3. . . . *this is my body . . . this is the chalice of my blood*
Before Jesus' body and blood are given up they remain interpreted within the structures of significance that prevail within the public domain. They are 'defined ontologico-categorially'[126] as being co-essential to Jesus' they-self, Jesus as son of Mary born in Bethlehem and raised in Jerusalem (the historical Christ) over Jesus Son of God crucified on Calvary and raised from the dead (the Christ

---

[123] Eros is not precluded in this 'taking action within me of my *ownmost self*. We may recall in the last chapter Pope Benedict saying 'the Greeks – not unlike other cultures – considered *eros* principally as a kind of intoxication, the overpowering of reason by a "divine madness" which tears man away from his finite existence and enables him, in the very process of being overwhelmed by divine power, to experience supreme happiness . . . *Eros* was thus celebrated as a divine power, as fellowship with the Divine' [Benedict XVI, *Deus Caritas Est*, §4.'. . . mundum ante aetatem christianam. Certissime congruentes cum aliis culturis, viderunt Graeci in illo *eros* ante omnia aliquam ebrietatem, nempe rationis ipsius oppressionem per "divinum furorem" qui hominem ad ipsius vitae limitem abripit et, quod sic potestate quadam divina percutitur, quam maximam beatitudinem facit ut ipse experiatur . . . Sic celebrabatur *eros* veluti divina quaedam vis, tamquam communio cum divina natura'].
Thomas Sheehan notes that Plato deployed the 'notion of *eros*' to name the 'excess-dimension', namely the 'kinetic nature of man' (*physis* and *kinesis*) that is lost, forgotten and covered over when man 'is read in terms of stability and appearance', when '*eidos* assumes the role of the primary characteristic of the beingness of beings' [Sheehan, *Karl Rahner: The Philosophical Foundations*, pp. 305–7].

[124] Kierkegaard says: 'Silence is the state in which the Individual becomes conscious of his union with the divine' [*Fear and Trembling . . . A Dialectical Lyric*, p. 129].

[125] M. Heidegger, *Sein und Zeit* (GA2), p. 298.
The political implications of transubstantiation become visible at this point: if my being is no longer determined by (or is no longer under the 'protectorship' of) the they but instead, following my sacrifice, responds to the proclamations (*stimme*) of a new and deeper sovereignty the powers and principalities sustained by the they feel threatened.

[126] M. Heidegger, *Sein und Zeit* (GA2), p. 71.

of faith). The Jews, when Jesus said he was 'the Bread which came down from heaven',[127] sought to discredit his claim by highlighting his earthly origins. They grumbled: 'Is not this Jesus the son of Joseph whose father and mother we know? How is it then that he saith I came down from heaven?'[128]

4. . . . *which will be given up for you . . .*

In giving up his body and blood Jesus is relinquishing his publicly interpreted being as 'Jesus the son of Joseph whose father and mother we know'.[129] The they of his 'they-self' collapses in his being-towards-death. The self, ordinarily passed over by everyday *Dasein*, now robbed of its lodgement and hiding-place, rises to life for the first time. Jesus becomes, in his giving up and going-out-of-the-world in the sense of dying, 'the Bread which came down from heaven'.[130] In my eating and drinking the same, a corresponding collapse and re-birth happens to me so that I cease being the earthly 'they-self' I was before and become the *Tanzenden Stern* (dancing star) descended from heaven. This is what St Paul means when he says: 'if, then we die with Christ, we believe that we shall share his life'.[131] The bread that has become the body, the wine that has become the blood, the me that has taken, eaten and drunk these, are now, after the giving-up, beings undetermined by fixed transcendental terms[132] but rather held out into the primeval void of *das Nichts*.[133] This shows in my non-relational betrothal to the other.

Where a road that is being laid breaks off, a pathway may nevertheless continue. The giving up of life provokes the question: what may be after death? The '. . . *will be given up*' speaks of an expectancy, an anticipation, which turns out to be the possibility of authentic existence, of understanding oneself no longer in terms of the they but of the uttermost potentiality-for-being. In the expectation, anticipation reveals to existence that its uttermost potentiality-for-being lies in sacrifice or in giving itself up. It shows contemptuous disregard for whatever social status or public position one has reached.

---

127 Jn 6.41 ὁ ἄρτος ὁ καταβὰς ἐκ τοῦ οὐρανοῦ.

128 Jn 6.42 Οὐχ οὗτός ἐστιν Ἰησοῦς ὁ υἱὸς Ἰωσήφ οὗ ἡμεῖς οἴδαμεν τὸν πατέρα καὶ τὴν μητέρα πῶς οὖν λέγει οὗτος ὅτι Ἐκ τοῦ οὐρανοῦ καταβέβηκα.

129 Jn 6.42 Ἰησοῦς ὁ υἱὸς Ἰωσήφ οὗ ἡμεῖς οἴδαμεν τὸν πατέρα καὶ τὴν μητέρα.

130 Jn 6.41 ὁ ἄρτος ὁ καταβὰς ἐκ τοῦ οὐρανοῦ.

131 Rom. 6.8. εἰ δὲ ἀπεθάνομεν σὺν Χριστῷ πιστεύομεν ὅτι καὶ συζήσομεν αὐτῷ.

132 It may be recalled from earlier that *Dasein* in this register approximates the holy being of divinity or higher life. Jesus for Nietzsche is a *'freien Geist'* ('free spirit'): 'he cares nothing for what is fixed: the word *killeth*, everything fixed *killeth'* [F. Nietzsche, *Der Antichrist*, (1990), p. 229. '. . . er macht sich aus allem Festen nichts: das Wort *tötet*, alles, was fest ist, *tötet*']. In this register of being we become *der Wahnsinn* (the frenzy) or the chaos that gives birth to the *tanzenden Stern* that is the *Übermenschen* (Superman).

133 There were divergent views in the medieval Church regarding the substance of the Body ranging from Berengar's position asserting it to be corporeal, to Paschasius' theology claiming it to be the risen Christ glorified and incorporeal [see especially David Macy's *The Theologies of the Eucharist in the Early Scholastic Period*, p. 72]. Following the Berengarian controversy, the orthodox Catholic view of the substance of Eucharistic species came to be defined in terms of the latter position.

When Jesus goes out to the 'not-yet' of his being (i.e. the authentic existence of transcendent, risen life) the 'that it is there' of his body and blood dissolves in coming face to face with the 'nothing' of the possible impossibility of existence. The uttermost possibility of existence is *sich selbst aufzugeben* (to give itself up). When Jesus came to this difficult realization in the Garden of Gethsemane, on the eve of his crucifixion, it was the cause of deep consternation for him – he was anxious unto death. To the disciples who accompanied him 'he began to be sorrowful and deeply distressed'. He said to them: 'My soul is exceeding sorrowful even unto death'.[134]

The giving up of life in dying, is an act of defiance in the face of the they's tendency to de-individuate death through their claim that dying belongs to nobody in particular. The giving up of life contests the prevailing and common-sense view that dying is a social inconvenience against which the public is to be guarded. It proves instead to be the highest act of living. It is truly 'pleasing'[135] to God and is the reason St Paul in his letter to the church in Rome advises his listeners the best way to worship God is 'to present their bodies as a living and holy sacrifice'.[136] There is something dangerous, giving rise to the dread of anxiety, in the giving up of life[137] so that life in its uncanniness may free itself from the iron grasp of tranquillized everyday existence.

5. . . . *the blood of the new and eternal covenant* . . .

This dying, signalled in the giving up of the body and blood (Jesus' being-towards-death), makes possible a sociality wherein others can be together in their authenticity, without assuming airs and affecting manners in their ownmost potentiality-for-being. In the resoluteness that being-towards-death effectuates we can authentically be with one another in a new and enduring non-relational[138] way of engagement. Big words, loud talk and noisy doings, the defining traits of filial association, are not characteristic of the new and everlasting covenant.

---

[134] Mt. 26.37 ἤρξατο λυπεῖσθαι καὶ ἀδημονεῖν . . . Περίλυπός ἐστιν ἡ ψυχή μου ἕως θανάτου.

[135] Rom. 12.1 εὐάρεστον.

[136] Rom. 12.1 παραστῆσαι τὰ σώματα ὑμῶν θυσίαν ζῶσαν ἁγίαν.

[137] This observation, following Heidegger, is borne out in the ethnographic research of anthropologists. In *Celebrations of Death . . . The Anthropology of Mortuary Ritual* for instance Richard Huntington observes the 'emotional reaction to death' of those left behind. Although he refers to biological death nevertheless his observations are not insignificant for understanding the reaction of the they to the ontological dying of the individual. He says 'surely one of the most prominent aspects of death is its potential for intense emotional impact on the survivors. The reasons for the strong response are almost as numerous as they are obvious. There is the simple but often searing fact of separation from a loved one. There is emotion at the realization that he or she will no longer enjoy the fruits of life. There is shock at the suddenness with which death often strikes out of nowhere. There can be fear for one's own life, and fear of the power of death in general. There may be anger at the persons or powers supposedly responsible for death. Finally there are numerous strong reactions to the corpse itself' [Huntington, *Celebrations of Death . . .*, (1987), p. 23].

[138] In the sense of not having any reference to a transcendental world of interpretative structures of significance.

Although my relations to others have been undone (i.e. relations to others in their inauthenticity) nevertheless, the undoing of these entanglements frees me to embrace them now in their authenticity and uncanniness enabling full participation in this wider sociality. Relations henceforth are not things I procure, contrive or engineer but are encounters into which I am pushed by the momentum of my ownmost being, agitating and appealing in conscience. Although death as the non-relational possibility individualizes, redeeming being from the superficialities of ordinary human engagement, *Dasein*, reinvented now as *Mitsein* (being-with) understands *das Seinkönnen der Anderen* (the potentiality-for-being of Others).[139]

6. . . . for the forgiveness of sins . . .

In listening and responding positively to the call, so that my *ownmost self* takes action in me simultaneously as the they of my they-self collapses, being-guilty likewise dissolves. The ontological damage (sin) inflicted upon my being-a-whole in my listening away to the they and neglect of the call of my ownmost potentiality of being, is corrected (forgiven) in my attentiveness and response to the call breaking through the clamour of the they's idle talk.

If being-guilty results from an incorrect hearing of *oneself*, or a misunderstanding of conscience's call (misinterpreted because muffled and drowned out by the clamourous they), in eating the body and drinking the blood the call becomes once again audible such that the self, in thrall to its ownmost possibility of existence, begins to take action in itself. My throwness into the nothing of my being, so that the uncanny releases like a vapour from containment, pushes me out to others in their uncanniness and nothingness.

7. Do this in memory of me.

To recall Jesus to our minds we must give up our bodies and shed our blood in our own being-towards-death since *no one can take the other's dying away from him*. Jesus' dying in sacrifice cannot absolve us of our own unique existential responsibly to do the same. We cannot be authentically ourselves in resoluteness nor let others 'be' in their ownmost potentiality-for-being unless we respond positively to the appeal of conscience in our *own* dying to the 'they'. We owe it to ourselves.

From out of the ruins of the they-self that uncanny part of me, hidden and covered up by the they who tranquillize its agitatons, re-surfaces. Its aspect is

---

[139] Heidegger's suggestion that being re-emerges following its death recalls Nietzsche's *Zarathustra* who says 'Now doth it come to pass that solitude itself becometh fragile and breaketh open, like a grave that breaketh open and can no longer hold its dead. Everywhere one seeth resurrected ones' [F. Nietzsche, *Also sprach Zarathustra* (1999), p. 87, 'die Einsamkeit selber mürbe wird und zerbricht, einem Grabe gleich, das zerbricht und seine Todten nicht mehr halten kann. Überall sieht man Auferstandene'].

terrifying to the they who, faced with the unfamiliar and concerned with its own survival, takes flight in horror. Conscience, calling *Dasein* forth (and 'forward') into its ownmost possibilities, testifies to this hidden and silent presence, that once lay undetected but which now stirs to life in an abrupt arousal. In dying I am spared the vanities, the tricks, the chattering, the secretiveness and busyness found in the idle talk and general opinions of the 'they'. In the Eucharist I am called back from the confused collective scream of the crowd or from the public idle talk of the they, into the reticence of my existent potentiality-for-being. Rescued from dispersion and scattering in the manifold, in resoluteness I am pushed into solicitous being with others. In short, sacrifice prompts authentic belonging-together.

Indeed 'this teaching is hard' but as Jesus said to those who were upset by it 'What if you should see the Son of Man ascend to where he was before? It is the spirit that gives life/the flesh has nothing to offer/ the words I have spoken to you are spirit/and they are life'.[140]

5.7.4 All that sheltered me is gone – final synthesis

It has been shown what Eucharistic presence looks like when investigated, not from a metaphysical standpoint or on the path of symbolism, but instead from out of the uncanny and holy being of man. A voice speaks in the deepest region of man's being, far beyond the machinations of the human intellect and beyond the boarders of the human psyche. Its sound instils dread for it speaks to the ordinary everyday self from the forgotten, concealed but fundamental foundation of being which is unfamiliar and strange. Because ordinarily its voice is drowned out by the hubbub of loud voices and general opinions, when finally it breaks through, the words that it speaks are almost incomprehensible, being so unfamiliar. To gather their meaning, being must be recalled from its dispersions so that, fully focused in resoluteness and finely tuned to this new sound, it can stay in the spirit's breeze doing what the caller summons. Possibilities that before were impossible are now conceived as abrupt momentums, initially provoking dread, as being awakens from tranquillized existence to the enquivering fullness of undispersed resolute life.

To conceive presence after metaphysics not in terms of symbolic meanings (however rich and varied these may be) but rather in terms of a call, the voice of

---

[140] Jn 6.63 τὸ πνεῦμά ἐστιν τὸ ζῳοποιοῦν ἡ σὰρξ οὐκ ὠφελεῖ οὐδέν· τὰ ῥήματα ἃ ἐγὼ λαλῶ ὑμῖν πνεῦμά ἐστιν καὶ ζωή ἐστιν.

conscience, is not a postmodern innovation but rather, as may be expected in a phenomenological investigation, a return to origins. In the garden of Eden God presences to Adam as a sound 'walking in the garden in the cool of the day'[141] and as a voice calling out 'Where are you?'[142] The effect of the call was to instil such terror and fear into the hearts of man and woman, they hid 'among the trees of the garden'.[143] The consequence of eating the forbidden fruit in disobedience to God's word was the closure of their spiritual eyes and the introduction of death into the human condition.[144]

The same voice that called out to Adam speaks within the Eucharistic moment. Instead of 'walking in the garden in the cool of the day' the holy moves now within the deepest and darkest regions of being. Its strange and alien call initially provokes dread because it cannot be domesticated within the familiar and habitual. If like Samuel though we say 'speak for your servant is listening'[145] dread transmutes into wonder as we come out from our hiding places to stand and dwell in our emptiness and nakedness before the living God. This coming out from behind the trees (unconcealment) and stripping-off of fig-leaves (uncovering) is *Dasein's* going-out-of-the-world in the sense of dying. It is *going-under* or sacrifice.

When we listen to the voice of conscience and undergo death in the sense of *Sterbens*, the death that entered the human condition on account of Adam and Eve's original act of disobedience to God's call, is once and for all eradicated. Whereas the eating of the apple in defiance of God's word erased the breath of God's spirit from Adam and Eve so that 'death spread to all men',[146] the eating of the flesh and blood of the Son of God in obedience to God's call fills man's lungs once again with the breath of God's spirit. In the Eucharistic moment the holiness of God comes to life within us for, as Jesus says, 'whoever eats my flesh and drinks my blood has eternal life'.[147]

In short Eucharistic presence, after metaphysics, is a paradox: it eradicates physical death from the human condition precisely through instigating ontological dying or sacrifice in which being departs from the concealments and cover ups of the they to become beingfulness or being-a-whole. Eucharist is the realization of our salvation and confirmation of the Psalmists' belief : 'the Lord is my light and my salvation whom shall I fear'.[148]

---

[141]   Gen. 3.8.
[142]   Gen. 3.8.
[143]   Gen. 3.8.
[144]   Rom. 5.12.
[145]   1 Sam. 3.10.
[146]   Rom. 5.2.
[147]   Jn 6.54 ὁ τρώγων μου τὴν σάρκα καὶ πίνων μου τὸ αἷμα ἔχει ζωὴν αἰώνιον.
[148]   Ps. 27.1.

Conclusion

In *The Eucharist* Edward Schillebeeckx is sympathetic towards modern theologians and their attempts to make Eucharistic presence more comprehensible. This is because 'the so-called modernists' are really deeply concerned with the problem of making the inviolable *dogma* itself once again relevant to the faithful of today by separating it from the framework of ideas within which faith can no longer thrive in the present age. Even though, Schillebeeckx recognizes, some epigones are clearly unable to show moderation their excesses nevertheless should not discredit the exercise in itself or call a halt to the genuine effort being made at the moment throughout the whole world (and especially in Western Europe) 'to understand the real content of "transubstantiation".'[1]

This book has examined the attempt of a French theologian, Louis-Marie Chauvet, to rethink the sacraments in the light of contemporary philosophical thought. Evaluating Chauvet's main work *Symbole et Sacrement*, in which he separates sacramental theology from the scholastic framework of ideas (through which conventionally it has been interpreted) and thinks it afresh after engaging with the thought of the German philosopher, Martin Heidegger, an attempt was made to answer the question: is it possible to continue thinking sacraments in an orthodox way after Nietzsche's exclamation *God is Dead!*?[2] This question was formulated in reaction to Chauvet's claim that, when sacraments are thought through a Heideggerian framework of ideas, the term 'transubstantiation' is no longer apt to express theologically the integral content of the Eucharist presence.[3]

---

[1] E. Schillebeeckx, *The Eucharist*, 2005 (1968), p. 28.
[2] F. Nietzsche, *The Gay Science*, (2007), p. 120.
[3] L.-M. Chauvet, *Symbole et Sacrement*, p. 400.

In the first chapter, Chauvet's reading of Heidegger was discussed. It was discovered that, although Chauvet consults primary texts and relies little on secondary literature on Heidegger, he omits nonetheless to take seriously the importance of *das Nichts* in Heidegger's reflections on metaphysics. This omission was attributed to Chauvet's suspicion of the apophatic tradition in theology, in particular pseudo-Dionysius' knowledge under the mode of unknowing,[4] and to a lack of appreciation of Heidegger's philosophical approach. It was demonstrated that phenomenology promises a new kind of knowledge, allowing us to see 'something that proximally and for the most part does *not* show itself at all'[5] because it 'lies *hidden*'[6] in sharp contrast to that which does show itself. In short, it allows what previously was unthinkable to be thought.

In the second chapter the trajectory of Chauvet's sacramental theology, beginning with Heidegger's thought, was mapped. Although Chauvet had succeeded in freeing himself to some extent from the categories of thought associated with medieval scholasticism, nevertheless he substituted in its place a Heideggerian framework of ideas that Chapter 1 had shown to be incomplete. The genealogy of Chauvet's theology from its philosophical foundations, through its foray into ethnological research to its eventual sacramental conclusions, was traced. Heidegger had enabled Chauvet to overcome a metaphysical view of sacraments by facilitating Chauvet's symbolic approach. This served as a primordial stumbling block, Chauvet says, to *Dasein*'s pretension to return to its origins, and to an exacerbated subjectivity that holds out the possibility of an immediate, face-to-face encounter with God. For Chauvet alliance with Jesus cannot be lived in an imaginary direct contact with him that presupposes his 'full' presence. The mystery of the sacrament is to be found (for Chauvet) in its function: it enables *Dasein*'s accession to the symbolic realm, always-already spoken before the subject comes into existence. This oblation, in the sense of the sublimation of 'narcissistic' tendencies, is not simply an event in the life of an individual for it refers man back to creation in the exigency of a counter-gift. In other words, when a metaphysical view of the sacraments is overcome a new understanding of ethics and sacrifice opens up.

In the third chapter, given the importance of the overcoming of metaphysics to Chauvet's sacramental theology (Chapter 2), together with his neglect of the nothing in his reading of Heidegger on metaphysics (Chapter 1), the notion

---

[4]   L.-M. Chauvet, *Symbole et Sacrement*, p. 46.
[5]   M. Heidegger, *Sein und Zeit* (GA2), p. 35, 'solches, was sich zunächst und zumeist gerade *nicht* zeigt' (emphasis in original).
[6]   M. Heidegger, *Sein und Zeit* (GA2), p. 35, '*verborgen* ist' (emphasis in original).

of *das Nichts* and the referent that it indicates was examined in some depth. By researching the influence of Rudolph Otto on Heidegger's thought, it was demonstrated that *das Nichts* shares many of the features of *das Heilige*. The suggestion was ventured that Chauvet's deep suspicion of an unmediated encounter with divinity, which he caricatures as the 'danger of sinking . . . in the quicksands of the "unutterable" and "touching",[7] is contingent on his by-passing *das Nichts*. In other words, his view (that God presences *symbolically* after Jesus' crucifixion and his Second Coming) would have been unsustainable had he not situated Heidegger's philosophy within the transcendental horizons of positivist systems of symbolic thought precluding altogether any consideration of *das Nichts*. In suggesting that the *topos* of God's encounter with man is to be found in *das Nichts*, wherein the terrifying majesty and awesomeness of the divine touches and transforms being, awakening a sense of *Dasein*'s uncanniness, it was suggested that Eucharistic presence after metaphysics is not located in a symbolic realm (as Chauvet upholds) but rather in the ontological roots of *Dasein*. Heidegger, thinking out of the domain of *das Nichts* that is foreclosed in Chauvet's reading of him, is clear that 'the experience of God and his manifestedness, to the extent that the latter can indeed meet man, flashes [eventualizes] in the dimension of being'.[8]

In the fourth chapter, having earlier determined the impossibility of bringing Heidegger's thought into conversation with theological questions without a thorough appreciation of *das Nichts*, a phenomenology of ethics was attempted. This was done because in Chauvet's sacramental system the subject 'verifies' what it has received in the sacrament through the return-gift of 'an *ethical* practice'.[9] In other words, the key to a postmodern understanding of Eucharistic presence[10] that does not depend upon the framework of metaphysics is found as much in the *ad-esse* of the members constituting the ecclesial body as it is in the *esse* of the Eucharistic species. It was demonstrated, following a consideration of Pope Benedict's first encyclical *Deus Caritas Est* and a close reading of Heidegger's lecture *Der Satz der Identität*, that ethics, thought within the horizon of the hidden (the *verborgen*) or *das Nichts*,[11] implies a radical ontology. It is from the strange and uncanny realm into which I am cast by the overpowering, which

[7] L.-M. Chauvet, *Symbole et Sacrement*, p. 130, 'menacé de sombrer . . . dans les sables mouvants de l' "indicible" et du "touchant"'.
[8] M. Heidegger, *Seminare* (GA15), p. 437, 'die Erfahrung Gottes und seiner Offenbarkeit (sofern sie dem Menschen begegnet) in der Dimension des Seins sich ereignet'.
[9] L.-M. Chauvet, *Symbole et Sacrement*, p. 288, 'une pratique *éthique*' (emphasis in original).
[10] That is, attempts to think Eucharistic presence after metaphysics and the death of God.
[11] That is, phenomenologically.

reverses the assault of *techne* against *dike*,[12] that the unbound powers of being come forth.[13] As these break-in, as I lose those qualities with which metaphysics has endowed me (the moment of sacrifice), I am impelled outwards towards the other, becoming more and more open and concerned with their happiness. It is here, beyond the sameness of everyday *Dasein*, in the decisive moment of the colliding of God and man in the midpoint of be-ing,[14] in the stillness of the passing of the last god,[15] that the command of the difference, reverberating in the peal of stillness,[16] gently impels.

In the fifth and final chapter an attempt was made to think Eucharistic presence, not from the metaphysical or symbolic realms but, from out of the district of *das Nichts* in the hope that the *verborgen* (what lies hidden) be brought to disclosure in some way. In search of the phenomenal content of the phenomenon of Eucharistic presence endeavours were made to answer the question: what is the manner and 'how' of Jesus' presencing after the crucifixion and before his Second Coming? It was demonstrated, given the *topos* of divine epiphany is the dimension of being, that for God to come fully into presence after the crucifixion there must be a *going under* or departure from the realm of beings thought metaphysically in their 'whatness'. This is sacrifice in the fullest sense because for Heidegger 'sacrifice is the departure from beings on the path to preserving the favor of being'.[17] Those who are *going under*, he insists, sacrifice themselves.[18] It was shown that, once the dimension of being has been accessed, the possibility of an immediate and direct encounter with God becomes real for it is here in the midpoint of be-ing (and not in the mediation of symbols) that the colliding of God and man takes place. In other words, Eucharistic presence is a fundamental ontological event occurring in the being of man and can not be spoken of in a postmodern way without reference to sacrifice or being-towards-death. It was shown that the moment of sacrifice is when I turn a deaf ear to the hubbub of idle talk in my being-towards-death.[19] It is then, through an attunement to the stirring of my own self or in listening to the appeal of conscience, that I enter the realm of being wherein God flashes. 'The call', Heidegger says, 'comes from the soundlessness of uncanniness, and

[12] M. Heidegger, *Einführung in die Metaphysik* (GA40), p. 176.
[13] M. Heidegger, *Einführung in die Metaphysik* (GA40), p. 172.
[14] M. Heidegger, *Beiträge zur Philosophie (Vom Ereignis)* (GA65), p. 416.
[15] M. Heidegger, *Beiträge zur Philosophie (Vom Ereignis)* (GA65), p. 406.
[16] M. Heidegger, *Unterwegs zur Sprache* (GA12), p. 29.
[17] M. Heidegger, *Nachwort zu: 'Was Ist Metaphysik?'* in *Wegmarken* (GA9), p. 310. 'Das Opfer ist der Abschied vom Seienden auf dem Gang zur Wahrung der Gunst des Seins.'
[18] M. Heidegger, *Beiträge zur Philosophie (Vom Ereignis)* (GA65), p. 397.
[19] M. Heidegger, *Sein und Zeit* (GA2), p. 235.

the *Dasein* which it summons is called back into the stillness of itself, and called back as something that is to become still'.[20] The call, which (like the Word) is the true knife of sacrifice, does not discourse in familiar words but rather in the uncanny mode of *keeping silent*. Sacrifice understood phenomenologically, then, is a surrender to 'the momentum of the push',[21] a yielding to the pressure of the orienting 'abrupt arrival'[22] in the midpoint of be-ing as the last god, in stillness, passes-by.

This book has shown, against Chauvet, that it *is* possible to continue thinking sacraments in an orthodox way after Nietzsche's exclamation *God is dead!* if for no other reason than Heidegger's philosophy, read in an unprejudiced way, has been shown to be not inconsistent with a Catholic understanding of sacrifice and thereby an orthodox understanding of Eucharistic presence. It has been demonstrated that Catholic orthodoxy, in particular within Eucharistic theology, does not require a metaphysical God to sanction and legitimize its various claims.

Further research

While investigating the central claim of this book, namely that it is possible to conceive the sacraments (without the subversion of Catholic doctrine) after the death of the 'stupendous concept "God"',[23] off-spring of 'the brain-sick fancies of morbid cobweb-spinners',[24] it became clear at certain junctures, that these conclusions might open up horizons for further research which, due to the limited space available, could not be pursued here. By way of conclusion therefore three possible areas for future research will be briefly outlined.

1. Ethics

Susan Parsons, editor of *Studies in Christian Ethics*, believes that in Heidegger's comments on the last god ethics is brought into a 'place of ultimacy before a cleavage, *die Zerklüftung*'.[25] This cleavage represents a 'rift or rupture of the

---

[20]   M. Heidegger, *Sein und Zeit* (GA2), p. 296, 'der Ruf kommt aus der Lautlosigkeit der Umheimlichkeit und ruft das aufgerufene Dasein als still zu werdendes in die Stille seiner selbst zurück.'

[21]   M. Heidegger, *Sein und Zeit* (GA2), p. 271, 'das Moment des Stoßes'.

[22]   M. Heidegger, *Sein und Zeit* (GA2), p. 271, 'abgesetzten Aufrüttelns'.

[23]   F. Nietzsche, *Götzendämmerung* (1990), p. 96, 'stupenden Begriff "Gott"'.

[24]   F. Nietzsche, *Götzendämmerung* (1990), p. 96, 'die Gehirnleiden kranker Spinneweber'.

[25]   S. Parsons, *The Last God as Disclosure of the Ethical . . . A Short Paper for the Seminar of* The Last God (2008), Unpublished paper, p. 2.

times'.[26] At the end of Chapter 4 it was shown that ethics, understood as a project of transformation, a project of disrupting our concepts and theories and the ways we act, could benefit from an engagement with Heidegger's thought. For instance, as Benjamin Crowe has recently argued Heidegger associates the search for authenticity in human lives (individual and collective) with destruction, that is, Parson's 'rift or rupture'. He says:

> destruction attempts to clear away obstacles to seeing what is 'genuine' about one's cultural and intellectual inheritance . . . Destruction is an activity that 'breaks into [*einschlägt*]' the present and 'unsettles [*erschüttert*]' it, freeing individuals from the burden of what passes itself off as 'common sense' at a particular time.[27]

2. Sacrifice

In his paper *Eucharistic Sacrifice and the Social Imagination in Early Modern Europe* William Cavanaugh believes that 'the confinement of the Body of Christ to the altar allows for the invention of "modern" politics based on the privatization of the organic-charitable body and the public assertion of the sovereign territorial state'.[28] If, as has been shown, the *topos* of Christ's Eucharistic presence is not exclusively confined to the altar, as it is when substance is not taken as *pragma*[29] involving the human subject, but is understood to be located additionally in 'the midpoint of be-ing',[30] what are the implications for politics? Can 'the privatization of the organic-charitable body'[31] and its corollary, 'the sovereign territorial state',[32] be sustained when Eucharistic presence is understood in a postmodern way as the colliding of God and man in the midpoint of be-ing?[33]

---

26 S. Parsons, *The Last God as Disclosure of the Ethical . . . A Short Paper for the Seminar of* The Last God (2008), Unpublished paper presented at a seminar on Heidegger's '*Last God*' at the University of Lancaster (16 June 2008), p. 2.

27 Benjamin D. Crowe, *Heidegger's Religious Origins* (2006), p. 264.

28 W. Cavanaugh, Eucharistic Sacrifice and the Social Imagination in Early Modern Europe, *Journal of Medieval and Early Modern Studies*, 31:3 [Fall 2001], p. 594.

29 *Pragma* signifies 'something with which we have to do, not so much something that we observe as something we encounter in our concernful dealings (*praxeis*)' [J. Macquarrie, *Thinghood and Sacramentality*, 1995, p. 18].

30 M. Heidegger, *Beiträge zur Philosophie (Vom Ereignis)* (GA65), p. 416, 'der Mitte des Seyns'.

31 W. Cavanaugh, Eucharistic Sacrifice and the Social Imagination in Early Modern Europe, *Journal of Medieval and Early Modern Studies*, 31:3 [Fall 2001], p. 594.

32 W. Cavanaugh, Eucharistic Sacrifice and the Social Imagination in Early Modern Europe, *Journal of Medieval and Early Modern Studies*, 31:3 [Fall 2001], p. 594.

33 M. Heidegger, *Beiträge zur Philosophie (Vom Ereignis)* (GA65), p. 416.

3. Liturgy

In *Experiénce et Absolu . . . Questions disputées sur l'humanité de l'homme* Jean-Yves Lacoste asserts that a phenomenology of the liturgy is concerned less with the order and ceremonies of divine worship and more with the logic that presides over the encounter between man and God.[34] To view the encounter between man and God phenomenologically means to uncover the wherein of this event which occurs no longer in an inessential dimension of 'Spirituality enriched by knowledge' but rather has its roots in our flesh.[35] Since Lacoste takes leave of Heidegger prematurely, believing the meeting of man and God in the fourfold to be a "'pagan moment of facticity,"'[36] it would be interesting to research the implications for a phenomenology of liturgy of staying with Heidegger. What happens to our understanding of liturgy when the *topos* of encounter is taken to be, not the non-place of 'the *eschaton*' or 'eschatological anticipation,'[37] but, the midpoint of be-ing, that is, the dimension of being itself? If the topology of encounter is thrown into turmoil with the overcoming of metaphysics and the subordination of the symbolic order, what are the implications for liturgy of Heidegger's writings on the last god and the *Geviert* understood, against Lacoste, as more than a pagan moment of facticity? Hemming's book *Worship as a Revelation* has opened up this inquiry.[38]

---

[34] Y. Lacoste, *Experiénce et Absolu* (1994), p. 2.
[35] Y. Lacoste, *Experiénce et Absolu* (1994), p. 26.
[36] Y. Lacoste, *Experiénce et Absolu* (1994), p. 24, 'moment païn de la facticité'.
[37] Y. Lacoste, *Experiénce et Absolu* (1994), p. 30, 'l'*eschaton* . . . l'anticipation eschatologique'.
[38] L. Hemming, *Worship as a Revelation* (2008).

Bibliography

Texts by Martin Heidegger

Gesamtausgabe 2, *Sein und Zeit*, Niemeyer, Tübungen, 1993 [17th edn]. Translated by Macquarrie, John and Robinson, Edward, as *Being and Time*, London, SCM Press, 1962.

Gesamtausgabe 4, *Erläuterungen zu Hölderlins Dichtung*, Frankfurt, Klostermann, 1991. Translated by Hoeller, Keith, as *Elucidations of Hölderlin's Poetry*, New York, Humanity Books, 2000.

Gesamtausgabe 5, *Holzwege*, von Herrmann, Friedrich-Wilhelm (edn), Frankfurt, Klostermann, 1977. First published as *Holzwege*, Frankfurt, Klostermann, 1950. Translated by Young, Julian and Haynes, Kenneth, as *Off the Beaten Track*, New York, Cambridge University Press, 2002.

Gesamtausgabe 7, *Vorträge und Aufsätze*, Pfullingen, Neske, 1954.

Überwindung Der Metaphysik in *Vorträge und Aufsätze*. Translated by Stambaugh, Joan, as *Overcoming Metaphysics* in *The End of Philosophy*, Chicago, University of Chicago Press, 2003 (1973).

Gesamtausgabe 9, *Wegmarken*, von Herrmann, Friedrich-Wilhelm (ed.), Frankfurt, Klostermann, 1976. First published as *Wegmarken*, Frankfurt, Klostermann, 1967. Translated by McNeill, William (ed.), as *Pathmarks*, New York, Cambridge University Press, 1998.

Gesamtausgabe 11, *Identität und Differenz*, Pfullingen, Neske, 1957. Translated by Stambaugh, Joan (ed.), as *Identity and Difference* in a bilingual edition, New York, Harper Torchbooks, 1969.

Gesamtausgabe 12, *Unterwegs zur Sprache*, Pfullingen, Neske, 1965 [Frankfurt, Klostermann, 1985]. Lectures from 1950 to 1959. Translated by Hertz, Peter D. (ed.), as *On the Way to Language*, San Francisco, Harper, 1982.

Gesamtausgabe 14, *Zur Sache des Denkens*, Tübingen Max Niemeyer Verlag, 1969. Translated by Stambaugh, Joan (ed.), as *On Being and Time*, San Francisco, Harper Torchbooks, 1972.

Gesamtausgabe 15, *Seminare*, Ockwadt, Curd (ed.), Frankfurt, Klostermann, 1986.

Gesamtausgabe 17, *Einführung in die phänomenologische Forchung*, Frankfurt, Klostermann, 1994. Translated by Dahlstrom, Daniel O., as *Introduction to Phenomenological Research*, Bloomington, Indiana University Press, 2005.

Gesamtausgabe 19, *Platon: Sophistes*, Schüßler, Ingleborg (ed.), Frankfurt, Klostermann, 1992. Translated by Rojcewicz, Richard and Schuwer, André, as *Plato's Sophist*, Bloomington, Indiana University Press, 1997.

Gesamtausgabe 20, *Prolegomena zur Geschichte des Zeitbegiffs*, Jaeger, Petra (ed.), Frankfurt, Klostermann, 1979. Translated by Kiesiel, Theodore, as *History of the Concept of Time, Prolegomena*, Bloomington, Indiana University Press, 1985.

Gesamtausgabe 40, *Einführung in die Metaphysik*, Jaeger, Petra (ed.), Frankfurt, Klostermann, 1983. First published as *Einführung in die Metaphysik*, Tübingen, Niemeyer, 1953. Translated by Manheim, Ralph, as *An Introduction to Metaphysics*, New Haven, Yale University Press, 1959.

Gesamtausgabe 53, *Hölderlin's Hymne 'Der Ister'*, Biemel, Walter (ed.), Frankfurt, Klostermann, 1984. Translated by McNeill, William and Davis, Julia, as *Hölderlin's Hymn 'The Ister'*, Bloomington, Indiana University Press, 1996.

Gesamtausgabe 54, *Parmenides*, Frings, Manfred S. (ed.), Frankfurt, Klostermann, 1982. Translated by Schuwer, André and Rojcewicz, Richard, as *Parmenides*, Bloomington, Indiana University Press, 1992.

Gesamtausgabe 60, *Phänomenologie des religiösen Lebens*, Jung, Matthias, Regehly, Thomas and Strube, Claudius (eds), Thomas, Frankfurt, Klostermann, 1995. Translated by Fritsch, Matthias and Gosetti-Ferencei, Jennifer Anna, as *The Phenomenology of Religious Life*, Bloomington, Indiana University Press, 2004.

Gesamtausgabe 64, *Der Begriff der Zeit*, Tübungen, Niemeyer, 1989. *Der Begriff der Zeit (Vortrag 1924)* translated by Mc Neill, William, as *The Concept of Time* in a bilingual edition, Oxford, Blackwell, 2005 (1992).

Gesamtausgabe 65, *Beiträge zur Philosophie (Vom Ereignis)*, von Herrmann, Friedrich-Wilhelm (ed.), Frankfurt, Klostermann, 1989. Translated by Emad, Parvis and Maly, Kenneth, as *Contributions to Philosophy (From Enowning)*, Bloomington, Indiana University Press, 1999.

Gesamtausgabe 66, *Besinnung*, von Herrmann, Friedrich-Wilhelm (ed.), Frankfurt, Klostermann, 1997. Translated by Emad, Parvis and Kalary, Thomas, as *Mindfulness*, London, Continuum, 2008 (2006).

Texts by Other Authors

Beckwith, Sarah (ed.), *Catholicism and Catholicity . . . Eucharistic Communities in Historical and Contemporary Perspectives*, Oxford, Blackwell Publishers Ltd, 1999.

Bergson, Henri, *An Introduction to Metaphysics*, New York and London, G.P. Pitman's Sons, 1916.

Boeve, L. and Leijssen, L. (eds), *Sacramental Presence in a Postmodern Context*, Leuven, Leuven University Press, 2001.

Caputo, John D., *The Mystical Element in Heidegger's Thought*, New York, Fordham University Press, 1986 (1978).

Casel, Odo, *The Mystery of Christian Worship*, New York, Crossroad Publishing Company, 1962 (1932).

Cassirer, Ernst, *The Philosophy of Symbolic Forms. Volume Two: Mythical Thought*, New Haven: Yale University Press, 1955.

Chauvet, Louis-Marie, *Symbole et Sacrament: Un relecture sacramentelle de l'existence chretienne*, Les Editions du Cerf, 1987. Translated by Madigan, Patrick S. J. and Beaumont, Madeleine, as *Symbol and Sacrament . . . A Sacramental Reinterpretation of Christian Existence*, Liturgical Press, Collegeville, Minnesota, 1995.

Crowe, Benjamin, D., *Heidegger's Religious Origins . . . Destruction and Authenticity*, Bloomington and Indianapolis, Indiana University Press, 2006.

Davies, Oliver, *A Theology of Compassion – Metaphysics of Difference and the Renewal of Tradition*, Grand Rapids, SCM Press, 2001.

Davies, Oliver, Janz, Paul D. and Sedmak, Clemens, *Transformation Theology . . . Church in the World*, London, T&T Clark International, 2007.

De Lubac, Henri Cardinal, *Corpus Mysticum*, 2nd Edition, 1949. Translated by Simmonds, Gemma, with Price, Richard, and Stephens, Christopher, as *Corpus Mysticum . . . The Eucharist and the Church in the Middle Ages*, London, SCM Press, 2006.

Gooch, Todd A., *The Numinous and Modernity . . . An Interpretation of Rudolph Otto's Philosophy of Religion*, Berlin, Walter de Gruyter, 2000.

Hemming, Laurence Paul, *Heidegger's Atheism . . . The Refusal of a Theological Voice*, Notre Dame, University of Notre Dame Press, 2002.

—, *Postmodernity's Transcending . . . Devaluing God*, London, SCM Press, 2005.

—, *Worship as a Revelation: The Past, Present and Future of Catholic Liturgy*, London, Continuum, 2008.

Hodge, Joanna, *Heidegger and Ehics*, London and New York, Routledge, 1995.

Hopkins, Burt and Crowell, Steven (eds), *The New Yearbook for Phenomenology and Phenomenological Philosophy*, Seattle, Noesis Press Ltd, 2003.

Huntington, Richard (ed.), *Celebrations of Death . . . The Anthropology of Mortuary Ritual*, Cambridge, Cambridge University Press, 1987 (1979).

James, William, *The Varieties of Religious Experience*, New York, Penguin Books, 1982 (1902).

Jonas, Hans, *The Gnostic Religion, The Message of an Alien God and the Beginnings of Christianity*, Boston, Beacon Press, 2001 (1958).

Kierkegaard, Søren, *Fear and Trembling: A Dialectical Lyric*, London, Oxford University Press, 1939.

—, *The Concept of Dread*, Princeton, Princeton University Press, 1957.

—, *Attack Upon 'Christendom'*, Princeton, Princeton University Press, 1968.

—, *The Concept of Anxiety*, New Jersey, Princeton University Press, 1980.

—, *Three Discourses on Imagined Occasions*, New Jersey, Princeton University Press, 2009 (1993).

Kovac, George, *The Question of God in Heidegger's Phenomenology*, Evanston, Northwestern University Press, 1990.

Lacoste, Yves, *Experience et absolu*, Paris, Presses Universitaires de France, 1994.

Langiulli, Nino, (ed.), *European Existentialism*, New Brunswick and London, Transaction Publishers, 1997 (1971).

Lyotard, Jean François, *La condition postmoderne . . . Rapport sur le Savoir*, Les Éditions de Minuit, Paris, 1979. Translated by Bennington, G. and Massumi, B., as *The Postmodern Condition: A Report on Knowledge*, Minneapolis, University of Minnesota Press, 1984.

Macquarrie, John, *Martin Heidegger*, London, Lutterworth Press, 1967.

—, *Heidegger and Christianity*, London, SCM Press, 1994.

—, *Thinghood and Sacramentality*, The Centre for the Study of Theology in the University of Essex, 1995.

—, *A Guide to the Sacraments*, London, SCM Press Ltd, 1997.

Macy, David, *The Theologies of the Eucharist in the Early Scholastic Period*, Oxford, Oxford University Press, 1984.

Marion, Jean-Luc, *Dieu sans l'être: Hors-texte*, Librairie Arthème Fayard, 1982. Translated by Carlson, Thomas A., as *God Without Being: Hors-Texte*, Chicago, University of Chicago Press, 1984.

—, *Prolégomènes à la charité*, E.L.A. La Différence, Paris, 1986. Translated by Lewis, Stephen, as *Prolegomena to Charity*, New York, Fordham University Press, 2002.

Martelet, G., *Résurrection, Eucharistie et Genèse de l'Homme*, Desclée, 1972. Translated by Corbishley, Thomas S. J., as *The Risen Christ and the Eucharistic World*, London, William Collins Sons & Co. Ltd, 1976.

McGuckian, M., *The Holy Sacrifice of the Mass . . . A Search for an Acceptable Notion of Sacrifice*, Hertfordshire, Gracewing Publishing, 2005.

Metz, J. B., *Glaube in Geschichte und Gesellschaft*, Matthias-Grunewald Verlag, Mayence, 1977. Translated by Corset, Paul and Schlegel, Jean-Louis, as *Dans L'Histoire et Dans La Societe . . . Essai de theologique fondamentale pratique*, Les Editions du Cerf, 1979.

Nietzsche, Friedrich, *Also sprach Zarathustra.*, Berlin, de Gruyter, 1999 (1968). Translated by Common, Thomas, as *Thus Spake Zarathustra*, Hertfordshire, Wordsworth Editions Limited, 1997.

—, *Jenseits von Gut und Böse*, Berlin, de Gruyter, 1999 (1968). Translated by Faber, Marion as *Beyond Good and Evil*, Oxford, Oxford University Press, 1998.

—, *Der Antichrist*, Berlin, de Gruyter, 1999 (1968). Translated by Hollingdale, R. J., as *The Anti-Christ*, London, Penguin Books Ltd, 2003 (1968).

—, *Zur Genealogie der Moral*, Berlin, de Gruyter, 1999 (1968). Translated by Diethe, Carol, as *On the Genealogy of Morality*, Cambridge, Cambridge University Press, 2007 (1994).

—, *Die Fröhliche Wissenschaft*, Berlin, de Gruyter, 1999 (1968). Translated by Williams, Bernard, as *The Gay Science* Cambridge, Cambridge University Press, 2007 (2001).

Olafson, Frederick A., *Heidegger and the Ground of Ethics . . . A Study of* Mitsein, Cambridge, Cambridge University Press, 1998.

Otto, Rudolf, *Das Heilige*, 9th German edition. Translated by Harvey, John W. as *The Idea of the Holy . . . An Inquiry into the Non-rational Factor in the Idea of the Divine and its Relation to the Rational*, London, Oxford University Press, 1950 (1923).

Parkes, Graham (ed.), *Heidegger and Asian Thought*, Honolulu, University of Hawai Press, 1987.

Pope Benedict XVI, *Gott ist uns nah. Eucharistie: Mitte des Lebens*, Augsburg, Sankt Ulrich Verlag, 2001. Translated by Taylor, Henry, as *God is Near Us . . . The Eucharist, the Heart of Life*, San Francisco, Ignatius Press, 2003.

—, Encyclical Letter *Deus Caritas Est*, Rome, Libreria Editrice Vaticana, 2007.

—, Post-synodal Apostolic Exhortation *Sacramentum Caritatis*, Rome, Libreria Editrice Vaticana, 2007.

Pope John Paul II, Encyclical Letter *Redemptoris missio*, Rome, Librereia Editrice Vaticana, 1990.

—, Encyclical Letter *Ecclesia de Eucharistia*, Rome, Librereia Editrice Vaticana, 1999.

Pope Paul VI, Encyclical Letter *Mysterium Fidei*, Rome, Librereia Editrice Vaticana, 1965.

Richardson, William J. S. J., *Heidegger: Through Phenomenology to Thought*, Dordrecht, Martinus Nijhoff, 1963.

Rockmore, Tom, *Heidegger and French Philosophy: Humanism, Antihumanism, and Being*, London, Routledge, 1995.

Schillebeeckx, Edward, *The Eucharist*, London and New York, Burns & Oates, 2005 (1968).

Schleiermacher, Friedrich, *Der Christliche Glaube nach den Grundsätzen der evangelischen Kirch im Zusammemhang dargestellt*, Berlin, Walter De Gruyter & Co., 1960 (1821). Translated by MacKintosh, J. S., as *The Christian Faith*, Edinburgh, T&T Clark, 1989.

—, *Über die Religion . . . Reden an die Gebildeten unter ihren Verächtern*, Stuttgart, Reclams Universal-Bibliothek, 2007 (1799). Translated by Coulter, Richard, as *On Religion . . . Speeches to its Cultured Despisers*, Cambridge, Cambridge University Press, 2006 (1988).

Schneeberger, Guido, *Ergänzungen zu einer Heidegger-Bibliographie*, Bern, Druck: Buchdruckerei A G Suhr, 1960. Containing *Beilage IV Arbeitsgemeinschaft Cassirer-Heidegger,* translated by Slade, Francis, as *A Discussion Between Ernst Cassirer and Martin Heidegger* in Langiulli, Nino (ed.), *European Existentialism*, New Brunswick and London, Transaction Publishers, 1997 (1971).

Scholze-Stubenrecht, W. and Sykes, J. B., (eds), *The Oxford-Duden German Dictionary*, Oxford, Clarendon Press, 1997 (1990).

Sheehan, T., 'Heidegger's *Introduction to the Phenomenology of Religion*, 1920–21' in Kochelmans, J. (ed.), *A Companion to Martin Heidegger's Being and Time*, Washington, University Press of America, 1986.

—, *Karl Rahner . . . The Philosophical Foundations*, Athens, Ohio University Press, 1987.

Vedder, Ben, *Heidegger's Philosophy of Religion . . . From God to the Gods,* Pittsburgh, Duquesne University Press, 2007.

Journals

Beattie, 'Insight Beyond Sight', in *New Blackfriars*, vol. 88, no. 1014, March (2007).

Blankenhorn OP, Bernhard, 'The Instrumental Causality of the Sacraments: Thomas Aquinas and Louis-Marie Chauvet', in *Nova et Vetera*, English Edition, vol. 4, no. 2 (2006).

Cavanaugh, 'Eucharistic Sacrifice and the Social Imagination in Early Modern Europe', *Journal of Medieval and Early Modern Studies*, 31:3, Fall (2001).

Dobszay, Lazslo, 'What might be called "The Roman Rite" or simply What is the "The Roman Rite"', unpublished paper, (2007).

Duffy, 'Benedict XVI and the Eucharist', in *Blackfriars Journal*, vol. 88, no. 1014 March (2007).

Hampson, Peter, 'Making Sense of Love', in *The Tablet*, 28 January (2006).

Hemming, Laurence Paul, 'After Heidegger: Transubstantiation', in *Heythrop Journal*, vol. 42, October (2000).

—, 'Transubstantiating Ourselves ... A Phenomenological Basis for the Theology of Transubstantiation', in *Heythrop Journal*, vol. 44, October (2003).

—, 'Polarisation and Liturgy', *The Pastoral Review*, vol. 1, January/February (2005).

—, 'A Transcendental Hangover: Lévinas, Heidegger and the Ethics of Alterity', in *Studies in Christian Ethics*, vol.18, August (2005).

—, 'Martin Heidegger and Being's Divinity ... an introductory discussion paper for a seminar on Heidegger's *Der Letzte Gott*', unpublished paper (2008).

Kirwin, Michael, Eucharist and Sacrifice, in *New Blackfriars*, vol. 88, no. 1014, March (2007).

Kubicki CSSF, Judith Marie, 'Recognising the Presence of Christ in the Liturgical Assembly', in *Theological Studies*, 65 (2004)

Macquarrie, John, Eckhart and Heidegger, in *The Eckhart Society Journal*, no. 2, Spring (1993).

Martos, Joseph, 'Book Reviews', in *Horizons*, 23/2 (1996).

McKenna, John H., 'Eucharist and Sacrifice: An Overview', in *Worship*, vol. 76, no. 5, September (2002).

Mickens, Robert, 'Labour of Love', in *The Tablet*, 4 February (2006).

Miller, Vincent J., 'An Abyss at the Heart of Mediation: Louis-Marie Chauvet's Fundamental Theology of Sacramentality', in *Horizons*, 24/2 (1997).

Mitchell, Nathan D., 'Mystery and Manners: Eucharist in Post-Modern Theology', in *Worship*, vol. 79, no. 2, March (2005).

Niebuhr, Richard, R., 'Schleiermacher On Language and Feeling', in *Theology Today*, vol. 17, July (1960).

Rahner, Karl, 'Introduction au Concept de Philosophie Existentiale Chez Heidegger', in *Recherches de Sciences Religieuses*, vol. 30 (1940). Translated by Tallon, Andrew, as 'The Concept of Existential Philosophy in Heidegger', in *Philosophy Today*, vol. 13 (1969).

Soskice, Janet Martin, 'Heart of the matter', in *The Tablet*, 4 February (2006).

Webb, Mary-Ann, 'Eros and Ethics: Levinas's Reading of Plato's "Good Beyond Being"', in *Studies in Christian Ethics*, vol. 19, August (2006).

Welte, Bernard, 'The Question of God in the Thought of Heidegger', in *Philosophy Today*, vol. 26 (1982).

Index

Made in the USA
San Bernardino, CA
02 December 2016